PRACTICING CATHOLIC

The Search for a Livable Catholicism

PENELOPE J. RYAN, PH.D.

HENRY HOLT AND COMPANY

NEW YORK

Henry Holt and Company, Inc. / *Publishers since 1866*
115 West 18th Street / New York, New York 10011

Henry Holt® is a registered
trademark of Henry Holt and Company, Inc.

Library of Congress Cataloging-in-Publication Data
Ryan, Penelope.
Practicing Catholic : the search for a livable Catholicism /
Penelope Ryan. — 1st ed.
p.   cm.
Includes bibliographical references and index.
ISBN 0-8050-4663-1 (alk. paper)
1. Catholic Church—Doctrines.   2. Ryan, Penelope.   3. Catholic Church—
United States—History—1965–   I. Title.
BX1751.2.R9   1998
282'.73'09045—dc21   97-51624

Henry Holt books are available for special promotions and
premiums. For details contact: Director, Special Markets.

First Edition 1998

Designed by Victoria Hartman

Printed in the United States of America
All first editions are printed on acid-free paper. ∞
1   3   5   7   9   10   8   6   4   2

To John and Jack

Contents

Acknowledgments

I am grateful to all those people who directly and indirectly encouraged me in this endeavor. To Madeleine Morel, Theresa Burns, Alessandra Bocco, and Lisa Lester, your patience and professionalism is deeply appreciated. For my school communities of St. Ignatius at Fordham University and the School of the Holy Child, your faith and encouragement has inspired me. Terry, Kiki, Annalea, and Marcia, thank you for your friendship. To my sister-in-law Mimi Lamb, without your subscriptions to the *National Catholic Reporter* I would not have had the imagination to see this book through. And, John and Jack, without your love and support this would not have happened.

Introduction

Several years ago my ninety-year-old, Irish/German Catholic Grandmother Coakley died. Until her retirement at seventy she had been a highly successful, professional businesswoman whose opinions had been sought and respected by her male colleagues decades before the feminist movement had begun. She was the Rosie the Riveter of the wholesale clothing business. I grew up believing that women could do and be anything they set their minds to because of my grandmother. She was bright, assertive, and strong, and one of the reasons was her Catholic faith. It had sustained her through the Depression, the death of her husband, and the deaths of all of her children. Her grandchildren were all she had left, along with a litany of vivid memories of the old days that we delighted in hearing. As soon as I was notified of her death, I traveled to my hometown, a suburb of Buffalo, New York, where the funeral services were to be held.

Despite the brutal winters and the mountains of snow that characterize Buffalo, or perhaps *because* of them, the people who live there are warm and kind. Buffalo is also very Catholic. Like many industrialized cities in the United States, it grew and prospered at the hands of Irish and Polish and Italian immigrants who brought little with them from their native countries other than their Catholicism. In a new and unfamiliar world their faith offered them stability, peace, and hope. They clung to it as a link to the past and as a bridge to the future.

My whole world was Catholic as I was growing up in the suburbs of Buffalo. It was like a blanket that enfolded my life, and this wake and funeral of my grandmother's brought back many memories of growing up Catholic. I went to Catholic schools and played with Catholic friends, and most gatherings of family and friends were centered around Catholic occasions like baptisms, Communions, and confirmations. Some of these old friends of my grandparents' were the first to enter the funeral home for her wake. Although my grandmother's husband and many of her friends had preceded her in death, members of the old Irish crowd were sufficiently numerous to enliven this event. When the O'Learys approached me at the wake to offer their condolences, they reminded me of the wonderful card parties my grandparents used to host on Saturday nights years before. These parties were filled with laughter, political bantering, and smoke from Lucky Strikes. At precisely 11:00 P.M. I helped my grandmother clear the tables of cards and set out a lavish buffet of ham and cheese, roast beef and potato salad, hearty pumpernickel bread. This minifeast had to be consumed by 12:00 midnight because that was when the fast began. If you were going to Mass and taking Communion the next day, on Sunday, which all of these good Catholics no doubt were going to do, no food or drink could pass your lips after midnight. That was the fast. The card parties, the food, the beginning of the fast made Saturday nights special, shrouded in warmth and mystery.

Kathleen, another one of my grandmother's cronies and also a Saturday-night cardsharp, commented on the green Connemara marble rosary beads that twisted around my grandmother's lifeless fingers as she lay in her coffin. After a moment Kathleen remarked in her Irish brogue, "Your grandmother was a good Catholic woman. Why, she loved the Church, said her rosary every day, went to all the missions and novenas, and offered to drive the rest of us as well. A good, holy woman." Everyone within earshot nodded approvingly. And so she was, if these were the measuring rods to determine how good a Catholic one had been.

These visitors to the wake stirred my memory as I recalled how I had often watched my grandmother late on a Sunday afternoon, when the dishes had been washed and put away after a big dinner, fingering these rosary beads. She had a small black beaded pouch in which she kept them. The pouch was placed on a kitchen shelf next to a twelve-inch statue of the Blessed Mother clothed in a soft blue mantle. On the wall opposite the statue hung a framed print of the head of a crucified Christ, blood flowing from the crown of thorns and sad brown eyes that seemed to follow us around the kitchen. Tucked behind the print were dried palms, left over from Palm Sunday. These and numerous other symbols throughout the house gave witness to the Catholicity of my grandparents' home. The Catholic Church is sacramental by nature and tradition; these outward signs were significant in the lives of my grandmother and friends, the faithful. They still are significant to many people, despite the fact that there are fewer of these sacramentals in use today. As the wake progressed that afternoon, each person who came to express condolences recalled a memory of my grandmother that attested to what I had always known: She was a good and faithful woman, she was a good Catholic.

The morning of my grandmother's funeral we arrived at Blessed Sacrament Church, which peculiarly smelled the same as it had twenty-five years earlier when I had been a parishioner here. Several generations of my family had been baptized here, received Communion here, gone to confession here, been confirmed and married here, and been buried from this church. Memories of Benediction and incense, the Stations of the Cross, and Latin hymns flooded my mind. I remembered purple cloths covering statues during Lent, meatless Fridays, and flowered hats on Sundays.

Since the liturgical reforms had gone into effect after the Second Vatican Council, many changes had occurred on the inside of the church. Gone were the high altar and the golden Communion rail at which the faithful had knelt to receive the sacred Host on their tongues. Gone, too, were the flickering vigil lights and the numerous statues of saints, the Sacred Heart, and the Infant of Prague, who had appeared in different dress for every liturgical season; purple for Advent and Lent, gold for the big feasts like Christmas and Easter, and white or green for the Ordinary Time of the year. The church seemed simpler now, less crowded and festive, and quieter than I remembered it. The stained glass windows remained, with events around the birth of Christ brightly depicted and the sun from outside casting patches of red and blue and gold light across the pews.

Once the funeral Mass had begun, I recalled how Father O'Toole had swaggered out onto the altar in vestments in the shape of a violin and how he would turn solemnly from the high altar chanting, *"Dominus vobiscum,"* which meant "The Lord be with you." The altar server would respond, *"Et cum spiritu tuo,"* which I thought sounded curiously like my telephone number. Father O'Toole would smell vaguely of whiskey as he handed out Communion, and sometimes he would put more than one Host on our tongues and we would giggle. I was too young then to understand the loneliness that could haunt a celibate diocesan priest.

In this church I had prayed to get souls out of Purgatory on November 2, the Feast of All Souls, and said prayers with big indulgences attached to them so that I myself would do as little time in Purgatory as possible. During Lent each year I had been encouraged to go to daily Mass in this church, memorizing all the Latin responses to the Mass, and it was here that I first had heard the litanies of the saints we were meant to imitate: Agatha, Theresa, and of course Maria Goretti, who was martyred because she refused to have sex with a man. After faith, hope, and charity, purity and virginity were the main virtues to be practiced. Impure thoughts and actions headed the list of sins we lined up to confess behind the heavy black velvet curtain of the confessional at the back of the church. Memories randomly filtered through my mind at this funeral as I recalled my world of growing up Catholic. It was a world stable and secure. This church was home and family for me. This was the world of the Church before 1960, before John XXIII and the Second Vatican Council.

My grandmother's funeral was celebrated with white vestments and hymns and prayers that emphasized a resurrection to new life, rather than with the black vestments and singing of the doleful "Dies Irae" that characterized funerals I had attended as a youth. A confession room where parishioners could, if they so chose, face the priest for confession, had replaced the small confessional with its black velvet curtain and sliding wooden doors where scores of us had lined up between 2:00 and 5:00 P.M. every Saturday. As my Grandmother Coakley's friends shuffled out of the pews to accompany her casket to its final resting place, I thought of all the Catholic practices and rites that had died or been transformed so dramatically, during my grandmother's lifetime and mine as well, that they were hardly recognizable.

These practices defined us as Catholics, set us apart. They gave us structure, a social and religious life as well: Mass on Sunday, novenas on Monday, the rosary on Thursday, Benediction with its chanting and incense on Friday, and confession on Saturday. The practices, symbols, signs and even smells brought order and sanctity to people's lives in the past. They shrouded us in a cloak of mystery and awe. Sometimes we understood why we were doing what we did, and sometimes we did it simply out of habit. Sometimes the practices were done out of love and devotion, other times they were done out of a sense of obligation or fear that we would lose God's love—or, even worse, go to Hell.

I wondered if the loss of many of the former practices had left a void in people's lives? Besides teaching theology as an adjunct at Fordham University for the past nineteen years, I also teach at a private high school for young women, where over the past two decades I have often seen a desire among young people to find a spiritual center, sometimes enhanced by what formerly would have been called sacramentals. I recalled how sixteen-year-old Maria Ricci recently asked if she could bring in some incense and a tape of prayers written by a medieval nun, Hildegard von Bingen, and set to chantlike music so we could meditate in a prayer and spirituality class I was teaching. Here was another generation finding comfort in an age-old practice. I also asked myself, why does the exacting obedience of cults, with sexual abstinence and fasting, appeal to so many young people today, when vocations to most religious orders have drastically diminished?

The good Catholic participated in the services and other important practices and listened attentively and followed obediently whatever the priests, bishops, and—most important—the Pope had to say, in the name of God. There was order to being Catholic. There was unity of belief and practice as we were reminded that one could go anywhere in the world and the Mass was the same, in Latin, whether you were in Europe, Africa, Asia, North or South America. We knew that every Catholic throughout the world followed the same rules. All that a Catholic needed to know about faith could be found in the Baltimore Catechism, a guide of what Catholics were to believe, made up of questions about the faith, followed by answers to be memorized. Those were the good old days when the good were assured of Heaven and the bad were on their way to Hell.

A high school friend of mine, Marty, who had spent hours in my grandmother's kitchen with me sipping root beer floats also attended Grandma Coakley's funeral Mass. By the time Marty and I were in high school, the first Catholic president, John Fitzgerald Kennedy, had been elected and Vatican II was stirring debate. The words *ecumenical*, *collegiality*, and *layperson* had been added to the common Catholic vocabulary. The Church was in the midst of *aggiornamento*, a modernization, which appeared as radical change at the time. Marty and I had spent some weeks after our junior year in an inner-city parish in Buffalo, where we learned that not everyone in the Church was white, and the concept of the Church as the People of God took hold in us. We discovered that being a Catholic meant something more than going to Mass and novenas and Benediction, the private practices that had defined and structured our Catholic lives. We discovered what it meant to be a Catholic in the world, in the family of humankind, genuinely concerned for the less fortunate and working with them to build better lives. Issues of peace and justice, living the Gospel values of compassion, understanding, and forgiveness took center stage in our quest to be good Catholics. Marty and I went on to take theology courses at Catholic University as undergraduates and began to feel a sense of responsibility for our Church. We examined the teaching of the Church in an intelligent, scholarly way.

Life in Washington, D.C., in the late sixties and early seventies—at the height of the Vietnam War and in the midst of the civil rights movement—filled my college days with peace marches and rallies. As my brother Bob marched through the jungles of Vietnam, I was marching to protest the immorality of this war. I met people like the priest activists Dan and Philip Berrigan and took a morality course from respected author/theologian Father Charles Curran. Curran was later dismissed from Catholic University and forbidden to teach at any other Catholic college because of his opposition to the Church's stance on birth control as set forth in the Pope Paul VI's 1968 encyclical *Humanae Vitae:* "On Human Life".* Because an encyclical is a papal letter circulated to the whole world concerning matters of dogma, social justice, or human rights, it is expected that members of the church accede to its teaching. This encyclical and Father Curran's dismissal became focal points for ensuing debate regarding not only the issue of artificial contraception but also the teaching authority of the Church. The documents from the Second Vatican Council had been published and were being studied. As students we had read Vatican II's Pastoral Constitution on the Church in the Modern World (*Gaudium et Spes:* "Joy and Hope")†, and had been assured that we as laypeople were important to the future life

---

* As is the Catholic Church's tradition, important statements and documents, including encyclicals, are issued in Latin and are divided into paragraphs. A document can be known by its Latin name, the English translation of that Latin title, or a more generic name based on its content. For the purposes of this book, both the Latin and English title of such Church documents are given in the text; duplicate citations consist of an assigned abbreviation based on the Latin title, followed by the paragraph number from which the quote is taken. Therefore, *Humanae Vitae:* "On Human Life" will hereafter be cited as HV. A list of important documents used in this book, and their abbreviations where applicable, appears in the Appendix.
† Hereafter cited as GS.

of the Church. It was exciting but frustrating as my contemporaries and I, high on idealism, met with conservativism.

Unlike many of my friends who dropped out of the Church, charging it with hypocrisy and lack of vision, I stayed with it, believing change would come. The change did come, but many would argue that it did not keep up with the dramatic changes in the world as a whole. Others still defend the Church, believing it needs to resist further modernization in protest of present-day society's "culture of death," as Pope John Paul II defined it in the 1995 encyclical *Evangelium Vitae:* "Gospel of Life".*

Despite the fact that in 1994 the Church published a long-awaited new Catholic Catechism, meant to be the definitive word on what was to believed and practiced by Catholics, and that the present Pope in his numerous encyclicals and statements has outlined what it means to be a good Catholic, there is nonetheless uneasiness about what the Church teaches on some issues and why. Perhaps the emphasis is on the *why*. What does it mean to be a "good" Catholic in the latter part of the twentieth century? Is it possible to take issue with certain teachings and still be a practicing Catholic? Were my grandparents, who unquestionably followed the dictates of the Church, better Catholics than those today who support the right of a woman to have an abortion under certain circumstances, or those who vocalize their dissent against prohibiting the ordination of women to the priesthood? In the past there were dogmas to which we unquestionably adhered; today there are questions and doubts about some of these teachings. In the past there was silent respectful obedience toward its teachers, today there is reasoned dissent. For many practicing Catholics, as well as those on the fringes, the desire to remain true to their religious roots and heritage is still an important part of their lives. But they also feel the need to sort the essentials of their Catholic faith from the nonessentials.

Defining oneself as a Catholic is no longer the simple task that

---

* Hereafter cited as EV.

it used to be. There are sixty million people in the country who describe themselves as Catholic; many of whom feel at odds with themselves about what the Church teaches, at odds with what they are hearing in homilies at Sunday Mass, and at odds with the proclamations coming from the Vatican. It is a time of inner and outer conflict as Catholics struggle with their consciences, their reason, and the secular culture of the modern world. What makes a "good" Catholic, and what do I have to do and believe to be a practicing Catholic? These are some of the questions we ask.

For some people the answers to the above questions are simple. One listens to the Pope and the hierarchy, attends Mass and Communion each week, and agrees with all the official teachings. For these folks, this is the simple recipe for a good Catholic. For others of us the answers are not so simple. We have been brought up to think, to use our reason, and to question in our search for truth. Yes, we listen to and try to assent to those teachings we believe are at the heart of our Faith, but we have doubts and concerns about others. Still, we continue to practice Catholicism. And there are those who have found themselves at times in conflict with the Church: Catherine of Siena, Francis of Assisi, Trappist Thomas Merton, Joan of Arc, Archbishop Oscar Romero of San Salvador, and countless others who have lived lives that have bettered the world. They have offered models of ways to live a meaningful life that encourage me and fill me with pride at being a part of this "communion of saints," the bond that all the faithful in heaven and on earth share. The Church has been home for them and is for me.

Not long ago, a classmate, housemate, friend, and theologian at Notre Dame, Catherine Mowry LaCugna, died after a brave fight against cancer. Katie and I studied theology together as Ph.D. candidates at Fordham twenty years ago and used to discuss through the night and well into the early morning some of the issues taken up in this book. Katie's theological expertise was the Trinity, which she was able to explain for modern Catholics as an interpersonal relationship of persons. Her personalist approach to this mystery disclosed a better understanding of the Trinity for us. A more personalist approach to many teachings of the Church has allowed us to feel more in touch with our Faith. This book promotes such an approach to some of the divisive issues Catholics face today.

Sadly, there are many Catholics for whom the Church has become irrelevant; it seems out of touch with their lives and human experience in general. They are angry and resentful about what they perceive as hostile attitudes held by the Church; priests who have married and no longer are allowed to administer the sacraments, women who feel called to ordination but are stymied in their efforts, divorced and remarried Catholics who receive Communion but have been told officially that they are not welcome to do so without an annulment, gays and lesbians seeking an institutional affirmation of love for their lives, and pregnant women who feel they have no alternative to abortion but know their Church's condemnation of the practice. These people feel abandoned by the Church they used to call family. They feel uncertain about their goodness as Catholics, in conflict about the difference between what the Church teaches on one hand, and what their hearts and consciences tell them on the other. We question the legitimacy in this day and age of a group of select celibate men governing and making decisions that affect millions of people's lives from birth to death. We wonder if it's time for laypeople to share in that power. How can one take seriously statements by the hierarchy when one-half of the Catholic population, women, are not represented in the decision making itself? Growing concerns over the number of priestless parishes, the aging American clergy, and the alienation of youth from the Church's practices have left us wondering about the future of the Catholic Church and cause us to ask for a reexamination of alternatives.

This book's intention is to thoughtfully examine some of these issues. When I first told friends and relatives that I was writing this book, many responded by seizing upon some event in their own experience and telling me how they just could not understand the Church's teaching on an individual issue. A man told me about an uncle who had left the priesthood to marry—but who still would make an excellent priest. A woman told me how her husband had gotten an annulment from their twenty-year marriage because he was a doctor at a Catholic hospital and wanted to remarry without suffering any loss of stature on the job. Another person told me about his struggle with his homosexuality, his faithful relationship with his mate of twelve years, and his desire to practice his Catholic faith. These were not selfish, small-minded individuals, but people who wanted to consider themselves good Catholics even though they couldn't embrace everything the Church is teaching.

Ideally the confusion experienced by Catholics ought to be alleviated by advice from a sympathetic member of the clergy or by a thoughtful and prayerful reading of the Scriptures, particularly the New Testament. Turning to the clergy for answers is not always as easy as it sounds because many Catholics feel priests are too busy or are out of touch with their world. Although there are countless devoted, well-educated, sincere priests who are in fact sympathetic to the plight of wondering Catholics, they are often hesitant to say anything that could be construed as deviating from official Church teaching. The process of finding a member of the clergy to confide in and then sorting out the questions and answers is a challenge, to say the least.

Going to the Scriptures for answers ought to be an option but often it is not for most Catholics because many are not only unfamiliar with but also downright uncomfortable with the Bible, despite the fact that the Second Vatican Council urged Catholics to make themselves at home with the Good Book. Prior to Vatican II, Catholics felt inhibited about reading the Bible. They were made to feel that individual reading and interpretation of the Sacred Scriptures could lead them into error and even sin because of their limitations as laypeople. Interpreting the Bible on your own was something Protestants did. My Protestant friends would walk down the street after Sunday church services with their white leatherbound, gilded Bibles tucked in the crook of their arm. By the time they were confirmed at twelve they could recite whole passages from memory. They knew where the Beatitudes could be found, the miraculous stories of the cure of the blind man as well as the multiplication of loaves and fishes. This all seemed somewhat forbidden to me as I was growing up.

When I was in college I took a Scripture course and was introduced to the New Testament in a way that has influenced my entire life. I learned the importance of understanding the times in which Jesus spoke and taught. I became aware of the concept of the *Sitz im Leben*, the context in which a particular biblical passage ought to be understood and interpreted. It was a simple idea, but I began to see the Scriptures and their relevance to everyday life in a whole new light. No longer did I view the New Testament, or the Old Testament, as something that had to be interpreted literally. Scripture does have layers of meaning related to Jesus' time, but teachings also have to be reexamined in every age. Understanding Jesus' Jewishness, the era in which He lived, became something of a challenge and a key to understanding his message.

For example, several years ago a friend of mine who is also a Jewish rabbi questioned me about something he had heard. A Catholic friend of his had told him that one of the reasons the Church could not ordain women was that no women were present at the Last Supper when Jesus ordained his apostles. The rabbi told me he understood that the ordaining had taken place at the Passover meal. He reminded me about the centrality of the family for Jews, particularly in regard to their feasts. The rabbi assured me that a group of Jewish men would not go off to celebrate the Passover without their wives and children. It has been this principle of the *Sitz im Leben* that has most inspired my college students over the years, shedding light on new ways of thinking about Scripture and their lives as Christians. This approach to Scripture has, in part, inspired this book. I believe most assuredly that God continues to speak to us through the Scriptures and also through our human experience. Examining one against the other offers us ways to reexamine the teachings and issues confronting us today.

Sometimes I can still hear the sound of my grandmother's rosary beads as she gathered them together and slipped them back into their pouch. She was a good Catholic, and I would like to think I am, as well. I have tried to bring an intellectual honesty to this examination of some of the issues facing us as Catholics. I have raised the questions born out of human experience and presented to me by countless students, friends, relatives, and acquaintances over the past twenty years as they try to reconcile themselves with the Church they love as home and family.

PRACTICING
CATHOLIC

1

CHARGING INTEREST,
DEALING WITH CHANGE

Several years ago I had an opportunity to give a talk in Buffalo. I called my Grandmother Coakley to tell her I would be in town for a day and asked her if I could take her out to lunch. She lives alone, loves to get out, and loves her grandchildren. The conversation went something like this:

"Hi, Gram, it's me, Penny. I'm coming to Buffalo next week and thought we could have lunch at the Sassafras on Tuesday. I'll come by and pick you up about twelve o'clock."

"Well, I don't know. You see, Tuesdays at eleven-thirty I get my hair done."

"Can't you get it done another day?"

"But I always get it done on Tuesdays, and Beatrice will be expecting me."

"Who is Beatrice?"

"Beatrice does my hair, and I'm a good tipper, or so she says. She depends on my tip."

"I'm sure she does, Gram, but I'm only going to be in town for two days, and I'm giving a talk on Monday. Maybe you could make the appointment for earlier in the morning or later in the afternoon."

"Not early in the morning. Irene and I go to Mass, then to

Denny's for breakfast. It's the only day Irene's husband will give her the car. Then she drops me off to have my hair done. The hair appointment can't be later in the day because I'd have no way of getting to it. Irene does her grocery shopping while I have my hair done and then comes back to pick me up."

"How about I take you to have your hair done after we have lunch? My flight doesn't leave till six-thirty."

"The problem is Hannah [that's a cousin, one of her only living relatives] always calls me at four o'clock on Tuesday. She'd worry if I wasn't home. Do you think I could be back by four?"

"I don't know, Gram. How long does it take you to get your hair done?"

(Pause)

"When will you be in town again? I would like to see you, but this is all so complicated, and I don't know if I can change all these things."

We did have lunch, after the hair appointment and before the phone call, but the fact of the matter was my grandmother did not enjoy change and, like many of us, did not deal with it well. For many people in the Church today, there is one way of doing things: the tried is true. In our *secular* lives, however, most of us have lived through such radical changes in every area of public life, communications, transportation, and information that expecting change because it is the norm has created a situation where often we fail to see the value of long-standing traditions. Of course, there is ultimately a balance to be struck, and that process provides much of the conflict that Catholics face today.

Being Catholic has always meant for me being connected to a large extended family throughout the world. This family has a rich heritage, rooted in the person of Jesus Christ, whose followers, through the power of the Holy Spirit, continue his life and mission, passing their lessons on to future generations. Our family Bible, the New Testament, has the names of men and women who have inspired us and given us guidance throughout the centuries. Our ancestors are a motley crew of saints and sinners who have enlivened us with their religious writings, inspired us with great works of art and architecture, and moved us with magnificent music. Our family rituals are festive celebrations of remembering and making Jesus present at the Eucharist, baptizing our children, and confirming young adults in this family of faith that we call Church. We witness the joyful union of married couples, ask forgiveness for our failings, strengthen the sick among us, and ordain men to unite us and assist us in living our faith. The sacramentals, whether they are stained glass windows, rosary beads, holy water, or candles, have always reminded me that this is an incarnational Church, grounded in the human, God becoming man. The Tradition, the teachings, even the obligations, have always made me feel securely related to this family, the Church giving me a specific identity. Being Catholic is not just a state, but a process of becoming more human as we strive to realize the ideals of peace, justice, mercy, and compassion that the Church's social doctrines encourage. The characteristics of the Church that I recognized from the Baltimore Catechism as One, Holy, Catholic, and Apostolic still fill me with pride, knowing that I belong to such a strong family. And wherever I have traveled throughout the world, when I see a sign in front of a building that marks it as Catholic—whether it is a chapel, a cathedral, or a university—I feel at home. Catholic becomes us as we become Catholic, and practicing this family faith is a challenge as well as a privilege of grace.

❖

NOT SINCE MARTIN LUTHER posted his Ninety-Five Theses in 1517, putting the Reformation into full swing, has the Roman Catholic Church gone through such radical change as it has experienced in the last thirty-five years. Everything from the liturgy to daily practices to Church organization has been subject to scrutiny, questioned, and in many cases changed since the Second Vatican Council began in 1962. Change is never easy even when it is welcomed. It means readjusting, giving up the familiar and comfortable, being inconvenienced, taking risks, and in some cases having to admit that the ways of the past may not have been the best. But, of course, change is necessary. It allows for growth and revitalization.

My husband works for IBM, a giant of the computer industry. For many years belonging to IBM meant job security. Everyone thought the company had a stranglehold on computer technology. But upstarts like Microsoft and Macintosh moved in on IBM, and they had fresh ideas and new approaches that gave IBM the appearance of a tired old dinasaur, soon to become extinct. The decline of its profits and stock in the eighties shocked many. It was time for change.

In April 1993, Lou Gerstner was appointed the new IBM CEO, and the next five years were dedicated to reevaluation. Some employees lost jobs, in a company that insisted such would never happen; factories closed, people relocated, retirement packages were handed out, the mainframe was downsized, and budgets were tightened. Employees lamented that this was not the company that they had joined twenty or thirty years earlier; some predicted its downfall. However, the fact of the matter is that today IBM is stronger and better equipped to meet the needs of the future. Changes introduced have given it a shot of new life. Profits are up, stock prices are climbing, confidence abounds. IBM met the challenge of change, but it is after all just a business. It has never claimed to be inspired by God (although some diehard loyalists may think it is!) or divinely guided in its policies, so the need for serious change to comply with the rapidly changing world of technology, though it may have been uncomfortable, was accepted and addressed.

Change within the Catholic Church, however, involves more than change within IBM. The Catholic Church as a religious giant of the Western world has for centuries relied on the power of Jesus' promises to guide it and to be present forever: "Behold I am with you always, until the end of the age" (Matt. 28:20), and, "I will ask the Father and he will give you another Advocate, to be with you always, the Spirit of truth" (John 14:16–17).* These promises

---

*The Bible used throughout this book is the *Catholic Study Bible: New American Bible* (New York: Oxford University Press, 1990).

promoted the idea that taking a new direction as a divine institution could come about only after much study and prayer; if the Holy Spirit and Jesus had inspired the Church in the past to take a certain stance in regard to a teaching or practice, then it is only under the guidance of the Holy Spirit that it can be reconsidered. The Church believes that her teachings are not simply the teachings of an ordinary group of men or women, but rather are guided by the presence and power of God. Because of this belief and these promises that Jesus made to the Church, breaking with the past is difficult to address, to enact, and to adjust to within the Church. To change something, therefore, requires hours of scriptural study, studying the teachings of the Church Fathers, and an examination of historical precedent to make sure whatever is changed remains true to the original message of the gospel and the constant teaching of the Church referred to as Tradition. If the Church has articulated specific teachings, such as priests cannot marry or divorced Catholics will not have their second marriage recognized without an annulment, that teaching is believed to have benefited from the special assistance of the Holy Spirit in its formation. When, over time, whether due to changes in society or the discovery of new scientific knowledge (as in our understanding of reproduction), a teaching or practice is questioned, the teaching authority of the Church seems threatened. The inevitable question is asked, "How can this be changed when it is part of the Tradition of the Church?" How can the institution justify changes that align themselves with the modern world? Haven't its teachings and practices been divinely inspired? In many instances, people's very faith is challenged when the Church faces change because the legitimacy of a particular teaching in the first place becomes an issue. An example of this was the longtime understanding, though not formally taught, that outside the Church there is no salvation. Generations of Catholics grew up believing that if you were not a baptized Catholic, the possibility of getting into Heaven was slim to nonexistent. We even had a place, Limbo, where unbaptized people who had led charitable, morally upright lives, and especially babies, could go if they died without baptism. It was peaceful there, but they would live for all eternity without seeing God. It was the firmly entrenched belief among Catholics that our Church was the one true Faith; *we* somehow had a monopoly on God's truths. How many Catholics have worried about the salvation of their non-Catholic relatives and friends? As a child I remember convincing a friend whose parents didn't attend any church that she would go to Hell when she died if she were not baptized. I conducted her baptism myself as an "emergency" baptism in my kiddie pool on a hot summer day in July. I also remember worrying late at night as I lay in my bed that my beloved Grandmother Ryan, who was a Methodist, would not be with the rest of the family in Heaven. My cousins and I would plot ways to get her baptized by a priest without her knowing it, since she was pretty firm about her own religious convictions and was not about to convert to Catholicism on her own.

Over time, within the Church, through contact with people of other faiths and an increased knowledge and appreciation of various world religions, a greater understanding led to the Ecumenical Movement, creating a dialogue in search of our common ground. The 1964 Decree on Ecumenism *(Unitatis Redintegratio)*, and the 1965 Declaration on the Relationship of the Church to Non-Christian Religions (*Nostra Aetate:* "In Our Age") from the Second Vatican Council, both indicated giant steps forward in recognizing the truth and beauty of these other ways to find God and encouraged respect and dialogue among all people of good faith. Does this mean that the Church was mistaken or misled in teaching that outside the Church there is no salvation? Does this mean that the Church erred? How could the Church err if inspired by God?

There are other examples of changes in the Church's teaching in light of new sociological understandings. In the first few centuries of the Church, to lend money and charge interest was forbidden to Christians and was referred to as the sin of usury. Because Jewish people did not consider this wrong, they accepted the task of lending money and consequently these lenders became very successful, astute bankers. Over time the Christian attitude about lending money changed.

An even more impressive example of change occurred regarding the Church's attitude toward slavery. In Jesus' day, slavery was a part of the social fabric of life, although nowhere does he speak of it. Saint Paul does, however. In his first letter to Timothy he writes: "Those who are under the yoke of slavery, must regard their masters as worthy of full respect" (1 Tim. 6:1). And in his letter to Philemon Paul says that he is sending his runaway slave back to him and urges Philemon to treat the slave like a brother (Philem. 1:11–13). Paul also admits that in Christ there is to be no distinction between slave and freeman (Gal. 3:28, 1 Cor. 12:13), but there is no condemnation of slavery in the New Testament, and as a result Scripture was used to justify slavery by later Christians. Even Saint Augustine, the esteemed scholar and writer whom the Church has always considered an enlightened teacher, could find reasons to support slavery in his times, as the fourth century gave way to the fifth. Eventually the Church saw slavery as an evil that had to be abolished and began speaking out against it. Today the Church has very strong views about the sinfulness of enslaving other human beings and has issued many statements on human rights, but this awakening has been a gradual process mirroring the self-awareness and conscience of Western society as whole. As a human community we all are more aware of innate dignity, and ensuring mutual respect has become a world mission as well as the mission of the Church. We have come a long way in the past one hundred years on issues such as this, but there is still work to do. How to rationalize and justify the change, how to examine the self-doubt, or face the credibility gap by suggesting that what was taught was not in people's best interest, is all a part of the challenge. This is not simply a matter of saying, "Whoops, we made a mistake, that was not a good teaching, and now we'll do something different." We have evolved, not just physically or technologically, but intellectually and spiritually. The Church needs to accommodate itself to the changes in our self-understanding, without losing its core Gospel principles and values.

There are people today who believe that the Church has changed too much, compromising its history and Tradition in the process. Church organizations such as Opus Dei—which advocates a return to the Latin Mass, old-style habits as the dress of men and women in religious orders, and an authoritative monitoring system for all education in Catholic institutions—cling tenaciously to the past. There are other people who feel that many of the changes that have occurred since the Second Vatican Council—such as greater participation by the laity in parish matters, the liturgical and sacramental reforms, and updated education programs—have enhanced the life of the Church, but enough is enough, and hadn't we better keep the status quo to prevent any further erosion of Church values and practices? There are still others who feel that the reforms since the Second Vatican Council have been stalemated, and that if we don't continue to change and grow with the times, the Church will become extinct. With concerns about the dwindling priest population, outrage at the scandals created by the annulment process, and a general disregard of the Church's birth-control stance, many Catholics wonder why the Church is unable to reconsider its teachings involving such issues. Various groups in the Church often pit themselves against one another, suggesting that members of the opposition do not have the best interests of the Church at heart, or that in essence they are not the Church of Jesus Christ. There is mudslinging and name-calling by and directed toward the "conservatives," the "moderates," and the "liberals." Skepticism and resentment divide members of the same Church. There is evidence, however, to suggest that the groups feel a common devotion to the Catholic Church despite the differences of opinion, to such an extent that they are willing to try to work things out.

A cursory glance at Church history tells us that the institutional church has always been challenged from within as well as from without by various groups, often on the issue of change. In the 1300s Pope Clement V was forced by the French king to live in Avignon, France, in what became known as the "Babylonian Captivity," or the Avignon Papacy. While in France Clement V appointed numerous French cardinals, the people who elect a Pope. For seventy years France and Italy fought over where the Pope should reside. At the end of this period, after seven Avignon popes,

Gregory XI did return to Rome as Pope. When he died, a new Pope had to be elected; an Italian was chosen. But when the French cardinals left Rome after the election, they concluded that they had elected the Italian under duress, and that they would elect another Frenchman as Pope to rectify the situation. Because of all the confusion and conflict over the Italian and the Frenchman both claiming to be Pope, the College of Cardinals in Rome decided to elect a third Pope, who was considered to be the legitimate Pontiff. But imagine what this must have done to the life of the Church at the time! Still, somehow it survived.

When Martin Luther posted his Ninety-Five Theses on the cathedral doors at Wittenberg, Germany, in 1517, he was basically challenging the Church to eliminate abuses such as the selling of indulgences, the lavish lifestyles of some of the bishops in palaces and grand estates far from their constituents, and superstitious practices like devotion to relics and saints on the part of Catholic laypeople to compensate for the distance they felt from the image of a God who far transcended their lives. The controversy and scandal that ensued haunts the history of the Church because of the lasting divisions that occurred, creating separate denominations within Christianity.

In any consideration of change, it is important to keep in mind that despite the fact that the Church is led and inspired by God, it is also comprised of human beings. The community of Christian believers is made up of mortals, people like myself and whoever else may pick up this book to read it. We make bad choices, we don't always consider the consequences of our actions, we often react out of fear, we can be shortsighted, mean-spirited, and proud. We have to redress our wrongs, reconsider chosen paths, and ask forgiveness periodically. We are far from perfect. Someone in a position of authority in the Church is not immune from the weakness of our common humanity. We would like to believe that the people in authority in the Church are somehow more saintly than the rest of us and we certainly expect them to set an example to the faithful, but the fact of the matter is that any priest or bishop, or even the

Pope for that matter, does not abandon the human baggage he carries with him when he is ordained a priest, appointed bishop or cardinal, or elected Pope.

Something that has always intrigued me is the portrayal of Peter
in the gospels. At one point Jesus says to him, "You are Peter and
upon this rock I will build my Church" (Matt. 16:18). And yet despite
the fact that Peter is singled out and recognized as having a primary
position in the founding and supervision of the Church, he is also
the man that evangelists portray as the one who denies Jesus three
times before his death and runs for fear of his own life. Surely after
all the time that Jesus spent with his apostles, he must have known
of Peter's human weaknesses, and yet Peter is the one who clearly
emerges as the individual to lead the early followers of Jesus. Even
though we expect Church leaders to be paragons of inspiration and
goodness, it is important that we remember their limitations as
humans. They make mistakes and stand in need of renewal and
change as do other members of the universal Church. That the
Church continues to exist after two thousand years of struggling
with human limits is testimony to the enduring faithfulness and
inspiration of the Holy Spirit promised by Jesus.

This discussion can now turn to some of the practical considerations involved when the Church is challenged to change a practice
or a teaching. Why is this process so complex? Any change with
regard to Church teaching or practice has to be examined against
the core of the Church life, which consists primarily of three elements: Tradition, Scripture, and magisterium. The Second Vatican
Council, announced in 1959 by Pope John XXIII, was convened for
the purpose of renewal and change in the Church. The Dogmatic
Constitution on Divine Revelation (*Dei Verbum:* "Word of God"),
spelled out the interlocking factors necessary to the careful examination that had to precede any suggested change: "It is clear that
sacred tradition, sacred scripture, and the teaching authority of the
Church in accord with God's most wise design, are so linked and
joined together that one cannot stand without the others, and that
all together and each in its own way under the action of the one
Holy Spirit contribute effectively to the salvation of souls" (para. 10).

Tradition, as the first principle mentioned here, refers to the content of the Church's teaching and practices handed down throughout the generations from the time of the apostles to the present. Tradition is an essential aspect of the Church's preaching, rituals, worship, and doctrines. The sacraments, devotion to Mary, and even the New Testament itself are products of tradition. The Scripture (both the Old and New Testaments) existed for many years as part of an oral tradition before ever being committed to writing. In fact, careful study of the Scriptures over the years has revealed that there were many layers of oral tradition woven throughout the Sacred Scriptures before the canon of Scripture was finalized. It is the concept of Tradition that finalized the New Testament itself: what was transmitted orally as part of the Tradition of the Church was considered of such importance that it *had* to be set down in writing.

An important distinction about tradition needs to be made here. There is Tradition (uppercase) and tradition (lowercase). Tradition (uppercase) includes the doctrines and teachings of the Church, which are part of what is described as the Deposit of Faith. The Deposit of Faith consists of those teachings based in Scripture and considered to be essential to Christianity, such as the fact that Jesus is the Son of God, that the Church is an instrument of salvation in the world, that Jesus is really present in the Eucharist, that the Holy Spirit is present in the life of the Church. These are dogmas of faith. But there are also traditions (lowercase) that are simply customary ways of doing things and, while they may be an aid to faith, are not essential to the life of faith. For example, customs adopted by the Church at a particular time are often conditioned historically and can lose their meaningfulness or appropriateness as time proceeds. These traditions are more easily changed than Traditions. For example, for many years—centuries in fact—women kept their heads covered in church because Saint Paul's first letter to the Corinthians states, ". . . any woman who prays or prophesies with her head unveiled brings shame upon her head" (1 Cor. 11:5). I can remember as a child putting pieces of Kleenex on my head to make sure it was covered when I went into Church. As time went on, this statement was understood as referring to a specific cultural tradition for women of his time and did not necessarily apply to women for all time. Gradually the tradition of wearing veils or hats to church came to carry less significance and was no longer expected. While there are women who wear hats to church today, it is more a fashion statement than a Church rule. Similarly, not eating meat on Fridays, receiving Communion directly on the tongue, and saying Mass in Latin were all traditions that were a part of the life of the Church for a time, but times have changed. Such traditions are subject to revision or even elimination because they are not considered to be essential to the faith, they are not necessary for considering oneself a practicing Catholic or even a good Christian.

It has always been a temptation for Catholics to confuse traditions not essential to the faith with Tradition, which *is* essential to the faith. I remember great debates in my Catholic high school about whether or not Mass should be allowed in English. Mass in Latin was considered essential to the faith by many people simply because this was the way it had been done for centuries; to change this tradition seemed close to blasphemy. I had a neighbor who said he would refuse to go to Mass if it was said in English. Back in the sixties it was determined that having Mass said in the language of the people, in our case English, was of greater benefit to the life and faith of Catholics than continuing to have it celebrated in Latin, so this tradition was changed. Some of the issues raising questions in the Church today, such as mandatory celibacy for priests, are candidates for this complex debate about what is essential to the life of faith.

Sorting out Tradition from traditions is not an easy task; rather, it must be done with prayer and scholarship. It is accomplished by the official teaching authority of the Church, sometimes referred to as the magisterium, which is made up of the Pope and the bishops assisted and informed by theologians, people who have been educated at Catholic universities throughout the world as biblical, systematic, moral, and historical experts in their fields of religious/theological studies. There are theologians who are trained to know and interpret the Scripture, which will be discussed as one of the three elements to be examined before change can be made. These theologians study the Scripture in such a way that they present all the nuances of a particular word or phrase as it was used at the time of Christ. This helps to establish the meaning of Jesus' words, what was being taught or communicated in *his* day, in order that we may apply it to our own time. The task of the theologian in the Church has always been an important one because it is through such scientific study that we better understand our relationship to God and our responsibilities toward one another. Many theologians today devote their entire lives to bringing God and humans together.

However, the Church also teaches that the theologian's job is to serve the magisterium, not dictate to it what is to be taught. Occasionally the magisterium and theologians can be at odds over a particular teaching or practice. Officially it is the magisterium that acts as the final teacher on matters of faith and morals, but if, after careful study, a theologian differs with a teaching and feels that it is a matter of conscience to make this known to others, a conflict may occur. Even Saint Thomas Aquinas was questioned by the magisterium at the time about his Aristotelian leanings. Because this book is about issues in the Church that affect a great many people and therefore are concerns of various theologians, some modern-day conflicts will be apparent.

Another important element in sorting out what is essential to faith is the experience of the Christian community itself. The term used to designate this element is *sensus fidelium*. Translated, this means the "sense or the reasoning of the faithful." The rationale behind the inclusion of laypeople in Church debate is that baptism has brought all Christians into the life of the Church and given them the gift of the Holy Spirit; their prayerful reflection and experiences of God and life, therefore, hold meaning for the Church. The *sensus fidelium* factored into the calling of the Second Vatican Council 1959 by Pope John XXIII. Unlike many of the previous Church councils that were called to refute errors and promote specific teachings, the Second Vatican Council was a call to respond to the "signs of the times." The Pope referred to Matthew 16:4 in his address

Humanae Salutis, convoking the 1962 Council on December 25, 1961: "Indeed, we make ours the recommendation of Jesus that one should know how to distinguish the 'signs of the times' " (Abbott, *Documents and Speeches,* 704). Thus he recognized that the experience of the faithful in the latter part of the twentieth century was necessitating, among other things, new forms of liturgical worship, a greater appreciation of other religious traditions, and a better understanding of what it means to be Catholic in the modern world. Many Catholics and non-Catholics alike hailed the greatness of Pope John XXIII and this council specifically for including the experiences and reasoning of the very people who needed reform for their life of faith. Worship, the importance of the laity, missionary activity, the education and training of priests, greater ecumenical dialogue, and religious freedom were just some of the issues addressed at this council, which ultimately produced sixteen documents, all pastoral in nature.

Christians believe that Jesus as the Son of God entered history as human, thus grounding the Divine in our Christian human world. He revealed God to his listeners through the vivid imagery of human experiences in stories such as those of the ten lepers who are healed, the woman who finds a lost coin, the Good Samaritan who helps someone who is robbed, seed that is scattered on the ground, the good shepherd, and the prodigal son. What his listeners heard and saw related to their everyday lives. Human experience, then and now, is a vehicle for understanding God's revelation.

❖

IN A SHORT ARTICLE THAT APPEARED in the *National Catholic Reporter* in 1994, Richard McBrien, respected theologian, former chair of the theology department at Notre Dame, author of *Catholicism*, and general editor of the *Encyclopedia of Catholocism*, stresses the importance of staying focused on what is really essential to being a good Catholic: loving your neighbor, not taking revenge, being humble and a peacemaker, and, of course, forgiveness. Father McBrien is a man steeped in his love for and knowledge of the

Church. That he highlights these values as reminders to what is essential about our faith reminds us that it is these principles that must be a part of the measuring rod for or against change, whether we are talking about birth control, a married clergy, remarriage in the Church, or ordaining women. Of course as we attempt to define measuring rods we must always take caution against oversimplifying change in the life of the Church. Change for the sake of convenience, because it is more comfortable, should not compromise the ideals. We cannot, and we should not want to, throw off traditional teachings and practices without careful, prayerful consideration of the consequences to the life of the whole Church.

It is our belief that the Holy Spirit has stayed with the Church and been present to her for all these past centuries and will continue to do so precisely because the Church continues to remain faithful to the original message of Jesus. There is a story in the Acts of the Apostles where members of the Sanhedrin, thinking that the followers of Jesus are a threat to their way of life, want to have some of the apostles put to death. But one of their members, a man named Gamaliel, cautions the others with these words: "So now I tell you, have nothing to do with these men and let them go. For if this endeavor or this activity is of human origin it will destroy itself but if it comes from God you will not be able to destroy it and you may find yourself fighting against God himself" (Acts 5:38, 39). I think about this when I am teaching Church history because it reminds me that despite the mistakes that have been made in the Church, the scandals created, and the sins committed, the Church has nonetheless endured and has been a positive influence and means of salvation for countless people. I like to think that it has endured not because it is of human origin but because it comes from God. Not so long ago the Church had the courage to acknowledge its guilt in not having done enough to prevent the Holocaust; the Church also has had to acknowledge its guilt for the part it played in the Eastern Schism, the separation of the Church in the East from the Church in the West, and its responsibility for the thousands of innocent people who suffered or were killed during the Crusades and the Church-sponsored Inquisition in Spain. The Church even has recognized its error in condemning Galileo. Being able to admit shortcomings and a limited vision at a particular point in history is part of what it means to be human. Being able to reevaluate and readjust means that we are confident of God's continued presence among us.

Two of the most effective outcomes of the Second Vatican Council were the encouragement of greater lay participation in the life of the Church and the encouragement of a better understanding of the Scriptures. As the laity came to see *themselves*—not just the institutional Church—as the People of God after the Council, they were willing to take on more responsibility for the life of the Church. Becoming catechists, Eucharistic ministers, deacons, and theologians gave many Catholics a new vision of the Church and their place in it. Many of us studying theology in the seventies were no longer willing for change to come from above, but rather we had the sense that as members of the Church we were a part of the agency for change and renewal. A transformation of the Church had begun after the Second Vatican Council and we expected it to continue. The majority of Catholics were enthusiastic and hopeful about this transformation. Our identification with the Church meant that our lives, our thoughts, our activities as laypeople were essential to the future of the Church.

The second effective outcome of Vatican II was a quest on the part of Catholics to rediscover the New Testament, in an attempt to remain faithful to the Gospel during these turbulent modern times. In fact, one of the most significant documents to come out of the Council was the 1965 Dogmatic Constitution on Divine Revelation (*Dei Verbum:* "Word of God"). Because of this document, Catholics were encouraged to become more familiar with the Sacred Scriptures, the third element, along with Tradition and the magisterium, to be studied when change is considered in the Church. As was mentioned in the introduction, prior to Vatican II the majority of Catholics were not familiar or comfortable with reading the Bible on their own, without the guidance or interpretation of a priest or theologian. We listened to Gospel passages read at Mass, we hovered around the television Sunday nights for Bishop Fulton Sheen's commentaries on the Bible, and we kept important papers and records in the Family Bible, which had a prominent place in the living room. But the Bible was something Protestants, not Catholics, were familiar with. I was in awe of my Baptist friend, Elizabeth, who could recite innumerable passages from the New Testament and who seemed to have a certain power and authority over me in so doing this. After Vatican II, Bible study groups became commonplace in parishes, and a movement to publish and distribute biblical study guides got under way. The more comfortable Catholics became with the Scripture, the more their understanding and vision of the Church began to change.

Even before Vatican II, in the latter part of the nineteenth century, both Protestant and Catholic biblical scholars had made great contributions in helping us understand the Bible as a source of revelation. Their insights and scholarship became known as biblical hermeneutics. These biblical scholars encouraged a way of looking at the Scripture that included contexts of language, history, and culture, thus enabling a better understanding of the intent of the biblical writer. Such *Sitz im Leben* recognized that each book of the Bible was written by a particular person, for a particular audience, with a particular purpose in mind. It was important then to recognize and study all these particulars to get a full understanding and appreciation of the depth of Biblical writings. The study of language was critical for understanding context, since words and their meanings change over time and geographical distance.

These new interpretations amounted to a revolution in biblical studies at universities around the world, spurring further change. No longer were the words of the New Testament to be interpreted in some narrow, literalist understanding. Their meaning and mystery now could be unraveled and meditated upon, prompting action. Catholics became more familiar with the Church in the Acts of the Apostles, which showed members of the Church participating fully in its life, and modern Catholics wanted to be a part of that experience, as well. A movement to revive the diaconate began, allowing laymen a more direct, personal involvement in the Catholic Church. Women realized how active members of their gender had been in the earliest days of the Church. Catholics have become familiar with the apparent lack of continuity between the way Jesus treated women and the inequality women experience in the Church today. A movement has begun to allow women a greater role in the life of the Church today, perhaps leading to ordaining them to the priesthood. In addition, Catholics became more aware of Jesus' concern and love for the poor and the outcast, and so a renewed social consciousness to alleviate some of the world's suffering evolved within the Church. Providing relief for suffering always has been part of the mission of the Church, but in the twentieth century such practice has taken on new meaning for a greater number of people. Soup kitchens and hospices for AIDS patients have opened. People also have questioned the context of Jesus' words on divorce and remarriage.

This new intimacy with the Scriptures somewhat parallels the effects of Gutenberg's printing press on Reformation-age Europe. The first book to be printed was the Bible; because educated people at that time finally could get a Bible and read it for themselves, they became aware of the discrepancies between what they found in this written word and the decadent lives of many of the clergy at the time. This new knowledge created a credibility problem concerning the authority in the Church, so that it was easier to sway people for political, economic, or religious reasons to follow one of the new Protestant movements. Similarly, a greater familiarity with the Scriptures since Vatican II, together with the influence of modern technology and science and our changing world, has caused modern Catholics to rethink and question practices and teachings. It would be naive to believe, with all the progress the world has seen in every area of life over the past thirty years, that Catholics would be immune to questions and discussion of issues that affect their lives, including Church matters. However one may love the Church, examining what one holds as a belief is only natural and to be expected.

The past few decades have not been easy on the Church. There are some people who feel disappointed that the changes begun at Vatican II somehow have come to a halt. There are people who twenty years ago were full of enthusiasm and hopeful anticipation about the Church, but who now feel discouraged and even defeated by recent stances the Church has taken and by the perceived penchant to end discussion on important issues. Many of my students simply feel that the Church is out of touch with the real world and point out alternatives to practicing their Catholic faith, such as Zen Buddhism or yoga. I tell them the Church needs their input and support to move forward, hoping this is true. And of course there are Catholics who feel that any more change is a compromise on what is essential to the Church, and further changes will completely erode the respectability of the Church. Mother Angelica—a nun in full traditional habit who unites such Catholics with broadcasts on her Eternal Word Television Network by haranguing against the liberal members of the Church who are searching for reform, and suggesting that this is the work of the devil—has quite a following of individuals who support her admonitions against any further changes in the Church.

As this book examines some of the issues that modern Catholics wonder about, it is important to always keep in mind not only why change is difficult for the Church to undergo, but also why change is essential. The preservation of the Gospel—and the values expressed therein—and the sacredness of Tradition in the Church are paramount; when those appear to be threatened, there is naturally going to be a backlash. Each of the controversies facing the Church today will be examined from an historical point of view to understand better how the position of the Church has evolved, what the problems have been and are in trying to change that position, and what resolution may be possible for acceptable change.

As we move toward the third millennium, I hold the firm conviction that people with different views on these issues are ultimately desirous of what is best for the Church. Applying the labels "conservative," "moderate," and "liberal" to various individuals or groups undermines the good intentions of the People of God. The unity of faith and belief in the promises of Christ to remain faithful within the Church, *the People of God,* are the real impetus for change or continuity. The world today needs the message of hope and salvation offered by the Church, which remains a compass for life as practicing Catholics continue their journey.

Pope John XXIII reminded people that the Church had already survived the winds of many turbulent changes. In his address convoking the Second Vatican Council he stated, "This will be a demonstration of the Church, always living and always young, which feels the rhythm of the times and which in every century beautifies herself with new splendor, radiates new light, achieves new conquests, while remaining identical in herself" (Abbott, *Documents and Speeches,* 706). Every age has brought new challenges, and somehow the Church has survived and offered to the world a message of hope and love. This is what is central; this is what is expected today.

2

WHO SAYS SO?:
AUTHORITY IN THE CHURCH
AND PAPAL INFALLIBILITY

G.O.D. There it was, just ahead of me on the New York State Thruway, emblazoned on a truck cruising along at sixty-five miles an hour. I accelerated to catch up with G.O.D. I wanted to get a glimpse of whoever was driving, so I pressed my foot to the pedal until I was finally beside this monstrous G.O.D. truck. The red-bearded man driving G.O.D. was a modern, heavier version of the image of Jesus that still illustrates some Bibles and religious books. I stared, he waved, I waved back. In smaller letters on the side of the truck it read GUARANTEED OVERNIGHT DELIVERY. Well, wasn't that what God was supposed to do anyway: guarantee delivery? Here was G.O.D. right in our midst, delivering the goods overnight. I felt assured of a safe journey to my destination as I drove along next to G.O.D., thinking. My thoughts hopped from G.O.D. to various other topics until they rested oddly enough on the state of authority in the Church.

For centuries it has been the common understanding among Catholics, and others, that the Pope is like God in our midst. Perhaps we don't believe this literally, but somewhere in the collective psyche of Roman Catholics is the understanding that the papal presence is unique, special, as close to God as we can get on Earth. We call him the Holy Father or Your Excellency. He refers to himself as the Vicar of Christ. He has been called Pontifex Maximus, meaning "the greatest bridge"—supposedly between God and man—a term that was used by Roman emperors who believed that they mediated between humanity and the divine. However, John XXIII chose to sign his name with the title Servant of the Servants of God, which has connotations quite different from Pontifex Maximus.

In the name of God, Pope Leo the Great was able to turn back Attila the Hun's advances on Rome in 452. In order to regain Jerusalem and the Holy Land from the Muslims in 1095, Pope Urban II, in the name of God, called the First Crusade, promising remission of temporal punishment for sins to those nobles and men who fought therein. The Crusades lasted several centuries, cost countless lives, and caused great destruction, but when Urban and subsequent Popes called people to serve, they responded as though it were a call from God himself. And down through the centuries, despite the fact that Popes have been rogues and sinners as well as saints, they always have wielded impressive authority over the people they shepherd. The current Pope, John Paul II, is no exception. He appears on the front page of major newspapers on any given day that he speaks or travels outside Vatican City. There are official Pope watchers in the media whose job it is to keep us informed on whatever he is doing. And though there are many individuals among the Catholic population who indicate they do not care what the Pope says or does, he is still a newsmaker, and his words and statements are publicized for everyone to read. Even politicians and statesmen know that an audience with the Pope is something of a coup for their career. He meets with Clinton and Castro, Yeltsin and Arafat.

The issue of authority in the Church today, who tells Catholics to do what and why, is a serious one because it is at the heart of much of the ferment and debate about other issues. It has caused a great deal of turmoil on a personal as well as communal level. Authority in general is more vulnerable to criticism than it has been in the past, so it was inevitable that the authority crisis would find its way into the Church.

Today the populace as a whole is more educated and has available a tremendous amount of information on almost any topic imaginable. Cruising through the television stations on any given evening, I am blitzed by news stations throwing information at me on topics ranging from the most recent cancer research and statistics to arctic air warming and its effects. The media and modern technology, especially here in America, deliver data and facts instantaneously to the public so that we can question, respond to, and debate situations on any issue presented to us. Many of us know that given the time and motivation we could become authorities on any number of topics—in the areas of politics, science, economics, technology, as well as religion. For example, my five-year-old nephew, Mike, can rattle off dates, dimensions, and species of dinosaurs and their extinction that dazzle his listeners. I am constantly amazed at not only how much more knowledge my students possess than what was available to me at the same age but also how much more independent their thinking is. It should be no surprise to us, then, that people in general are less likely to accept, without questioning, statements or teachings on the basis of what is perceived to be a limited authority.

Anyone who has taught on a college campus in the last ten years knows that today's students are very skeptical and critical of any presentation of material suggesting that a certain theory is the final word, whatever the topic. We have lived through numerous idea revolutions where one theory has been replaced by another. It was inevitable, in view of the present cultural situation, that authority in the Church as it has been known and understood for centuries would undergo the same challenges and scrutiny that authority in other areas of life has experienced. Ecclesiastical, or Church, authority and papal authority have suffered something of a battering in recent years. While it has always been subject to misunderstanding and confusion, papal infallibility, with a Pope deciding what

Catholics should do or not do, is considered a total anachronism by many today.

Present generations have been raised with the ideals of democratic principles, insuring the active participation of people in governing and taking responsibility for their own lives. People decry a violation of human rights where democracy does not prevail and where self-determination is denied. Within the past decade, we have witnessed the fall of communism in Eastern Europe and Russia and the demise of apartheid in South Africa. Who can forget the image of people literally chipping away at the Berlin Wall or the image of the mile-long line of people in Soweto, South Africa, waiting to cast the first ballots of their lifetime? Generations living today have campaigned for civil rights and freedom for all of humankind. In the past twenty years children's rights and women's rights have been championed nearly everywhere. Pope John Paul II and the bishops frequently speak out against issues of injustice, as do leaders of other religious traditions. In 1995, when Pope John Paul II visited the United States, he chided us on our poor treatment of new immigrants. When individuals feel that they are being held back, their opinions not considered, their freedom of speech limited, there is an outcry.

Like the information explosion, this cultural geist of freedom and responsibility has affected the Church. When a tenured professor, Mercy Sister Carmel McEnroy, was dismissed without due process in May 1995 from the institution where she was teaching for signing an open letter, sponsored by the Women's Ordination Conference and published in the *National Catholic Reporter*, Nov. 4, 1994, asking the Pope to reconsider the issue of women's ordination, many Catholics were troubled and rallied to show their support of her. In 1995 the Vatican withdrew its approval of translations of the Bible and lectionaries that U.S. and Canadian bishops had worked on for several years and approved. American Catholic bishops were upset that their authority was undermined in this way by the Vatican, and some were publically critical of what had happened. When the Congregation for the Doctrine of the Faith, the official Roman Catholic body of bishops assigned the duty of safeguarding the faith from false teaching and defending the Church against heresy, issued a statement that the teaching against the ordination of women is to be understood as infallible, it was met with disbelief by many theologians and laypeople. At their annual meeting in June 1997, the Catholic Theological Society of America drew up a formal statement questioning the Vatican's stance on upholding the refusal to ordain women with a claim of infallibility and asked for more study, prayer, and discussion on this issue. In September 6, 1994, an open letter to John Paul II was published and signed by people from thirty-two countries, representing tens of thousands of people who take issue with the Vatican teaching on contraception. On June 24, 1995, the *New York Times* reported that there had been an attempt to get one hundred thousand Catholics in Austria to sign a petition to protest the Vatican's rulings on mandated celibacy for priests, sexual morality, and the ordination of women. A similar movement occurred in Germany. In June 1995 forty bishops in the United States, an ad hoc committee of NCCB, met to endorse a twelve-page statement challenging their peers, other bishops, to take a more proactive, less subservient stance in relationship to the Vatican. The statement reminded the bishops that they were not meant to be mere auxiliaries of the Pope, but that their role was to act in communion with him. Bishop Thomas Gumbleton of Detroit has suggested that Catholics ought to mobilize for change in an open, healthy, adult way, to let their voices be heard, asking the Vatican for more say in Church matters. (His work toward progress in the Church is discussed in greater detail in chapter 7.)

One of the main problems in the perception of Church authority today is the feeling that while on the one hand the Church champions human rights everywhere, on the other hand it also controls the lives of its members and is threatened by open discussion of issues related to those lives. For instance, in 1997, Bishop Fabian Bruskewitz of Lincoln, Nebraska, threatened to excommunicate anyone belonging to a group known as Call to Action. This is a national group of Catholics who come together to study and discuss various topics such as a married clergy and the ordination of women to the priesthood because they feel a need for examining these topics responsibly. Throughout the year they hold meetings where they celebrate the Eucharist and listen to speakers. It is made up of Catholic men (some of whom had to give up their active ministry in the priesthood because they married) and women who are dedicated to living out their Christian lives in light of the gospel message of justice, equality, and love. They feel called in good conscience to act upon beliefs in order to make the Church more attentive and responsive to the world today. These people are good, practicing, but questioning Catholics; when a bishop states that he will excommunicate them rather than sit down and dialogue with them, it appears that he is motivated by fear of losing control or authority. Church decisions and statements are for the most part made by a group of celibate men whose daily experiences often differ widely from those of Catholics dealing with a modern society. Increasingly, Catholics who have been raised in an atmosphere where personal freedom is considered an inalienable human right find it difficult to give quiet acquiescence to whatever the Pope and the magisterium dictate. Blind obedience is a concept of the past.

There are many Catholics who are highly educated and very well read and who are unwilling to blindly accept the Church's teaching authority on certain matters without asking questions and seeking out the reasons behind the various teachings. It is not that they don't appreciate and respect the teaching office of the Church, but they have been brought up to think, to reason, to question, and search after truth.

Take the issue of annulment, raised in Sheila Rauch Kennedy's book, *Shattered Faith*. After a twelve-year marriage to U.S. Congressman Joseph Kennedy II that produced two sons, Sheila Kennedy was appalled to discover that through annulment her marriage would be considered nonexistent. Though she herself is an Episcopalian, she gives voice to the questions of countless Catholics who wonder about the annulment process. (Her situation is discussed in greater detail in chapter 6.)

Catholics today who ask questions are not necessarily any less faithful or loyal, nor do they consider themselves to be less Catholic than their ancestors who unconditionally accepted the Church's teachings. There are many Catholics who practice their faith by going to Church to celebrate the Eucharist, who attend Bible study or prayer groups, who participate in parish councils or choirs, who contribute time and money to Church functions, but who find themselves increasingly at odds with some official teachings. It does't mean that they are antimagisterium, selfish, or uncaring. These are people who have been taught to use the gifts of intellect and freedom they have been given by God to seek the truth. Since Vatican II Catholics have been raised with the belief that they are the Church. The Church is not merely a building or the exclusive possession of its leadership. Of course, any group of people with a purpose needs organization and leadership, and the papal office establishes unity for the Church and is a position respected throughout the world. But the Church is the People of God, and assuming responsibility for who we are seems only natural. True, the Church is not a democracy, but neither is it meant to be an autocracy.

❖

IF WE WERE TO EXAMINE CHURCH HISTORY, we would see that every generation has had its problems with authority in the Church. We have only to look at the eleventh-century schism between Rome and Constantinople, when in 1054 the papal representative, Humbert, who later became Pope Stephen IX, excommunicated Michael Cenelarius, the Eastern Patriarch, over the issue of papal authority. We can turn to the turmoil and arguments of the Reformation, whether Martin Luther's problems with Pope Leo X or Henry VIII's conflicts with Pope Clement VII.

One hundred years ago the Modernist crisis began to haunt the Church. Spurred on by science, technology, and the rational movement, which examined religious faith in view of Modern culture, the Vatican was kept busy condemning philosophers and theologians who questioned traditional metaphysical thought. Though this began as only an intellectual orientation among a select number of people wrestling with questions posed by a rising scientific community, the Vatican responded by insisting that all candidates for ordination to the priesthood take an anti-Modernist oath before they could be ordained. A Church-sponsored spying organization, Sodalium Pianum, was established, though later condemned by Pope Benedict XV. The magisterium viewed the Modernist crisis as a threat to the Deposit of Faith, understood to be the teachings of Jesus as found in Scripture and the Apostolic Tradition, and in particular the doctrines and dogmas that define the Church as Roman Catholic. So conflict with authority in the Church is nothing new.

Perhaps some of the problems with authority in the Church today also relate to the present Pope, John Paul II, whose firm hand has guided the Church for almost two decades. He has been a symbol of hope, a sign of contradiction, an enigma, an "army of one" as *Time* magazine called him when they named him Man of the Year in 1995. His reign has involved much controversy and conflict. His immediate predecessor, John Paul I, died suddenly after only thirty-three days as the Church's highest ranking prelate; Paul VI, who preceded John Paul I, will long be remembered as the Pope who promulgated *Humanae Vitae*, the encyclical that reaffirmed the condemnation of all artificial means of birth control. Before Paul VI, John XXIII was Pope, a giant in his own right, who called for opening discussion to let in the fresh breath of the Holy Spirit and convened the Second Vatican Council. Many Catholics look nostalgically upon that Pope as the man who moved the Church into the twentieth century. This man inspired hope, creativity, and excitement in the Church. The present Pope and John XXIII often are contrasted, especially since John Paul II, according to some of his critics, seems to have stalemated the reforms begun at Vatican II. The present Pope considers our age a "culture of death," as he referred to it in his 1995 encyclical *Evangelium Vitae:* "Gospel of Life." He intends to celebrate the millenium as Pope, and he may well do so despite his poor health and frail appearance. Over half of the baby-boomer Catholics in this country have grown up with this Pope, although he has alienated many of today's Catholics throughout the world because of his strong stance on such key issues as birth control, married and/or female priests, and Communion for divorced and remarried Catholics. Many Catholics feel left out of his Church, despite the fact that they are not willing to give up ties to their religion and some continue to practice their faith by going to Mass and Communion.

Many of these same marginalized Catholics applaud his attempts to make the industrialized world more conscious of its social and economic responsibilities to the Third World, the disadvantaged, and the handicapped. Of his twenty-seven encyclicals, many have dealt with the Gospel ideals of creating a more just social order for all. Pope John Paul II stands as a bulwark against the materialism and greed for profit that motivates much of society. In many respects he has been the conscience of the latter part of the twentieth century: deriding us for our lack of family values, our fascination with violence, and our lack of respect for human life, sharing with us his concern for the unborn, the elderly, the dying, and the politically oppressed peoples of the world. His words are often not easy to listen to because they cause us to elevate our personal thoughts and activities, including how little we sometimes offer to one another. John Paul II has been a man of steel in his singular defense of absolute moral imperatives in a world rapidly turning to moral relativism, and one has to wonder if in some ways the world isn't better for his presence. Sometimes when I am reading of his world travels in the paper I am deeply impressed by his genuine love and concern for those he visits, whether it is the people of his native Poland struggling with their newfound democracy or the people of an African nation dancing in native costume at liturgical celebrations while he taps his fingers to the beat of a drum.

Still, he remains a source of confusion. In his own words he is a sign of contradiction, setting himself up as a modern-day prophet against this "culture of death," and he seems unfazed that his demanding moral message upsets so many. On the one hand this Pope appointed the Harvard legal scholar Mary Ann Glendon, a

Catholic, to head the Vatican delegation to the United Nations Fourth World Conference on Women in Beijing, in fall 1995, convened to draw attention to and examine the discriminatory policies and abuses against women throughout the world; he also issued the Letter of Pope John Paul II to Women, July 1995, an apology for any part the Church has played in marginalizing women. Two months previous to this, his *Evangelium Vitae* encyclical juxtaposed the culture of death that surrounds us with the admonition to remain countercultural, condemning the use of artificial birth control, abortion for any reason, as well as euthanasia, and exhibiting disapproval over the death penalty. His eloquent words about the dignity and greatness of women in the July papal letter of apology were overshadowed when he responded to the growing debate over his 1994 encyclical *Ordinatio Sacerdotalis* ("On Reserving Priestly Ordination to Men Alone"), which denies discussion of the possibility of ordaining women to the priesthood, by approving another statement issued by the Congregation for the Doctrine of Faith in October that suggested that the teaching on this issue was infallible.

Whether one likes him or not, he has had significant political as well as religious influence on the Western world. In the weeks and days before his fifth trip to the United States in the fall of 1995, every newspaper in New York City, where he was to visit, and the surrounding metropolitan area, where I live, ran articles about the Pope. There was a media blitz on TV and radio, recounting his speeches during this five-day whirlwind trip. His popularity was at a fever pitch, one newscaster describing it as "Popemania." His seventy-two trips to more than one hundred different countries have made him something of a statesman in the twentieth century, like no other religious leader before him. On two separate occasions, he has been invited to speak before the General Assembly of the United Nations, where his words became a part of history. The United States appoints an ambassador to the Vatican to ensure good diplomatic relations with the papacy, which underscores the political importance of the Vatican in the world. Even Mikhail Gorbachev, the former Soviet leader, said that he played a pivotal role in the fall of communism. "Everything that has happened in Eastern Europe in these last few years," he wrote in 1992, "would have been impossible without the presence of the Pope" (Kwitny, *Man of the Century,* 592). The Pope's alliance with the Polish group Solidarity and his public support of Lech Walesa—and the right of workers to organize—were integral to the chain of events between 1989 and 1991 that freed East European satellites from Soviet rule and started them on the way toward more democratic societies. He overruled the local bishop and ordered nuns out of Auschwitz in 1996 because their presence grievously offended Jews, and he probably has done more than any other Pope or individual to heal the centuries of wounds between the Jewish and Catholic communities, even asking forgiveness for any anti-Semitism that the Church consciously or unconsciously may have permitted to occur.

In September 1994 a United Nations meeting on the problems of world population was held in Cairo. A special papal delegation was sent in an effort to protect the Church's interest and teachings against birth control and abortion. They sided with a Muslim delegation, refusing to have these issues bulldozed. This caused quite a furor among many people who felt that the presence of this delegation stalemated some important discussions such as the feminization of poverty, the fact that the great majority of poor in the world community are women and children who have little opportunity to improve their lives because they do not have the voice or the means to claim power. In some Third World countries women still do not have rights, even over their own bodies. Human rights groups had advocated greater access to birth control for their Third World women, but the Vatican expressed strong objections to this possibility. Some felt that the Vatican did not belong at the conference at all. Pope John Paul II, determined person that he is, made sure that his message on the sacredness of human life and the evils of birth control would be heard. And despite projections of overpopulation in Third World countries, the mistreatment of women there, and the threat of diseases such as AIDS, transmissible from pregnant mother to child before birth or during unprotected sex, his message was heard, loud and clear: No form of artificial means of birth control is acceptable for Catholics, and abortion is always morally objectionable. The Pope's power had a significant effect on this meeting because he intimidated people who might otherwise have given voice to what they truly believed; unexpressed convictions could not be acted on.

If Pope John Paul II has remained such a singularly undaunted individual entrenched in tradition, it may be in part because of his own personal history. Born Karol Wojtyla, he is a man who has experienced loneliness, pain, and the death of loved ones many times. His mother died in childbirth when he was nine. His only brother, a doctor, contracted a fatal disease from one of his patients and died when Wojtyla was only twelve, and at the age of twenty he was orphaned by his father's death. He has had to stand alone, depending upon himself for much of his life. He grew up in Krakow, thirty-three miles from what would become the death camp of Auschwitz, so that his memories of childhood must be mingled with thoughts of man's inhumanity to man. In fact, in 1942 the Nazi Gestapo arrested twenty-two-year-old Karol Wojtyla in a roundup of Polish dissidents. He was released because he worked in a limestone quarry, considered vital wartime labor. The other men with him were executed. Two years later Wojtyla was hit by a German truck and left for dead. Somehow, to the surprise even of the doctors, he survived despite being unconscious for nine hours. He had to study secretly to become a Catholic priest and lived most of his life under the shadow of communism in his beloved Poland, where he was unable to practice his ministry openly. Some people have suggested that this influence of communism has strongly affected his spiritual and moral message. It is as though he sees himself as a prophet meant to speak out against communism and other evils that plague the world today.

Even when he was elected Pope, he stood alone as the first and only Pole to ever receive this honor. In May 1981, Pope John Paul II had an assassin's bullet rip through his stomach, but after the loss of five quarts of blood and six hours of surgery, once again he defied death. In 1992 he had a precancerous tumor removed from his pancreas, and more recently he underwent a hip replacement. Still he carries on.

All of these experiences have obviously affected the messenger and his message. The confrontations with death, his commitment to his faith despite the open hostility against religion in communist Poland, and his own personal pain and suffering have made him a man willing and able to stand alone, to take a position and hold on to that with the tenacity of a lion defending her cubs. In addition, he seems to have a great sense of himself as a man with a unique destiny, having arrived at the papacy despite all of the things that could have limited him or cut short even his life itself. This is a man assured of the presence of God in his life and of his abilities to overcome even the most daunting obstacles.

The Roman Pontiff has a unique place among world religious leaders. His is one of the only positions left in the world in which one individual is considered to have a type of absolute authority. The term *papal authority* can seem almost enigmatic to people in a world that regards democratic principles and forms of government as the ideal. Unfortunately, many people misunderstand the authority of the Pope as absolutist power freed from any constraints. In actuality the Pope too is subject to authority. It may sound simplistic to say that the Pope is subject to the authority of God as it is revealed in Scripture and Tradition, and that he must also take into account the authority of bishops before making pronouncements, but understanding these facts is essential to an understanding of the position of the Pope in the Church. The Pope is not supposed to be an autocratic ruler, and he would never claim to be. His position is really that of a servant to the Word of God, and his job is to attempt truthfully and reverently to interpret this Word for the Church.

While the Protestant Churches rely almost exclusively on the Sacred Scriptures for inspiration and authority, as channeled through people like Martin Luther and documents like the Augsburg Confession, the Roman Catholic Church holds that Scripture *and*

Tradition—those teachings and practices passed down through generations by official statement—are the means of revealing God to the world and therefore are authoritative for the life of the Church. The Second Vatican Council affirmed this when it issued the Dogmatic Constitution on Divine Revelation (*Dei Verbum:* "Word of God"):

> The task of authentically interpreting the word of God, whether written or handed on, has been entrusted to the living teaching office of the Church, whose authority is exercised in the name of Jesus Christ. This teaching office is not above the word of God, but serves it, teaching only what has been handed on, listening to it devoutly, guarding it scrupulously, and explaining it faithfully by divine commission with the help of the Holy Spirit. (para. 10)

The concept of the teaching office of the Church has come to be identified with emanating from a hierarchy, episcopate, or magisterium made up of the Pope and the bishops, who by virtue of their Church position are charged with this role.

The tradition of a teaching office and the Pope evolved gradually. The teaching office began to develop in the first century when the Church was trying to establish an identity. In any group, it is normal for someone or a few people to assume leadership in order to organize and ground the rest. Leadership and authoritative teaching were granted naturally to the apostles who had been actual eyewitnesses to the life and teaching of Jesus. There was no New Testament as such to depend upon as a guide or teaching tool for first- and second-century Christians, although there were collections of Jesus' words and letters from the apostles and Paul circulating among Christian communities. Official teaching relied on the living, spoken words handed down by the apostles. Church teaching was validated by showing a line of succession to an apostle. This became essential especially when groups such as the first- and second-century Gnostics, who held that there was a secret knowledge of salvation for a select few, began to influence and confuse many early

Christians; Saint Paul in his letters makes frequent reference to such false teachers. To combat fraudulent discourse in the first three centuries, the bishops, whose title derived from the Greek for "supervisor," were charged with the role of presiding over the Eucharist and supervising Church organization and teaching. Authority was passed on successively through an ordination rite called the laying on of hands, by which bishops could claim a living link to the past, directly related to Christ and his teaching. Apostolic succession became a part of the Tradition of the Church.

The idea of the Pope as having supreme authority is extremely complex but is rooted in the position of the Bishop of Rome, "Papa" as he came to be called (later Pope), as a successor to the apostle Peter, cast in a primary role by Jesus and then by the apostles and disciples in the New Testament. In Matthew 18:18–19 as well as other places in the New Testament, Peter is recognized as the leader among the apostles. He is mentioned first in most of the lists of apostles, he is often their spokesperson, he is the first apostle to be witness to the Resurrection, and in the Acts of the Apostles, a type of history of the earliest days of Christianity, he is deferred to on important matters of judgment. Because Peter lived the last days of his life in Rome, the center, so to speak, of the Western world, and was said to be martyred there, the Bishop of Rome followed in the line of Peter. Even though there were other important centers of early Christianity—such as Antioch in Asia Minor, which also claimed Peter as its founder; Alexandria, the great hub of Greek and Roman culture and learning; as well as Constantinople, the new capital of the Roman Empire—it was the Bishop of Rome who emerged as the head of the Roman Catholic Church.

As persecutions of the early Christians occurred in places like Rome because followers of Jesus were seen as a threat to the established Roman religions, and "false" teachings or heresies such as Gnosticism abounded, looking to the Bishop of Rome for support and guidance became commonplace among Christians. In addition, the need to organize as more people became followers of Jesus meant that a model for governing the Church had to be established.

The model adopted was the one most familiar at that time, that of the Roman government. Cities and their surrounding areas were divided into dioceses. Roman dress, which can still be seen in liturgical celebrations today, the Roman language of Latin, and the Roman juridical system of tribunals became the way of life in the Church. As the Roman Empire was increasingly besieged by barbarian invasions, and as the need to establish an authoritative body to determine the moral order of life for Christians (the sacramental order) was felt, the bishops of the Church assumed roles similar to that of the Roman magistrates, with the Bishop of Rome having the most importance. Advisors to the Bishop of Rome, the magisterium, also found their name and their model in the Roman magistrate. After Emperor Constantine moved the center of the Roman Empire to Byzantium in 330, renaming the city Constantinople, the people in the Western part of the empire still looked to the Bishop of Rome as a focus of unity for the Church, which had spread throughout the known world and became the official religion of the Empire.

It was probably not until the fifth century, with the very strong-willed, charismatic Leo I (d. 461), who claimed that Peter spoke through him, that the authority of the Bishop of Rome was seen as definitive in matters regarding the universal Church. Even then, this idea was rejected by the Eastern leaders of the Church around Constantinople and thus began a growing controversy between the two sections of the Church.

As centuries passed, Christianity became the means used by tribal kings and rulers to unify the people of Europe, and the position of the Pope as the head of the Church took on greater importance in their lives. By the early Middle Ages religion and government had become so intertwined that in some instances they were almost indistinguishable. Clergy collected taxes, settled disputes between neighbors, carried out punishments for crimes. They presided over large estates, were in charge of educating the nobles, and were patrons of the arts. The Frankish king and father of Charlemagne, Pepin the Short, in 754 gave the papacy a tract of land in central Italy, covering about a third of the country, to rule. Pope Stephen II and subsequent Popes then became temporal as well as spiritual leaders over these lands, known as the Papal States, and some of the Popes spent more time managing their lands and wealth than attending to the spiritual needs of their people. The history of successive papacies reads like a melodrama of intrigue as holders of the office searched for its identity. Some Popes supported emperors and kings, others fought them, some even led military expeditions. Pope Formosus (d. 896) was exhumed after his death, propped up in full papal garb, put on trial for his misdeeds by some bishops, and finally thrown into the Tiber River. Leo V (d. 903) was thrown in prison after only thirty days as Pope and then murdered, while John XI (d. 936) is generally regarded as the illegitimate son of Pope Sergius III. John XII (d. 964) was elected at the age of eighteen only to be deposed years later by a Roman synod. Then came the Renaissance Popes, many of whom led dissolute lives, fathering children and living so extravagantly that they were a scandal to the people. To be sure, there were also many good, holy, sincere men who occupied the chair of Peter, for example, Leo VII (d. 939), who promoted clergy reform; Gregory X (d. 1276), remembered for trying to bridge the gap between the Church in the East and the Church in the West; and Innocent V (d. 1276), a Dominican scholar concerned about clerical education and rehabilitation. By the high Middle Ages, however, with the election of Leo X (d. 1521)—notorious for personal extravagance, military campaigns, and the construction of Saint Peter's in Rome, which led him to use the services of the infamous John Tetzel to sell indulgences in order to pay off his debts—the final scene had been set for the Reformation. One of Martin Luther's chief calls for reform involved not only the clergy but also the papacy itself. In the 1530s, there was a general recognition both within the Church as well as outside of it that corrective measures and renewal were absolutely essential; accentuating the spiritual and moral authority of the Pope was paramount.

The Council of Trent, called by Pope Paul III in 1545 to restore order to the Church after the Reformation, passed decrees spelling out exactly what was to be believed and practiced by Catholics. The council aimed to clear up any confusion between what the Protestant reformers were teaching and what was to be practiced by Catholics throughout the world. An Inquisition was launched to punish false teachers, and an Index of Forbidden Books was drawn up to prevent Catholics from reading material contrary to Church teaching. At the same time, the movement insisting on the absolute teaching authority of the Pope became entrenched to prevent further erosion to the unity of the Catholic Church.

The next several centuries saw a rise in nationalism all over Europe, an Age of Discovery, political revolutions on both sides of the Atlantic, the Enlightenment, and a steady influx of scientific ideas and discoveries that were minor revolutions in themselves in the Western world. It was almost inevitable that by the nineteenth century a Church council would be called to shore up beliefs and practices against the threat of the Modern spirit, which included materialism, atheism, and rationalism. In 1864 Pius IX published a Syllabus of Errors listing and condemning those of Modern thinking, and several years later he convened the twentieth general, or ecumenical, council, of the Church—Vatican I (1869–70)—to confirm solemn opposition to the evils of Modern thinking and also to promote a definition of papal infallibility.

The role of the Pope was still a very controversial issue at the time of Vatican I, the end of the nineteenth century. How to keep the Church unified amid a barrage of new ideas, how to make sure the Church remained true to its teachings, and how to keep the Church unified despite the diversity of its people were questions that all seemed to converge in the papacy. It was the belief of many, particularly among the magisterium, that what Christianity needed was an affirmation in no uncertain terms of the strength of its teachings and the absolute authority of those who do the teaching, particularly the Pope. Despite the fact that the supreme teaching authority of the Pope was generally accepted, some objected to passing the First Dogmatic Constitution on the Church—of Christ *Pastor Aeternus*, meaning "Eternal Shepherd"—formally stating that the Pope could speak infallibly on matters of faith and doctrine. Of the 774 participants at this council, one-fifth were opposed to making such a statement, and out of protest, 61 of this number left Rome before the final vote. The constitution was formally proclaimed, however, decreeing the pope as the chief teacher and ruler of the Church. *Pastor Aeternus* specifically states:

> When the Roman Pontiff speaks *ex cathedra*, that is, when as the pastor and teacher of all Christians in virtue of his highest apostolic authority he defines a doctrine of faith and morals that must be held by the Universal Church, he is empowered through the divine assistance promised him in blessed Peter, with that infallibility with which the Divine Redeemer willed to endow his Church. (*Encyclopedia of Catholicism*, 664)

This is not saying that the Pope *personally* is infallible but rather that he gives expression to the infallibility that is a gift to the whole Church. In other words, the Pope cannot speak *personally* and expect Catholics to accept his dogma, nor does infallibility depend on the gifts of a *particular* Pope. He speaks for the Church and from the Church, as a servant to the Church. Vatican I placed several restrictions on the exercise of papal infallibility: One, the Pope must be speaking ex cathedra, which means he must make a formal statement that he is speaking as the head of the Church. Secondly, he must be putting forth a teaching of faith or morals, not a teaching on practice or discipline. Thirdly, it must be very clear that he intends to bind the whole Church to belief and adherence to the teaching. All three of these elements must be present and clearly stated. In fact there are to date only three truly infallible statements: *Pastor Aeternus* itself, the dogma of the Immaculate Conception (that Mary was conceived without Original Sin), and the teaching of the Assumption of Mary, body and soul, into Heaven.

Because the issue of papal infallibility was still a concern at the time when John XXIII called Vatican II, this topic was addressed at the council. Vatican II issued a further clarification in its Decree on the Bishops' Pastoral Office in the Church (*Christus Dominus*:

"Christ the Lord"). First, it insisted that the college of bishops, either assembled in council or dispersed throughout the world, could teach infallibly in communion with the Pope. This was meant to show that infallibility was not the prerogative of just the Pope, but embraced the collegiality of all the bishops so that infallible teaching was clearly that of the *whole* Church. As the Decree states:

> For their part, the bishops too have been appointed by the Holy Spirit and are the successors of the apostles as pastors of souls. Together with the supreme pontiff and under his authority, they have been sent to continue throughout the ages the work of Christ the eternal pastor. Christ gave the apostles and their successors the command and the power to teach all nations, to hallow men in the truth and to feed them. Hence through the Holy Spirit who has been given to them, bishops have been made true and authentic teachers of the faith, pontiffs, and shepherds. (para. 2)

The Vatican meant to affirm the teaching role of all the bishops and the importance of dialogue among all the bishops before setting forth any kind of teaching, much less that labeled infallible. When in May 1994 Pope John Paul II issued the statement *Ordinatio Sacerdotalis*, indicating that the Church did not have the authority to ordain women to the priesthood, there was controversy about whether this way was to be understood as an infallible statement. When Cardinal Joseph Ratzinger as head of the Sacred Congregation for the Doctrine of Faith on behalf of the Pope issued an October 1995 statement that it was to be received as infallible, many Catholics were skeptical and some were outraged. The argument given against its infallibility, as recently as June 1997, in a paper issued by the Catholic Theological Society of America (mentioned in chapter 1), was that members of the body of bishops were not in concert about this teaching on women's ordination, and in fact many disagreed with it. How, then, could it be infallible?

While many issues in the Church may cause consternation—

whether birth control, divorce and remarriage, or women's ordina-tion—this issue of papal infallibility is key. When Catholic theologians or laypeople feel cut off from further discussion, questioning, or explanation, we wonder about an authority that dismisses members with the implication that the Pope is running the Church with an iron hand. I have frequently heard students and friends make the statement "But only God is infallible." Brian Tierney, a theologian who has written a comprehensive study on papal infallibility, *Origins of Papal Infallibility, 1150–1350*, feels that infallibility is theo-logically incorrect because it has not been a part of the constant teaching of the Church, but rather is something that evolved slowly over time due to historical conditions. We know that even leaders of the Church are members of the human community—and as such are inherently weak, often failing to act on the potential created by God for us, prone to selfishness, self-deception, and oppressive rela-tionships. So it is difficult to say that even with divine assistance an individual or a group could adequately define something as infallible for all time. Given the fact that all of our human statements, even those found in Scripture, are limited by human understanding and interpretation, how could any words, at any time, be considered free from error? Even at the time that Vatican I was defining papal infalli-bility, the question was raised about Popes who had erred in issuing statements over the centuries. There were and still are questions about how the concept of papal infallibility cripples ecumenical dialogue.

Our Jewish, Protestant, Muslim, and Buddhist brothers and sis-ters find it somewhat presumptuous when Catholics state that the Pope can speak infallibly. Most Catholics themselves do not under-stand the full meaning and conditions and consequences of this concept. I have yet to hear even a pastor attempt to openly and hon-estly explain exactly what is meant by papal infallibility to his congre-gation. That I grasp it is due only to the fact that I went on to graduate school to study theology.

The concept of infallibility has created a credibility gap, leading some individuals to dismiss the Pope altogether or dismiss any

Church teachings because they perceive a presumptuous, elitist attitude underlying myriad other issues. In short, they consider the Church's teaching authority as out of sync with the rest of the world, which encourages questioning, dialogue, democracy, and creativity. Unfortunately, the role of the Pope, originally a symbol of Church unity, has become a symbol of disunity for many.

We live in an age of searching for the truth. Many of us know that the truth is always a little ahead of us in terms of what we can realize and comprehend, that truth is not necessarily something we grasp once and for all but something that grasps us. Given the diversity of the human community, there is always something more for us to discover. The problem perhaps lies not in a lack of belief that absolute truths do exist, but rather in the fact that we are always in the process of pursuing them and they seem just beyond our reach.

The Pope is the presence of God in our midst on our journey through life, but so are the rest of the bishops and each baptized member of the Church who make up the People of God, the Body of Christ. As we travel along, it is important that we listen, search honestly, and read the signs of the times so that we can guarantee delivery of the good news.

3

DON'T BAPTIZE THEM
IF YOU WON'T ORDAIN THEM:
WOMEN, ORDINATION,
AND THE CATHOLIC CHURCH

There is a Hebrew prayer that begins, "I thank you, God, that you have made me a man rather than a woman." When I asked a rabbi about this particular phrase, he told me that the prayer really was not meant to slight women, or to suggest that in God's eyes it was somehow better to be a man than a woman, but that the prayer of thanksgiving was offered as such because only males were allowed to officiate at Hebrew services in ancient times. The prayer was simply that of a man who was grateful that his creation as a male rendered him able to serve God at the altar.

Today there are women rabbis within Reform Judaism to lead services, sharing a special relationship with God because of this privilege. However, many women, in particular within the Roman Catholic tradition, are still denied the opportunity to stand in that special relationship to God at religious services. Few people would go so far as to verbalize the idea that women are less worthy than men in this regard, but in fact this idea of women's secondary status is not foreign to Catholics—indeed, not foreign to many in society as a whole. Despite the fact that the Pope and the Vatican in encyclicals laud the gifts made by women to the Church, as Pope John Paul II did in a Letter to Women issued in June 1995, the bare truth is that ordaining women to the priesthood will not even be considered by the Church hierarchy, which has gone so far as to suspend discussion or debate on the topic. So, despite the recent accolades heaped upon the female of the species by the Vatican, what women are reading between the lines is that we are still not good enough to serve God as priests. A biological difference seems to gives one-half of the human race a unique place in relation to God.

Even when women *have* been accepted to ordination in other Christian denominations, they often are denied some of the opportunities that their male counterparts are offered in their service to God. One would expect that the religious life would provide an environment free of the secular limits placed on women. Pope John Paul II in his Letter to Women acknowledges, "Women's dignity has often been unacknowledged and their prerogatives misrepresented ... often relegated to the margins of society and even reduced to servitude," and he personally apologizes in this letter for any role the Church has played in this subjugation. He also recognizes that "when it comes to setting women free from every kind of exploitation and domination, the gospel contains an ever relevant message which goes back to the attitude of Jesus Christ himself" (para. 3). Yet it seems hauntingly hypocritical while claiming that we are all one in Christ—"There is neither Jew nor Greek; there is neither slave nor freeperson; there is not male or female. For you are all one in Christ Jesus" (Gal. 3:28)—to also declare that the Church does not have the authority to ordain women to the priesthood, as in the letter *Ordinatio Sacerdotalis* in 1994 (discussed in greater detail later in this chapter).

There is a long history of considering women inferior to men in some religious traditions. Much of Western civilization is based on a patriarchal mode of organization and operation, including the Judeo-Christian religious tradition. A patriarchy is a social organization marked by the supremacy of the father in the clan or family, the legal dependence of wives and children on the father, and the reck-oning of descent and inheritance in the male's line of the family. Patriarchies probably developed in ancient times, when the survival of the tribes of humankind was a constant struggle, and roles for survival were assigned to various members of the group based for the most part on biological considerations. Women bore and nur-tured the children. Because such activity confined them to the home for long periods of time, they were also given the task of keeping the fire going at the hearth and other chores associated with the dwelling. It was "natural" in ancient times for women to take care of the children, cook, and keep the house. Men, on the other hand, were forced out of the house to hunt and provide for those who had to stay home. These originally were tasks for sur-vival, but over the centuries they became so closely associated with maleness or femaleness that to cross the line, perform tasks not tied to one's gender, was taboo. This is not to say that women never hunted and men never stayed home, but such activity for long periods of time was not typical. As years passed and human-kind became less nomadic and more sedentary, male tasks evolved to become watching over the land, controlling its produce, pro-tecting the group from invaders, and dealing with outsiders. Women continued to be confined to tasks around the home. The broadened social arena experienced by men led to a perception that men were "in charge," and gradually the idea of women as dependent on the male, as the "weaker" sex, was ingrained into the collective psyche of civilization. The fact that women in general are smaller and weaker physically (though usually they tend to have more endurance), also translated into a view of them as inferior to men.

The case for a patriarchal system of organization and attendant perceptions of women was furthered in the Judeo-Christian tradi-tion through the religious myths found in the book of Genesis, which were intended to explain the origin of the world and creation of humankind, as well as the introduction of evil into the world. These explanations have had an enormous influence on the way that men and women have been viewed and understood, not only in the Judeo-Christian tradition but in Western society as a whole. For centuries these myths were taken as God's Divine Word, to be interpreted literally.

There are actually two accounts of the creation of the world and of humankind in Genesis. They are somewhat contradictory or complementary, depending on one's point of view. The first creation account comes from the priestly tradition, which was intent on showing God's holiness and power over all creation. It starts at chapter 1 and continues through chapter 2, verse 4a, with God creating the world from nothing at the beginning of time. For five days God separates night from day, the skies from the water, and makes all the birds, fish, animals, and plants that fill the earth. All that he creates is good. On the sixth day God creates humankind, man and woman together: "Then God said, Let us make man in our image, after our likeness. Let them have dominion over the fish of the sea, the birds of the air, and the cattle and over all the wild animals and all the creatures that crawl on the ground. God created man in his image; in the divine image he created him; *male and female* he created them." (Gen. 1:27; emphasis mine). In this account humankind arrives as the pinnacle of creation, man and woman are seen as good, and in fact *together* man and woman reflect the image of God. There is an equality and a solidarity between man and woman, who are made in the likeness of God here.

But this balance is often overlooked in light of the second and more colorful creation account, which biblical scholars tell us is from another tradition, the Jahwist, which had the duty of explaining why, if creation comes from God and is good, there is sin and disobedience in the world.

This second account begins at chapter 2, verse 4b, in Genesis, with God creating man out of dust at the beginning of the process of creation. Seeing that man is lonely, God begins making creatures who could serve as man's helpmate. After several unsuccessful attempts at creating a satisfactory helpmate—"The man gave names to all the cattle, all the birds of the air, and all the wild animals; but none proved to be the suitable helpmate for man (Gen. 2:20)—God puts man in a deep sleep, takes a rib from his side, and molds it into a woman: "This one shall be called 'woman' for out of 'her man' this one has been taken" (Gen. 2:23). It is from this second creation account that the idea of woman as supplementary or complementary to man is derived. Here woman is not only created *after* man, but is taken from his side. Later in this same creation myth there is an attempt to explain the origin of evil, and of course woman is the source of evil into the world.

Everyone knows the familiar story in which a snake slithers around a tree, calls to the woman Eve, and is able to seduce her into taking a bite from the fruit of the forbidden tree. Poor weak Eve. She then hastens off to seduce the man into sharing her sin of disobedience—or pride, as some theologians interpret it. After eating the fruit Adam and Eve are subsequently banished from the Garden of Eden, and to the woman God says: "I will intensify the pangs of your childbearing; in pain you shall bring forth children, yet your urge shall be for your husband and he shall be your master" (Gen. 3:16). To the man God says: "Because you listened to your wife and ate from the tree I had forbidden you to eat, Cursed be the ground because of you. In toil shall you eat its yield all the days of your life" (Gen. 3:17).

Eve is morally weak because she gives in to the devil, and she is viewed as a seductress because she involves man in her sin. The man is made master of the woman, pain and work are associated with sin, and the husband is remonstrated for listening to his wife. A literalist interpretation of this creation account enabled people for centuries to subjugate and discriminate against women, and denigrate her role in society. It is human nature to look for scapegoats to blame for one's problems and failures. Early Fathers of the Church, as well as more modern commentators, have used this text as fuel for their tirades against the wiles of women. Few people looked to the first creation account to see that the image of God is reflected as man and woman together, not separately. It is together that they continue the creative power of God at work in the world. An honest examination of this first text reveals that man and woman are both good in themselves as the creation of God and that neither is above the other.

I remember as a child of about ten, the first day of school in September, walking with my friends when a group of boys loomed in front of us. The leader of the pack yelled that Eve and girls were the reason we all had lost our summer vacation and had to go to school. If Eve hadn't given in to the Devil's temptations, we'd still be living in the Garden of Eden, he stated matter-of-factly. I agreed with him at the time and felt a certain shame in my ancestor Eve, that she hadn't been a bit stronger in the face of the Devil's temptings. I felt partly responsible that we all were on the way to school instead of the park.

Even today we are inclined to take a childlike, literal view of these texts. After all, this is God's Word; isn't what was spoken and recorded in Scripture the truth? One only has to consider the furor that swept the religious world when Darwin and other scientists suggested that the creation of the world took more than seven days and that the human race as we know it today evolved from more primitive beings. Some people still interpret the Bible literally or at least pick and choose which passages they will interpret literally for their own particular purposes. It has taken thousands of years to understand the place of women in life and society as equal to that of man, as having the same stature and place before God, an equality recorded in the first creation account. The problem, however, is that while this may be known and accepted intellectually, the truth of it is not implemented as a part of everyday life. Discrimination against women on the grounds that they are not capable of leadership outside the domestic arena still affects many aspects of life.

Nowhere is this more apparent than in the issue of women's ordination—or nonordination, as I think of it—to the priesthood in the Roman Catholic Church. After the close of the Second Vatican Council in 1965, in part because of the council's Dogmatic Constitution on the Church (*Lumen Gentium:* "Light of Nations"), emphasizing the universal call to holiness of *all* of God's people (para. 14), a movement advocating the ordination of women to the priesthood grew within the Church. Members of the Leadership Conference of Women Religious (LCWR), and even laywomen, were speaking out and making inroads into many aspects of the Church's life other than the more traditional roles they always had filled. For centuries they had been responsible for religious, educational, and medical institutions and programs, missionary activity, and social work. Often these roles were assumed by women in religious congregations whose vows of poverty, chastity, and obedience had freed them to dedicate their lives to service in the Church. But Vatican II's Dogmatic Constitution on the Church highlighted the importance of the *laity* for the life of the Church: "These faithful are by baptism made one body with Christ and are established among the people of God. They are in their own way made sharers in the priestly, prophetic, and kingly functions of Christ" (para. 31). The constitution did not make a differentiation here between *men* and *women* in referring to the laity. Laywomen had always played an important role in the Church: for example, Paul makes mention of women like Phoebe, who ministered to the Church at Cenchreae (Rom. 16:1); Lydia and Chloe were active supporters of his ministry (Acts 16). Now for the first time since the earliest days, of the Church, women as a whole began to realize that they had special gifts and talents and insights to bring to Catholicism. After all, they shared in the "priestly, prophetic, and kingly functions of Christ." In the early days after that council more women began studying theology and enrolling in courses to help them develop their talents and prepare to serve the Church. Hope abounded, with many individuals believing it was only a matter of time before women would be admitted to ordination, especially when Protestant denominations began this movement in the early seventies.

At the same time, of course, the secular women's movement was in full force, promoting the rights of women at work, demanding better health care and day care for women, and publicizing the need to give women the dignity and respect that is accorded to men in every area of life. Sexual harassment and abuse of women became issues, and women's studies courses found their way into colleges and universities, offering education on topics ranging from the over-looked contributions of women in history to the enslaving stereo-types women had endured for centuries.

A button I saw someone wearing over twenty years ago read, DON'T BAPTIZE THEM IF YOU WON'T ORDAIN THEM. Baptism makes us all children of God, with no distinction between male and female, no exclusionary clauses: "For all of you were baptized into Christ, have clothed yourself with Christ. There is neither Jew nor Greek; there is neither slave nor freeperson; there is not male or female. For you are all one in Christ Jesus. And if you belong to Christ, then you are Abraham's descendents, heirs according to the promise" (Gal. 3:27–29). The button prompts the questions: "If we are all baptized equally into the life of Christ, if we are all one in Christ, then how can we deny a full sharing in the sacramental life of the Church to any of its members? Why bother to baptize women at all if the Church does not really believe in their full equality with men? How does one *justify* denying women a call or vocation to ordination? Isn't a universal call to holiness sufficient grounds to demand that women who believe themselves called to serve the Church as ordained ministers be given the right to become priests?

In 1975 the first Women's Ordination Conference was held, and the following year WOC became an official organization, with Ruth Fitzpatrick its first full-time employee and president. Momentum for women's ordination was building, and true to form, the Vatican knew it had to respond. Also true to form, the Congregation for the Doctrine of the Faith released in October 1976 an official teaching, the Declaration on the Question of the Admission of Women to the Ministerial Priesthood, referred to as *Inter Insignores* (meaning "among the characteristics").

This document stated that women could not be ordained to the priesthood because the Church did not have such authority, an argument resting on three major premises. First, Jesus had not chosen women to be among his twelve apostles, and therefore women could not have this special privilege of entering into the inner sanctum of associates as ordained priests who mirrored the twelve apostles. Second, because the long-standing tradition of the Church had never allowed the ordination of women, the Church did not have the authority now in the twentieth century to do so. Third, because women physically did not resemble Christ as a man, they could not represent him sacramentally at the altar or at any other sacraments. *Inter Insignores* immediately touched off a tremendous amount of anger and debate. Women felt betrayed. Women were gaining equality with men in other segments of society, but here in the Church the Vatican was committed to keeping women in what the hierarchy thought was their place. The debate fostered biblical and theological research supporting or opposing the Church's teaching. The debate continued with the formation of theological study groups within major academic associations such as the Catholic Theological Association and with the creation of other, grassroots groups to promote discussion and encourage a rethinking of this issue by the teaching authority of the Church. Some people, myself included, believed that with modern biblical research on our side, we could convince the Vatican that this particular teaching was well within the Church's ability to reexamine and change. Certainly, the Church had changed its position on other major issues in the past, such as slavery.

Feminist theology was unfolding, examining many practices in the Church that alienate and subjugate women. The noninclusive language used in liturgy and sacraments, referring to God as male, was criticized, and change was demanded. The theologian Rosemary Radford Ruether put it succinctly when she said that women in the Church suffered from "linguistic deprivation and eucharistic famine" (*Women-Church,* p. 5). Recently at Mass I was jarred when I heard myself in chorus with the rest of the congregation during the recitation of the Nicene Creed: "For us *men* and for our salvation came down from Heaven" (emphasis mine). I thought of the centuries in which this basic statement of faith had been proclaimed throughout the world. And despite the fact that we might argue that the word "men" is used generically, nonetheless it still leaves out half of the human race. There are dozens of examples like that in the celebration of the Eucharist and other sacraments. When the new Catholic Catechism, which was intended to be an official guide for the faithful on what was to be believed and practiced, was published in the United States in 1994, the fact that it still used noninclusive language *twenty years* after attention had been drawn to the importance of inclusion struck critics as proof that the Church was becoming increasingly out of touch with the modern world. At a meeting of religious educators I attended in 1995, I learned that few people had ordered the Catechism as a teaching tool, partly on the grounds that the writers had ignored requests that it use more inclusive language. My students in a girls' high school are very sensitive to texts that exclude them by using words that are male-gendered; they want to be included. In section 1484, which deals with the sacrament of penance, the new Catholic Catechism reads: "Christ is at work in each of the sacraments. He personally addresses every sinner: 'My son, your sins are forgiven.' He is the physician tending each one of the sick who need him to cure them. He raises them up and reintegrates them into fraternal communion." A section such as this raises the questions: Why does it always have to be sons who are forgiven? and Why do we have to be raised to a "fraternal" communion? Women, even young ones, are sensitive to such things and trying to go into long explanations about why the wording is such does not satisfy them.

Disillusionment was evident in feminist theology, which pointed to the fact that it was a group of celibate men who talked about and ruled upon the most intimate details of human life, including sex, marriage, and reproduction, without the knowledge, experience, and insight of one-half of the human race. There are no women at papal synods involved in writing encyclicals or other documents, even on issues that relate to family life. There are rarely women at ecumenical councils or national councils of bishops, where important teachings are promulgated and Church matters discussed. Occasionally a token female is included in such a grouping, but she has little real influence. The roles and duties of making official statements and rulings are assigned to an all-male clergy. When a child is baptized into Christianity and specifically into the Catholic faith, there is not distinction made between the way that a male child is baptized and the way that a female child is baptized. The words and actions of the sacrament are the same. They both are baptized into full membership within the Church, equal before God as his children. They are both created in the image and likeness of God, and they are both full participants in all of the sacraments of the Church save one, ordination to the priesthood.

The same year that the Pope issued *Inter Insignores* the Pontifical Biblical Commission, an official group of biblical scholars and theologians, many of whom are priests themselves, stated that there was not enough evidence in the New Testament to either support or disallow the ordination of women, leaving the door ajar to continue examining the issue. In fact, it cited places in Scripture where women helped to found Churches, functioned in public worship, taught, and prophesied. Twenty years later, in a March 18, 1996, speech delivered in Rome by the Reverand Douglas Brown, a representative in Rome of the worldwide Anglican Communion, he admitted that the Pontifical study was used as evidence to support the ordination of women to the priesthood in the Anglican Church. It was suggested that Jesus' choice of twelve men was a choice of twelve *people* and not a question of gender as such. Wasn't the choice of the twelve ultimately to witness to the life and resurrection of Jesus? And since women were in fact witnesses to Jesus' life, and specifically in three of the gospels the first people to witness the Resurrection, weren't they equally worthy of witnessing to his life and Resurrection *today*? The choice of twelve men to follow him on a day-to-day basis may have been merely the culturally acceptable norm of the time; it would have been rare for a woman to adopt the nomadic existence of the apostles.

Theologians cite Jesus' close relationship with many women in the gospels, countercultural at the time, in itself a freeing and saving element in his ministry. He ate with women (Luke 10:38–42); touched those who were considered unclean (Luke 13:11–14) and outcasts, like prostitutes who came to wash his feet (Luke 7:36–40);

forgave women, like the one caught in adultery, whom the Pharisees wanted stoned (John 8:3–11); cured them, like the woman who had been hemorrhaging (Luke 8:40–48); and made obvious friendships with them, like Mary and Martha (Luke 10:38–42; John 11:11–44). He used them as positive examples in his parables and teaching (Luke 14:20–21; 15:8–10; 18:1–8; 21:1–4). What would seem ordinary to us today in terms of the way that Jesus related to women must have seemed extraordinary to his contemporaries, and was in fact a position for which he was criticized by the scribes and Pharisees. Nowhere in the Gospels does Jesus ever exclude women or allude to them as inferior to men. So why must we think that Jesus would desire that they be excluded from the ministry of the priesthood today? Still, the official Church holds tenaciously to the argument that Jesus did not call a woman to be an apostle and that women were not included at the Last Supper when Jesus ordained the twelve.

While the Gospels do not mention women at the Last Supper, it seems unlikely that Jesus, given his Jewish heritage, would pull the apostles away from their families for the celebration of the Passover, which was in fact the meal being celebrated at the Last Supper. When I was being interviewed over the phone by a young Jewish man working for *New York* magazine about a course I was giving at Fordham, he was curious about why women could not be ordained based on the fact that they were not ordained at the Last Supper.

"Do you think," I asked him, "that Jesus would have asked his apostles to leave their families and celebrate the Passover with him but *without* their wives and children?" "Well, no," he responded, similar to a discussion I'd had with a Jewish rabbi, previously cited in the introduction. "Passover is a family celebration. Of course the wives and children would have been there." "My point exactly," I said to him. "Just because the women aren't mentioned *doesn't* mean they weren't there." It is a biblical literary device to count only the men in certain situations or to make mention of only their presence. This is the case in the Gospel of Mark (6:44), where the author of Mark's Gospel records that Jesus fed five thousand "men." (Obviously, we can assume that women and children were there, as well.) So while the Gospel accounts tell us only of the apostles' presence, any Jewish person would tell us that Passover is a time of family celebration. The women prepare and serve the food; the youngest child asks the questions that are part of the Passover ceremony, or Seder. If Jesus was true to his Jewish heritage, as we have every reason to believe he was, then the wives of the apostles and others close to Jesus would have been present at this event when he said, "Do this in memory of me." These words of Jesus long have been held by the Church as the words commissioning or ordaining Jesus' disciples to repeat this meal as a memorial of Jesus' life, death, and Resurrection. If what happened at the Last Supper was an ordination rite, and if we can hold out the possibility that women were present, then perhaps Jesus did mean to include women when these words were uttered. The fact that Leonardo da Vinci did not paint women in his portrayal of the Last Supper does not mean that they were not necessarily present. It is hard to believe that these men would prepare the meal, set the table, light the candles, read the Old Testament account of the Passover, without their families. So who was Jesus addressing when he said, "Do this in memory of me"? Couldn't it have been the entire group of people gathered to celebrate the Passover with him? Obviously, this is a hypothetical question, one that cannot be answered here and now or even ever, but there is simply not conclusive evidence in this biblical account to suggest that Jesus' actions and words at the Last Supper were meant to be a signal for *only* an all-male clergy to be ordained and to rule the Church as we know it today.

If nothing is definitively stated, one cannot use Scripture to defend a definite point of view. What is written may not be *all* there is to say about a given story or teaching. The Gospels are actually silent on what Jesus intended for the future of his followers. They are silent about many aspects of Jesus' life, including the first thirty years or so. We cannot fill those gaps with what we would like to appear there, but if there is compelling reason to believe that something was most likely the case, as in pointing out that there were perhaps women present at this Passover celebration, then we can't rule out the possibility altogether. There were no priests as we know them in apostolic times. One could argue that Jesus did not intend to ordain these men priests at the Last Supper in the way that we know the priesthood today. The apostles and those who followed them adjusted their organizational structure and customs to suit the needs of particular times. In fact, the orders of deacons and bishops preceded that of presbyters, or what we call priests today. Just as changes occurred in the early Church to accommodate the growing needs of the faithful, so should that same confidence in the presence and power of the Holy Spirit to guide the Church be used as an argument to attempt to meet the needs of *these* times.

The fact that all the apostles were Jewish also comes up in the debate about ordaining women. In the earliest days of the Church, it was argued that one could become a follower of Jesus only by becoming a Jew first because it was believed that Jesus had come as the Messiah to fulfill the promises and prophesies made to the Israelites. Gentiles were uncircumcised and considered unclean because they did not live according to the dietary laws. This major controversy faced by the early Church is recounted in the Acts of the Apostles, chapters 10 through 15. Although an original criterion for witnessing to Jesus and celebrating the Eucharist was that of being Jewish, a council with Peter and Paul and the other apostles was called at Jerusalem to examine this qualification. It was decided that Gentile converts would not have to be circumcised and would be able to follow a modified version of the Jewish Law. Subsequently, Gentiles were allowed to represent Jesus at the Eucharist. If the practice of admitting Gentiles rather than just Jews to ordination was changed, then why can't women instead of just men be ordained?

Even Saint Paul, who is sometimes accused of being a misogynist, acknowledges the importance of women in the early Church. While Paul asks women in his letters to keep silent at meetings and to cover their heads, he also lists the names of many women who help him in his ministry, including Phoebe, an "authoritative leader," and

Junia, "outstanding among the apostles" (Rom. 16:1–3), which shows that women had leadership roles in the early Church, too. Even very early in the Church's history, however, women began to be excluded from most leadership roles. Unlike Jesus, who was able to move beyond the cultural conditioning of his time, later followers and leaders still were bound to their patriarchal thinking. Many of the early Fathers of the Church, like Tertullian or Clement of Alexandria (A.D. 150–211), who wrote that a woman should be ashamed when "she thinks of what nature she is," were influenced by the Fall motif of Scripture, which views the mother of all women, Eve, as responsible for the introduction of sin into the world, and helped to perpetuate the idea of woman as morally inferior to men. The thought of women leading and guiding a community would have been exceptionally difficult for these men to accept. Rather, to justify keeping women in a subordinate position, the early Church Fathers turned to Paul's often-quoted words: "Wives should be subordinate to their husbands as to the Lord. For the husband is head of his wife just as Christ is head of the Church . . . so wives should be subordinate to their husbands in everything" (Eph. 5:22–24). We know that at some time early in Church history men took complete control of the organizational and decision-making aspect of the Church, and so the even earlier tradition of women assuming positions of leadership was lost. But there has never been a formal teaching in the Church that would prevent women from being ordained. So despite the fact that the hierarchy claims that this has been the "constant teaching" of the Church, the real fact of the matter is that the Church has never had such a teaching until the twentieth century.

To be sure, the teaching today against the ordination of women relies on some Scholastic scholarship from the Middle Ages, namely that of Thomas Aquinas. Aquinas's objection to the ordination of women relied on the notion that women are *naturally* unable to receive the sacrament of orders because the sign quality of the sacrament cannot be found in her, a sign that indicates eminence and authority. She is in a situation of inferiority and subjection, not

necessarily because of her sex, but because of the way she was gen-
erated after Adam, and because men have greater discretion, not
having been tempted and not having given in to the devil's seduc-
tion. But Aquinas's writings were never made a teaching as such.
There was no official teaching prior to the twentieth century about
not ordaining women. It is the practice of not ordaining women to
the priesthood that is a part of the tradition of the Church and not a
Tradition of teaching. Even Thomas Aquinas, the great theologian
and Doctor of the Church, can be accused of perpetuating culturally
conditioned, un-Christ-like thinking about women.

To change a teaching that has been a part of Tradition in the
Church is one thing, but as we all know, the Church has frequently
changed its position on various practices throughout her history.
When advances in human knowledge or culture have occurred, the
Church has adjusted accordingly. The Church Fathers and Scholastic theologians justified slavery as a legitimate institution within the
"fallen order of nature" (Augustine, *City of God,* 694). Today the
Church sees any form of slavery as abhorrent. Indeed, the Church
has changed her understanding on the subject of women itself, and
we would be hard-pressed to find a serious theologian agreeing with
Aquinas.

In the fall of 1995 the *New York Times* (as reported in the
National Catholic Reporter, Dec. 1, 1995) published an article stating that some women and married men were ordained in Czechoslovakia during the Communist regime when the government had
put severe restrictions on the Church and its priests and threatened
to cut off the sacramental life to the people. This practice would
contradict the statements made in the Declaration on the Question
of Admission of Women to the Ministerial Priesthood issued by Pope
Paul VI in October 1976 and reiterated in 1994 in the pontificate of
Pope John Paul II—*Ordinatio Sacerdotalis:* "On Priestly Ordination", whose primary argument for excluding women from ordination was the supposedly unbroken tradition of restricting the
priesthood to men. The Vatican has since said that if such ordinations indeed took place, they were not valid; nonetheless, if there

was a need and the Church in Czechoslovakia ordained women to the priesthood, then the tradition was broken.

There is also the ecumenical dimension of this issue. The Declaration on the Question of Admission of Women to the Ministerial Priesthood states that it has been "the constant practice of the Church" not to ordain women, that this is "God's plan," "belonging to the Church's Divine Constitution" (para. 4, 5). The Church therefore sits in judgment on the ordination of women in other Christian Churches. As early as 1852 the Congregational Church ordained its first woman, Antoinette Brown. In the 1950s Methodism admitted women to ordination, and in 1976 the Anglican Church moved to admit women to the sacrament of orders. We can be sure that these changes were made only after careful theological study and prayer within the Christian tradition. They were not easy moves for these Christian Churches, but were done with the conviction that they were being guided by the Spirit who is larger than our human notions of sexism. What must our Anglican brothers and sisters think when they read a papal pronouncement proclaiming the nonordination of women as God's will, part of the "Church's Divine Constitution," and that we do not have the authority to ordain women? (It ought to be noted that a number of Anglican priests, some of whom were married, defected to the Catholic Church in their disapproval of women's ordination within their own Church.) The declaration seems to imply that other Church's ordinations of women have been a mistake or at least misguided. Such thinking does little to promote ecumenical efforts or good feeling among various Christian groups. Some Roman Catholic women who have felt a call to the priesthood have left to become Anglican priests.

The third argument on which the nonordination of women rests is perhaps the most preposterous to our present way of thinking: that women do not bear a natural resemblance to Christ; they don't have the same biological apparatus and therefore cannot be ordained. This is referred to as the *in persona Christi* argument. It is the most insulting, and the most theologically dangerous, because it suggests that maleness brings with it special privilege and grace denied in femaleness, that ordination is a matter of biology rather than theology. I have already countered this argument to some extent when quoting Paul's letter to the Galatians, saying in Christ "there is not male nor female." Christianity believes that the person of Christ incarnates God. The Incarnation is at the heart of Christianity, with God taking on human flesh, becoming human. The important concept here is *human*, not male. The process of the Incarnation took place in a womb, formed under the heart and within the body of a woman, seemingly without the help of a man, since this was done by the power of the Holy Spirit, as the teaching on the perpetual virginity of Mary suggests. It was woman who gave birth to the God-man, Jesus, so the question can legitimately be asked, what is it that makes women less capable today of bringing Christ sacramentally into the world, or of making God sacramentally present in baptisms, reconciliation, marriages, ministering to the ill? Denying women these tasks is contradictory to what has happened historically according to Christian tradition. If we really are to seize upon this *natural* argument, then a case could be made that *woman* is more of a natural symbol for what is occurring at the Eucharist. In one sense women embody what the sacraments are meant to convey: bearing life, giving new life and nourishment. I stated earlier in this chapter that the first creation account clearly shows that *together* man and woman image God. What is to be said of the sacrament of the Eucharist when only one-half of that image is allowed in the officiation at that sacramental celebration or *any* sacramental celebration? The crucial question here is whether human sexual differences ought to carry such theological significance. The controversy boils down to the issue of whether the nonordination of women is a matter more of biology or sociology rather than of theology.

Saint Augustine argued that the sacraments were the Church's acts and did not depend on the holiness of the minister (*Letters*, volume 2, 100–102). Later this argument was called *opus operatum* or *ex opere operato*, meaning "from the act itself." The sacraments communicate God's presence in and of themselves. Since the sacraments carry grace not dependent on the minister, then the *sex* of the minister should not matter. The sacraments, the grace and presence of God that come through them, belong to the whole Church. The life of God, the communication of Christ to the world, is not and should not be dependent on one's sex.

As time went on and consciousness in general was raised on such issues as hiring and job discrimination, the shortchanging of girls and women in the classroom, the soaring problem of poverty and single mothers, and domestic violence and rape, more women and men of the Church began to question why even within their religious tradition, women were second-class citizens. Further study, writing, and debate has ensued over the past twenty years since the Declaration on the Question of Admission of Women to the Ministerial Priesthood was issued. The arguments for the ordination of women have grown stronger and become more widely accepted, even among male members of the clergy. A 1992 Gallup poll reported that two-thirds of American Catholics favored opening the priesthood to women, an increase of 20 percentage points from seven years previous. At the same time the decline in male vocations to the priesthood has taken its toll on the sacramental life of the Church. There is growing concern about whether the Vatican's resistance to the woman's ordination issue will begin to crumble out of practical considerations: the decreasing number of priests to minister and celebrate the Eucharist before a theology for the ordination of women develops. Few would want the reason for change to be purely practical.

In 1994 Pope John Paul II issued his own statement on the ordination of women, which reiterates the declaration by Pope Paul VI, but with an addendum. This *Ordinatio Sacerdotalis:* "On Priestly Ordination" meant to resolve all doubt and to bring to conclusion any more debate on this matter, states: "Wherefore, in order that all doubt may be removed regarding a matter of great importance, a matter which pertains to the Church's divine constitution itself, in virtue of my ministry of confirming the brethren [cf. Luke 22:32], I declare that the Church has no authority whatsoever to confer

priestly ordination on women and that this judgement is to be definitively held by all the Church's faithful" (para. 4). End of discussion?
Not at all! The debate raged on and became further embroiled with
the whole issue of papal authority. We wondered how it was that the
Pope thought that he could end the discussion and debate on an
issue that had become so important to the life of the Church. It was
one thing to issue a statement but quite another to suggest that this
was the end of discussion and debate. The secular press, as well as
religious press, took hold of this opportunity to question not just
the ordination issue, but also papal infallibility, a married clergy, and
a host of other issues.

And then in November 1995, the unthinkable happened. Because
of the confusion and outrage that the 1994 document had brought
about in the minds of many Catholics, and because the *Ordinatio
Sacerdotalis* had not quelled the discussion and debate, the Vatican
Congregation for the Doctrine of the Faith issued another statement
confirming that the nonordination of women was a part of the
Deposit of Faith and was considered an infallible teaching. This was
done by the Congregation, headed by Joseph Cardinal Ratzinger, in
response to a question about *Ordinatio Sacerdotalis*. The question
was whether the teaching that the Church has no authority whatsoever to confer priestly ordination on women, which is presented in
Ordinatio Sacerdotalis, is to be held definitively, and to be understood as belonging to the Deposit of Faith. The response from the
Congregation was: "In the affirmative. This teaching requires definitive assent, since, founded on the written word of God, and from
the beginning constantly preserved and applied in the tradition of
the church, it has been set forth infallibly by the ordinary and universal magisterium" (as quoted in *Commonweal* [Dec. 1, 1995]: 6).
This statement instantly set off a series of responses ranging from
disbelief to outright rage. The *Boston Globe* reported in late
November 1995 that the statement was made out of fear that a
bishop or bishops may have been thinking of ordaining women,
despite the previous teachings, and that this drastic stand by the
Congregation implied such a step would be heretical. As mentioned
in chapters 1 and 2, in June 1997 the Catholic Theological Society of

America issued a report, "Tradition and the Ordination of Women," commissioned by its board of directors and written by a six-member task force after consultation with Catholic theology faculties across the country. It does not enter into whether the church should ordain women but addresses whether church teaching enjoys the level of authority and freedom from possibility of error ascribed to it by the Vatican Congregation for the Doctrine of the Faith. The study recognizes that traditionally women were not ordained as priests but says the argument that the traditional practice is decisive is open to question in this case because so much of it was based on the conviction of female inferiority, which the Church now rejects. The report calls for further study, discussion, and prayer regarding this question.

The intertwined issues of women's nonordination and infallibility served only to point out that fact. An ecclesiastical male elite has the Church in a stranglehold. As was discussed in the previous chapter, isn't the argument of infallibility to be used only when the worldwide episcopate unanimously agrees on a teaching as belonging to the Deposit of Faith? There is no evidence that such unanimity on the part of the worldwide episcopate exists in regard to the theological reasoning for the nonordination of women. Neither is there agreement about whether or not this should belong to the Deposit of Faith, along with such teachings as Jesus' being both Divine and human, his redeeming us through his death and Resurrection, and his sending of the Holy Spirit to make us children of God. Already some bishops and priests, as well as theologians, had spoken out in support of the ordination of women. Thomas Fox, in his book *Sexuality and Catholicism*, lists a number of bishops and theologians who departed from Rome on this issue: Bishops Francis Murphy, Rembert Weakland, Kenneth Untener, Matthew Clark, and John Cummins (*Sexuality,* 206–7).

In addition, a statement was issued by more than two hundred Jesuit leaders from around the world that, while falling short of actually affirming the ordination of women, advocated the "explicit equality of women and men" and the "genuine involvement of women in consultation and decision making in our Jesuit ministries" (as quoted in *Sexuality*, 247–48). Coming from one of the most influential groups of Catholics today, this statement recognized not just that women are equal to men but that they ought to be in solidarity with them in all facets of ministry.

Far from dispelling questions concerning the ordination of women, this latest statement has created a further credibility gap in the minds of many of its faithful about the teaching authority of the Church. The incredulity with which this statement was met further has entrenched people into their own positions and has probably driven a greater wedge between members of the Catholic Church on various other issues, such as mandated celibacy for its priests and birth control.

Just a week prior to the latest statement, the Women's Ordination Conference held its first official meeting in twenty years in Arlington, Virginia. Over one thousand people attended, including two bishops. To show how far and divisive this issue had become, the keynote speaker, Elisabeth Schüssler Fiorenza, argued that the ordination of women would solve nothing in the Church and that nothing short of a major deconstruction of clericalism, patriarchy, and hierarchy would do. The Harvard Divinity School scholar spoke bluntly at the WOC, saying, "Working for any place in the hierarchical authority structure only further perpetuates an inherently unjust system" (as quoted in the *National Catholic Reporter* [Dec. 1, 1995]: 10). The theme of the conference was a "Discipleship of Equals," but those attending soon broke into two camps, one advocating work within the present system for change and reform, and the other equating ordination with *sub*ordination and organized around the belief that the Gospel vision of democratic equality could never be realized within "kyriarchy" (Ibid., 24), Schüssler Fiorenza's term for a male-dominated Church, pyramidically structured, based on a Roman Imperial model. Writing in the fall 1995 issue of *New Women, New Church*, feminist theologian Mary Hunt put it this way, "The ordination question has evolved from the unthinkable in the 1970s, to the obvious in the 1980s, to the passé in the 1990s."

So the debate continues on this issue and does not look as

though it will have a simple resolution in the near future. What is certain is that the Vatican has backed itself into a corner by stating that its position on women's ordination is an infallible statement and part of the Deposit of Faith. A shift in that position will be very difficult without creating an even greater credibility gap. Furthermore, the attempt to cut off debate has created greater problems for the Church. This is not a matter of salvation in and of itself, and yet it has forced some of our most intelligent theologians to take up this cause. To still be entrenched in this argument at this point in history is unfortunate. There are thousands of Catholics without priests, and therefore without the sacraments and the grace that such presence confers; refusing to ordain women who feel called to fill the male vocation gap compromises the Church's priorities and opens the door for its obsolescence. For many of us who have grown up Catholic and love the Church for its salvific vision in Christ, this debate is counterproductive for everyone involved. The Church should move beyond this argument and concentrate its efforts on communicating the Word of God Incarnate to all peoples.

What also seems important to me is the reminder that any vocation, ordination included, is a call and a gift, not merited, but given freely by the Holy Spirit, who blows where she or he wills. As a seventh grader I was given a holy card by a favorite teacher, Sister Assumpta. The card read:

> *I wish I had a vocation,*
> *I heard a little girl say.*
> *Well, a vocation is given to you today.*
> *For God does not speak among thunder,*
> *Calling his chosen few,*
> *But quietly leads us to wonder,*
> *why we may not follow him too.*

Early in my life I had discovered that a vocation is God's doing. The women's ordination issue is not just a matter of rights or of vindicating past injustices toward women, but is rather a matter of the Holy Spirit who invites individuals to service within the Church.

Whatever stipulations we as humans place on that call ought to be very well thought out and based firmly on the Word of God; otherwise, we risk overriding the grace of God. An article that most touched me while researching the issue of women's ordination was a brief commentary made by the Reverend Mrs. Fleming Rutledge, the pastor of Grace Episcopal Church in New York City. She wrote for *Commonweal*, a respected Catholic journal of opinion,

> In the nineteen years since I was ordained, first to the diaconate and then to the priesthood of the Episcopal Church, it has never ceased to seem extraordinary to me that I should be ordained at all, that any human being should be entrusted with [to quote the apostolic letter] the mission of the incarnate word himself. A stance of wonder and amazement is always appropriate with regard to Holy Orders. Another ordained Episcopal woman recently wrote, in another context, "I am more comfortable with those who oppose my ordination out of loyalty to their understanding of God's will than those who cheer me on, out of a humanistic, social agenda. Ordination is obedience to a call or it is nothing" (quoted in *The Living Church*, June 12, 1994). We will be in trouble whenever and wherever we start thinking of ordination as a right to which we are entitled, rather than an unmerited and unexpected gift of God's mercy. (*Commonweal* [July 15, 1994]: 12)

Love, patience, and the conviction that it is the Holy Spirit who determines the call to ordination will see the Church through any future determination on this issue. Ordination is not a man's right anymore than a woman's right. It is the privilege bestowed upon those who have been called by the Holy Spirit. Though I personally don't feel called to be ordained to the priesthood, I know women who are. I have watched women who felt this call so strongly that they embraced the call in other Churches where it is recognized and welcomed. I daresay that these women make wonderful ministers to their congregations and that the Roman Catholic Church is poorer for not having their presence. I have listened to women preachers who could move a congregation to worship and action equal to that inspired by any man I have heard. It is the truth that makes us free; God's Word, not the sex of the person proclaiming it.

Sometimes I like to think that humanity is still in progress, and therefore the Church is still in progress. I used to have a little sign on my desk that read PLEASE BE PATIENT, GOD ISN'T FINISHED WITH ME YET. Two thousand years may seem like a long time, from our present perspective, for an institution to have been around; in actuality, when we look at the history of humankind, over eight million years, we still may be living in the early days of the Church. If we can imagine that the world and the Church may exist for hundreds of thousands of years more, then we can be consoled by the idea that we are part of the earliest evolutionary growing pains of a Church trying to come to terms with its identity in Christ. Someday Paul's words may be true in actuality: "There is neither Jew nor Greek; there is neither slave nor freeperson; there is not male or female. For you are all one in Christ Jesus" (Gal. 3:28).

The issue of woman's ordination has brought to light the whole history of the Church's attitude toward women. It has made us more keenly aware of the need to change the language that is used in liturgy and sacraments, the need to have women participating in decision-making, and the need to recognize in deed as well as word the dignity of what it is to be a woman. Like other controversial issues it has created a sense of uneasiness among many of the faithful about how the hierarchy sees itself in relationship to the world. Women especially, even if they have no desire to be ordained to the priesthood, see this as another instance where the Church seems to be out of sync with the modern world. Hopefully, the reason for ordaining women in the future won't be desperation to fill priestly positions not being assumed by men but will be the Church's recognition of the full humanity of all people imaging God to the world.

4

CELIBACY AND THE
PRIESTHOOD:
MANDATE VERSUS CALLING

One of Jesus' first miracles in the Gospels of Matthew and Mark is the cure of Peter's mother-in-law. Although the Gospel writers never really tell us what she was cured of, other than that she had a fever, comedians probably could have a field day with what ailed her. The point here is that Peter had a mother-in-law, which means he also must have had a wife, and probably children. Peter was a family man. We know that he had a job as a fisherman to support his family. Peter was obviously not celibate. Spouses and children are important within Judaism, as they are in most cultures; because Peter and the other apostles were Jewish, we can imagine that some of the other apostles were probably married as well.

As was mentioned in chapter 1, tradition has it that Jesus' words, "You are Peter and upon this rock I will build my Church" (Matt. 16:18), conferred upon Peter the primary authority for leading Jesus' followers. Jesus did not seem to be bothered by Peter's commitment to his wife and family when he called Peter to follow him or when he gave him the role of being the Rock on which he would build his Church. The other apostles looked to him for leadership, and it was his successors who were seen as the people to continue to lead the Church. Peter as a married man ministered to his community in apostolic times. As a married man he led the first church council at Jerusalem, and as seen in the Acts of the Apostles Paul and the others abided by Peter's judgment on important matters of faith and practice. This married man was dedicated to his work and mission of spreading the Gospel and establishing Christian communities, and he finally was martyred in Rome for this faith. Peter left quite an example of leadership and dedication for the faithful to follow. He also is a model of human weakness: After promising Jesus he would remain with him in time of suffering, Peter denied him three times to save his own skin. Peter is an inspiration to many who see in him a reflection of their own humanity. As my grandmother used to say, Peter is proof that God can write straight with crooked lines. I can remember many times listening during Mass to homilies in which the priest would talk about the fact that even though Peter had denied Jesus before his death, Jesus still chose him to be the leader of his following. This idea that Peter was one of us, a real person who was married, had a family, exhibited weaknesses, was comforting and told me one didn't have to be perfect to become a saint. Then, in biblical times, celibacy was obviously not a requirement for following Jesus or for being chosen for a role of leadership. Today, however, celibacy, renouncing all physical sexual relationships, is a requirement for those responding to the call to serve the Church as priests and has become another one of those debatable issues for Catholics.

Very few people would dismiss the fact that celibacy is or could be a value in serving the Church. Dedicating oneself wholeheartedly to one's work or goals has always been seen as a noble ideal. There are many priests who live full lives as celibate men and who are an inspiration to those they serve. I can think of dozens of priests and monks I have met over the years who seemed happy and confident as celibate men; who were and are open, sincere, and concerned about others. But I can also recall a few who obviously were struggling with the commitment to celibacy that the priesthood demands of them. I have known numerous priests, including the rector of a seminary, who have sought female companionship and sexual involvement openly. The issue here is not the value of celibacy; it *can* be a value. The issue is whether celibacy has to be bound intrinsically to ordination to the priesthood in Roman Catholicism. Should celibacy be mandated if an individual feels called to the priesthood, called to serve the Church in a sacramental way?

Mandated celibacy is the issue. There are those who feel that celibacy is a particular gift, or charism. Even the Second Vatican Council defined celibacy as a gift from God in its 1965 Decree on Priestly Formation (*Optatam Totius*). There are some people who feel very strongly that a life of selfless dedication requires celibacy as an important means to that end. They are willing to forgo intimate, sexual human relationships in order to give themselves completely to the service of the Church. But if celibacy is a gift, a charism that one is called to, can it and ought it be *required* for everyone who feels called to the priesthood?

Mandated celibacy has become an issue in part because of the declining number of vocations to the priesthood, seemingly related to the celibacy requirement. Many young men see the priesthood as something they might consider, but they are unwilling to commit themselves to a celibate lifetime. It is estimated that twenty thousand men have left the priesthood in the United States in the past twenty-five years, and nine out of ten of these have married since their departure. Many left *specifically* to get married. Mandated celibacy also is an issue today because increasingly a celibate clergy is viewed as aloof and out of touch with the struggles of ordinary people. Couples who seek marital counseling, young people who are confused about their own sexuality, and men and women caught in abusive relationships often find it difficult to go to a priest for advice, wondering how a man committed to a life of celibacy could possibly understand such problems. It is an issue because in reality many clergy who publicly profess to leading a celibate life have been and/or are involved in sexual affairs. It is also an issue because of the number of homosexuals being drawn to the priesthood and because of the scandals caused by the numbers of priests who have been accused of being pedophiles. Finally, it is an issue because in some areas of the world where the Church is growing, such as the cultures of Africa and South America, celibacy is viewed very negatively, and vocations to the priesthood in those regions are suffering because of this requirement. Each of these problems will be examined in greater detail as we examine the issue of priestly celibacy.

Since Vatican II over one hundred thousand priests worldwide have resigned the priesthood, many over the issue of celibacy. The vast majority of these men have married and have had families. Many of those would gladly serve the Church in a ministerial capacity today if allowed to do so. Some in fact do serve as Eucharistic ministers, teach in Catholic colleges, serve on parish councils, and participate in numerous other Church-related activities, but they have still been forced to relinquish their priestly activities because of the issue of celibacy. In the Latin rite, celibacy has been the law of the Church since the twelfth century. Before then it had been preferred, but not mandated. There are exceptions, as was the case several years ago (already mentioned in chapter 3 with regard to the issue of women in the Catholic priesthood) when a number of married Anglican priests, disillusioned over the fact that their Church was ordaining women, were admitted to the Roman Catholic Church with full priestly privileges. This angered some of the Catholic men who had been forced to give up their priesthood when they married but who still feel a call to serve the People of God as ordained ministers.

There are both religious and social reasons for why celibacy became mandated in the Church, but there do not seem to be theological reasons. At various times throughout European history, sexual intercourse was considered a lowly human activity to be performed only within the context of marriage and then only for the purpose of procreation. This thinking prevailed in the Church for centuries. The Church law that made celibacy the rule for priests coincided with an evolution in thinking by which the priest came to be viewed as set apart, privileged, in a special and superior state of life, rather than the servant to the people of God that Jesus so apparently in the Gospels is preparing his apostles to be: "I have come not to be served, but to serve and to give my life as a ransom for many" (Matt. 16:12); and "I am among you as one who serves" (Luke 22:27).

While the Church has made strides in affirming the sacredness and beauty of sexuality within marriage in the past thirty years, particularly in the Vatican II document on the Church, it inadvertently has suggested that marriage is a lesser state in life by upholding its requirement that one cannot serve God in the Church through priesthood except while celibate. Saint Paul's analogy of Christ's love for the Church as the love shared between husband and wife is not allowed to be lived out in actuality by those who minister most completely to the Church.

The history of celibacy in the Church is interesting, to say the least. The Old Testament, the Scripture that Jesus and his followers relied on for their understanding of what God expected of the human community, does not present celibacy as a particular virtue. In fact, within Judaism, the first command God gives to Adam and Eve in the garden is to be fruitful and multiply (Gen. 1:28), and this order was taken very seriously. Marriage, family, and of course sexual relations were considered important aspects of the covenant between God and man. Continuing one's lineage through children was a sign of humankind continuing the creative power of God in the world.

That married love symbolizes the covenant relationship God has to his people especially can be seen in the Book of the Prophet Hosea: "I will make a covenant with them on that day ... I will espouse you to me forever. I will espouse you to me in right and in justice, in love and in mercy; I will espouse you in fidelity and you will know the Lord" (Hos. 2:18, 21, 22). The Song of Songs underscores this theme. The opening lines (Song of Songs 1:2–4) introduce a poem of erotic love, which the Hebrews saw as an expression of not only human love but of God's love for his people:

> *Let him kiss me with kisses of his mouth!*
> *More delightful is your love than wine!*
> *Your name spoken is a spreading perfume—*
> *that is why the maidens love you.*
> *Draw me!*
> *We will follow you eagerly!*
> *Bring me O king to your chambers.*

All of the Old Testament heroes, from Abraham to Moses to David, were married. Remaining celibate is not even a consideration in the Old Testament.

In the New Testament the situation changes somewhat. While Jesus seems pleased to use the metaphor of a wedding feast for the Kingdom of God, performs his first miracle at a wedding in Cana, and delights in the presence of children, he himself does not seem to be married. There are authors who have attempted to present a case for Jesus as a married man, but the fact of the matter is, the Scriptures are silent in this regard. Surely, someone as important as a wife or child, even if a death had occurred prior to Jesus' beginning of his ministry, would not have been overlooked totally by the writers of the Gospels or the letters. There would have been ample opportunity for these New Testament writers, if Jesus had been married, to say something in this regard.

Jesus' actual words on sex or marriage are quite limited. At one point, when Jesus is being questioned about divorce, the idea of remaining unmarried comes up: "His disciples said to him, 'If that is the case of a man with his wife, it is better not to marry.' He answered, 'Not all can accept this word, but only those to whom it has been granted. Some are incapable of marriage because they were born so, some because they were made so by others; some because they have renounced marriage for the sake of the kingdom of heaven. Whoever can accept this ought to accept it' " (Matt. 19:10–12). This quotation serves the purpose of showing that Jesus suggests celibacy as a good when it is related directly to serving the Kingdom of Heaven; Jesus also suggests that celibacy is a gift, a charism ("only those to whom it has been granted"), and not something one can simply decide to do on one's own, or something that can be mandated.

There are also a few places in his letters where Saint Paul refers to celibacy. It is important to note in reading the following such passage that Paul seems certain that the end of the world and the final coming of the Kingdom are close at hand, will occur during his lifetime, and so he advises: "For the world in its present form is passing away. I should like you to be free of anxieties. An unmarried man is anxious about the things of the Lord, how he may please the Lord. But a married man is anxious about the things of the world, how he may please his wife, and he is divided. . . . I am telling you this for your own benefit, not to impose a restraint upon you, but for the sake of propriety and adherence to the Lord without distraction" (1 Cor. 7:31–35). It was a commonly held belief at this time while Paul was preaching that the Kingdom of God was about to become an immediate reality, and that Jesus would return in glory soon, as is seen in Paul's letter to the Thessalonians: "For the Lord himself with a word of command, with the voice of an archangel and with the trumpet of God, will come down from the heaven and the dead in Christ will be raised first. Then we who are alive, who are left, will be caught up together with them in the clouds to meet the Lord in the air" (1 Thess. 4:16, 17). This eschatological perspective influences a number of different teachings in the early Church. If Paul and the early Christians thought that the end of the world was coming, they would believe that it was very important to be totally focused and dedicated in preparing for Jesus' coming and the fulfillment of the promises about the establishment of the Kingdom of God.

This eschatological perspective is attributed even to the words of Jesus himself: ". . . in the same way, when you see these things happening, know that the Kingdom of God is near. Amen I say to you, this generation will not pass away until all these things have taken place . . . Be vigilant at all times and pray that you have the strength to escape the tribulations that are imminent and to stand before the Son of Man" (Luke 21:31–32, 36). Saint Paul's teaching on remaining unmarried, then, is a clear indication that the purpose of remaining celibate involves the ability to be undivided, without distraction from the things of the Lord, so that when he returned one would be prepared. It is understandable that celibacy in the New Testament would be seen as a good *if* the Kingdom of God is to be established within one's lifetime. Paul encourages celibacy for those who can embrace it, but he also recognizes that the grace of celibacy is not given to all, and those who could not live it should marry to avoid sin (1 Cor. 7:1–9, 27, 28, 36). Because of the eschatological perspective, and because seemingly neither Jesus nor Paul was married (1 Cor. 7:7), early on in Christianity, embracing a celibate life became a means of imitating Jesus in an exclusive way and a means of devoting oneself completely to the Kingdom of God. Celibacy was a respected and valued option in living the Christian life during the first century, but we have no indication that it was seen as the preferred or superior way of life. Ironically, in Paul's first letter to Timothy Paul states that a man who aspires to be a bishop should only be married once, and "must be able to manage his own household, keeping his children under control" (1 Tim. 3:2–3). This is a good quote in support for a married clergy.

However, by the second century the influence of the philosophy of Gnosticism, which taught that things of the material world, including anything related to sex, were base and even evil, began to have a significant influence on Christianity. To live on a spiritual plane unencumbered by physical desires was by far the ideal goal, according to the Gnostic teaching. As was mentioned in the previous chapter, the low opinion of women as seductresses of men's passions also added to a certain negativity regarding anything sexual. The first two centuries of the Church were marked by political and religious persecutions of Christians, who had come to be viewed as a threat to the established way of life. Martyrdom was encouraged in part because it was a release from this material world into life with Christ and also because some still held to the idea that this world was about to pass away because of the imminent coming of the Kingdom. Christian writers gradually began to discourage anything binding individuals to the passions and lusts of this life, especially sex.

Hermits, like Antony of Egypt in the second century, who went off to the desert to live devoted to prayer, fasting, and abstinence, were viewed as living witnesses that the Kingdom of God had established itself on earth. Historically, celibacy first emerged in Christian consciousness as a *freely chosen* way to express the desire to pursue a life totally focused on Christ. There was nothing obligatory about it, and it was not a condition of service to the Church or clerical office. Celibacy persisted during the earliest centuries of Christianity as an individual and nonsystematized practice among priests, laymen, and women. It was not legislated. In the fourth and fifth centuries, orders of monks and nuns living a celibate life began to flourish. Monasteries were begun throughout Christendom in the West as well as the East.

But around this time, too, Augustine of Hippo, who would define and synthesize what was considered essential to the faith, began to teach. He was a brilliant man whose turbulent youth and espousal of Neoplatonism deeply affected Christian thought. Neoplatonism gave Saint Augustine's thought and writings a dualistic tendency of antithetically separating and categorizing into closed compartments all of the main components of life: material/spiritual, body/soul, light/darkness, good/bad, male/female. He looked back upon his own troubled youth—which had been spent in wild revelry, according to his own account, and even involved fathering a child—as weak and sinful. In his famous *Confessions*, a type of autobiography, he speaks of his life as once lived in darkness and sin, and he displays a deep mistrust of the physical being, knowing full well from personal experience how it gives in to temptation and sin. Augustine seems almost obsessed with reminding his readers how easily man is tempted and succumbs to sin, especially sin of a sexual nature. Consequently, following Augustine's example, a growing body of theological writing dichotomized sexuality, with virginity as a good (spiritual) and lust as a necessary evil (physical), primarily meant for the procreation of children. This theme—coupled with the low esteem that theological writings granted to the female, who was portrayed as the vessel through which evil was introduced into the world—bolstered the case that celibacy was the favored way of life among those who truly wanted to follow and serve Christ and to avoid earthly wickedness.

At the same time devotion to the Blessed Mother, Mary, a virgin, began to take on a life of its own, establishing her as a real icon within Christianity. She began to appear in Christian art and literature and devotional prayers; she became the woman to love as well as emulate. The perfect Christian woman without sin, she had never given in to the passions of the flesh; as a virgin she had remained pure and blameless. All Catholics were encouraged to be like the Blessed Virgin Mary. Celibacy and virginity were ingrained further as the favored way of life as devotion to Mary continued to grow over the centuries.

To repeat, no universal law *required* celibacy for priests or bishops in these early centuries of the Church. Eventually laws were passed requiring that priests abstain from sex before celebrating the Eucharist, that they could not marry after ordination, and that they should not remarry after the death of a spouse. Despite a fairly consistent teaching suggesting celibacy as the preferred way of life for priests, it wasn't until Gregory VII (1073–85), who was bent on reforming the Church, that it began to be seen as a requirement. In the early Middle Ages, when clergy with children began passing on Church lands to their sons and bestowing titles upon them, thus eroding the financial as well as spiritual base of the Church, a married clergy was a source of scandal and a liability. Legislation was passed mandating celibacy for priests, and the Second Lateran Council (1139) imposed celibacy as a requirement for ordination to the priesthood. As has been demonstrated, however, celibacy for the priesthood has *not* been a constant teaching of the Church, one of the criteria used to determine if a practice can be changed.

The issue of celibacy in the East took a different turn. The Eastern Church, which includes Greek and Russian Orthodoxy, allowed priests, deacons, and other clerics to marry, but only prior to ordination. Celibacy was encouraged in the East for the clergy but if one thought that he would prefer to marry, he had to do so before ordination. Bishops were chosen from among those who remained celibate. According to an orthodox friend, the logic is that the family is so valued that the duties and responsibilities of a Bishop may take away from the time a man could spend with his family. These rules still apply today; the difference in attitudes toward celibacy for priests remains one of the points of division between the Church in the East and the Church in the West.

Martin Luther and the other Reformers took exception to celibacy in the fifteenth century. Basic to Luther's thinking was his concept of the "priesthood of all believers," which was in part a reaction to the hierarchical structure of the Roman Catholic Church at this time. As Luther saw it, with cardinals living like princes and bishops living like nobles, the time had come to simplify the Church. He believed that a priesthood removed from the people was not good. It was his purpose to remind people that because of our baptism we are all one in Christ and therefore all share in his ministry. Of course there are ordained ministers in the Lutheran Church who are celibate, as there are in other Protestant denominations, but they are not expected or encouraged to remain celibate. Neither is celibacy considered a greater state than marriage. In 1522 Martin Luther condemned celibacy, since it could give the impression that individuals who embrace this way of life are somehow better than Christians who do not.

As the centuries proceeded, right up until the twentieth century, most Roman Catholic theological writings stated that celibacy was a more perfect state than marriage. Consider this statement from the First Vatican Council in 1869: Anyone who "says that it is not better and more godly to live in virginity or in the unmarried state than to marry, let him be anathema," that is, cut off from the Church (Ranke-Heinemann, *Eunuchs for the Kingdom of Heaven,* 114). Even though Vatican II's Decree on Priestly Formation (*Optatam Totius*) asks seminarians to be aware of the duties and dignity of marriage, it also states: "Let them [seminarians] perceive as well the superiority of virginity consecrated to Christ" (para. 10). Nowhere in the Gospels, with the exceptions cited previously in this chapter, can this belief in the superiority of virginity or celibacy be supported. Nonetheless, this was a rather prevalent understanding among Catholics for many years. Growing up in the sixties, my friends and I were convinced that living a life of celibacy, remaining a virgin, was a surer way to Heaven than getting married. More often than not, however, we viewed it as a sacrifice of physical pleasure rather than as the gift of being totally devoted to Christ and the Church.

This point of view diminished with the Second Vatican Council, but the persistent teaching has been that one can best serve the Church in a ministerial fashion as a celibate person. In June 1967 Pope Paul VI, after refusing to allow a relaxation of mandated celibacy at the Second Vatican Council, issued the encyclical *Sacerdotalis Caelibatus:* "On the Sacredness of Celibacy" or "On Priestly Celibacy" in which he praised celibacy as a "dazzling jewel" and reaffirmed the Church's celibacy requirement for priests. Pope John Paul II continues to teach that celibacy is a requirement for the priesthood.

The problem, however, is that many Catholics, clergy as well as laypersons, view the requirement of celibacy for the priesthood as out of touch with present-day reality. There are and have always been those people who believe that it is precisely the mission of the Church to act as a beacon of light in times of darkness, to stand in direct opposition to cultural values that seem not to be in line with Gospel values. With such emphasis on free sex, self-gratification, and hedonism in society today, there are those who see the espousal of celibacy as an expression that sex is not the be-all and end-all that the secular media would have us believe. Celibacy stands as a value that encourages self-sacrifice, service, and discipline.

Celibacy, while it is a value, is no more of a value than marriage in the Gospels. It is a gift, another option for those who seek to live dedicated to Christ. As a result of Vatican II, a vision emerged of the Church as part of the world, not separate from it; as sharing in the life of all of the People of God. The opening statement of the Pastoral Constitution on the Church in the Modern World (*Gaudium et Spes:* "Joy and Hope") gives testimony to this: "The joys and hopes, the griefs and anxieties of the men of this age, especially those who are poor or in any way afflicted, these too are the joys and hopes, the griefs and anxieties of the followers of Christ. Indeed, nothing genuinely human fails to raise an echo in their hearts" (para. 1). Here Catholics are being urged to embrace the world and everything genuinely human. In the past, celibacy was often viewed as superior precisely because it separated people who sought holiness from the world. With Vatican II, however, the emphasis shifted; real value exists in becoming involved and sharing humankind's anxieties and hopes—remaining in the world, not living apart from it. What appeared as countercultural in the past is seen now as a divorcing of oneself from the real world, as non-Incarnational.

Many religious orders after Vatican II began simplifying lifestyles by moving out of huge, fortress-style convents and abandoning religious garb, viewed as willful separation from the people. They moved into smaller homes in actual neighborhoods and adopted "regular" clothing in an attempt to become more at one with the People of God, not remaining apart from them. Value came to be placed on the gifts of the laity to the Church, and many of us began to think that a day when laypeople could take an active role of leadership in the Church was not far in the future. One of the consequences of this atmosphere of change was a reassessment of celibacy. As men left the active priesthood to marry, they began to pursue a life of holiness as husbands and fathers, newly convinced that the passions of the flesh could be navigated in a mature manner, keeping them close to God. I have heard individuals ask the question, how could a man with a vow of celibacy understand my sins as a husband and father? I am of the opinion that a celibate priest is capable of understanding the sins of a married man, or a married woman for that matter, but the point here is that in today's world the value of celibacy is little understood by most people, while the value placed on marriage and family has increased. There is in fact so much emphasis placed on marriage and family by sociologists, educators, and even politicians that those who remain unmarried in our society often feel left out, unfulfilled.

There are various reasons why mandated celibacy and the priesthood should not be continued as mutually inclusive. The pragmatic reason is the present shortage of priests: Men are not responding to a call to the priesthood in large part because of the issue of celibacy, and many priests have left their ministry because of celibacy. A 1990 study in the United States found celibacy to be the biggest roadblock for men entering the priesthood. As a religious educator, I have changed my teaching about love and sexuality dramatically over the past twenty years. No longer is the emphasis on mistrusting one's passions and temptations because they could lead one to sin, as many of my contemporaries and I were taught. That sex is a gift from God, a celebration of our sharing in the love and creativity of God in a committed relationship, has become a common theme in my teaching. In my course "Human Sexuality and Christian Marriage," I emphasize marriage as a metaphor for Christ's love for the Church and as an analogy to the Kingdom of God. Imagine what must go through the mind of a young man who has been taught that his sexuality is good, that it is a part of his dignity as a human person, but that a vocation to the priesthood must rob him his right to marry, to celebrate life in intimate sexual expression, as well as deny him the joys of bringing life into the world as a parent. For many young men today, mandated celibacy is viewed as a contradiction to the ideals of the Kingdom of God they have learned. They do not see why married life should be considered a hindrance to their service in the Church. As one young man said to me recently, "If a married man with a family can run the country, why can't a married man run a parish or a diocese?" Perhaps this is a simplistic question, but the issue of celibacy as it relates to the decreasing number of vocations to the priesthood is critical throughout the world. As was mentioned earlier in this chapter, this is particularly true in some Third World countries, where being celibate is viewed negatively because it seems to contradict the natural, creative powers of life. In

countries in Africa and Latin America where the Catholic populations are growing, the numbers of vocations to the priesthood
because of mandated celibacy will not be able to keep up. It is
reported that in some of these countries the priests are in fact married and carrying on with their ministry despite the requirement.

In 1995, 522 men were ordained to the priesthood in the United
States, 83 fewer than in the previous year. This downward spiral
gives no indication of changing course. Once the object of awesome
reverence, the priesthood now is looked upon by some with pity
and by many with concern. There was a time when mothers prayed
that one of their sons would have a vocation to the priesthood, but I
know no one who feels that way today. However, if I thought that
my son could have a vocation *as well as* an option to marry and have
a family I might pray for that. Meanwhile, priests and bishops who
remain in the clergy are under continued pressure to provide a
sacramental life for the growing Catholic population—a responsibility that is becoming more and more difficult to fulfill.

Richard Schoenherr, a University of Wisconsin sociologist, has
been studying the declining number of priests for twenty five years.
He reports that we are in the midst of a "full blown crisis," recording
statistics about a reduction in the number of diocesan priests from
thirty-five thousand in 1966 to a projected twenty-one thousand in
2005, while the Catholic population is expected to rise from sixty
million to seventy-four million in the same time period. Not only are
there fewer priests, but the remainder are getting older. Schoenherr
suggests that the sacramental life of the Church is compromised by
the mandate of an all-male celibate clergy. He argues that marriage
would provide benefits for both priests who choose to marry and
the people they serve: "To be authentically religious, Catholic ministry must open itself to the charismatic, transforming power of marriage, as well as celibacy" (*Full Pews and Empty Altars*, 23–26).

Most Catholics, in fact, seem to have little problem in accepting
the concept of a married clergy. A 1993 Gallup poll showed 72 percent of Catholics favoring optional celibacy and 64 percent supporting the opening of orders to women. A National Federation of

Priests Councils' poll the same year indicated that 58 percent of active priests contend that celibacy should not be required of diocesan clergy. The fact that celibacy has been drawn into a legalistic framework by being mandated does not detract from its positive goodness and the generosity it provides to the Church. But to link it irrevocably with a vocation to the priesthood counteracts its potential productiveness. Celibacy is a gift that has to be interiorized and lived faithfully; it is not something to be mandated. As something that one *has* to do, it can become a burden, a sacrifice that weighs heavily upon the human heart and psyche, especially for an individual who is expected to spend long hours alone, with little support, and few people to share his daily life with him.

The fact of the matter is that required celibacy in many instances simply does not work, and while it may appear to the majority of Catholics that celibacy is an interiorized, lived reality among the clergy, this is often not the case. There are people who feel that sexual problems among priests, which never fail to titillate the media, are linked to the mandate of celibacy; many priests are unprepared for a lifetime commitment to celibacy and so approach that commitment only halfheartedly. In recent years the Church has been plagued by legal battles involving the issue of pedophiles among its priestly ranks. The number of priests who have been discovered and charged as sexual abusers of children has been alarming. This has had devastating effects on the reputation of the priesthood in general and has added noise to the issue of whether or not celibacy to the priesthood is something that ought to be required. One diocese in the United States almost had to declare bankruptcy after settling all the legal fees for its priests' indiscretions, and in the summer of 1997 the diocese of Dallas was required to pay $120,000,000 in damages to eleven former altar boys who had been molested by a priest. Added to the scandal of the clerical pedophiles is that of priests who are and have been involved in adult homosexual and heterosexual relations. Since 1985 the U.S. bishops have been agonizing over reports that 20 to 40 percent of candidates for the priesthood are gay, which the Vatican considers a "disorder."

Homosexual priests are not necessarily any more likely to break a promise of celibacy than are heterosexual priests, but remaining celibate in an all-male environment on a daily basis might prove an even greater struggle if one were gay, especially given the living situation of diocesan priests, who reside together in a rectory. Young homosexual men can be drawn to the priesthood because it provides an environment where they are in almost constant company with other men.

Celibacy requires a level of maturity that can sustain a professional and integrative approach to relationships with other men, women, and children that is not always a part of the training and formation of priests. At times the Church has taken celibacy for granted, as something simply expected of its candidates to the priesthood. When and if there has been a problem with celibacy, it often has been seen as the *individual* priest's or seminarian's problem. Richard Sipe, psychologist/sociologist, who has been working with priests on the celibacy issue in their personal lives, reports in his book *Sex, Priests, and Power: Anatomy of a Crisis* that at any given time at least 50 percent of priests, bound by the law of celibacy and publicly claiming the identity "celibate," are in fact practicing celibacy (*Sex, Priests, and Power*, 61). Of course, this statistic suggests that the other 50 percent are *not* practicing celibacy. Sipe uses a broad definition for the absence of any sexual gratification, including everything from masturbation to sexual intercourse. Still, these numbers are alarming. His estimates may be overstated, but through years of counseling and working with priests he nonetheless has identified a problem among those who have taken a vow of celibacy. He suggests that living out one's sexual desires is an integral part of human life and that to give this up takes a tremendous amoung of maturity and willpower; celibacy is a sacrifice that many men called to the priesthood are simply not capable of sustaining for a lifetime.

Nowhere is the problem of mandated celibacy more evident than in the experiences of the members of an organization called VOCAL, Victims of Clergy Abuse Linkup, known today simply as LINKUP. In October 1992 Jeanne Miller organized a conference for Catholic survivors of sex abuse by clergy. Her organization represents about forty-five hundred such victims. The awe and reverence attributed to the priesthood and its "pure," unselfish, idealized form of love has caught many victims of priestly sexual activity in a web of deceit, shame, guilt, and silence. The projected image that priests have of being close to God, set apart, has enabled many of them to perpetuate the misconception that sex with them is something sacred and beyond the realm of the "natural" world. I have read stories of women who were sexually active with priests who somehow thought that what they were doing was special and beyond censure. The priests themselves may come to believe this about their sexual involvement with others and thus are able to divorce their sexual activity from their humanity. When celibacy within the priesthood is described as a "dazzling jewel," those who possess it may consider themselves privileged. The fact that the priesthood carries with it sacred powers, including the forgiveness of sins, making the presence of Christ real in the Eucharist, creates the impression that priests' behavior is somehow beyond normal standards of judgment.

Richard Sipe writes about this phenomenon, touching upon the psychological effects of this attitude on the men and women and children with whom priests become sexually involved: Priests often retreat behind their collar, "maintaining their status and privilege within the celibate system while they relegate their women to the status of backstreet wife" (ibid., 137). Sipe records many stories of women who, after going to priests for counseling or confession, become entangled in relationships with them and end up feeling demeaned and used. There are numerous stories of young boys who have been abused by priests only after the cleric has told them that what they are doing is all right precisely *because* they are involved with a priest. Some priests have been able to rationalize their sexual activity by splitting it off from their priestly lives, seeing it as a part of their natural humanity and therefore even necessary for their effective service to their people. These are men who have never really dealt with their sexuality and have been able to live a double life at the expense of others. Sexual behavior among priests violates the trust of the faithful who believe them to be celibate.

Sipe also states that celibacy can be used as a part of the whole power structure of the Church. It separates the priesthood from the rest of the faithful in such a way that it creates the illusion that priests are superior in some way to the rest of us, and ultimately that males are superior to females. Perhaps the celibacy issue has helped to contribute to an atmosphere of mistrust toward anything sexual and at the same time made sexual issues appear tantamount in Church rulings and decrees. In 1995 Bishop Emerson J. Moore of New York died of AIDS. For many weeks, even months, the cause of death was not mentioned by the archdiocese. When Cardinal O'Connor finally spoke about this death, he was more willing to accept that it was related to drug use than he was to suggest that the AIDS virus had been transmitted sexually. The suggestion, of course, was that being a drug user was far more acceptable than being involved sexually with another person. Bishop Moore's colleagues were willing to remember that, in fact, he had struggled for many years with his sexuality, as well as the problems he had with drug addiction.

It is easy to overlook the fact that celibacy is not some sort of an abstraction, but rather an embodied reality lived out in human vessels with emotions and hopes. It involves a whole person, not just the cognitive and rational aspects of the person, so it must be an integral part of one's entire life, something freely chosen. Not to satisfy the deepest longings of the human heart, to give love and receive it back in an intimate and exclusive manner, not to satisfy the desire by some for children and family, can leave a void in a person's life, inevitably to be filled by something else. That something "ought" to be the pursuit of holiness and service to others. Celibacy is a value when it serves as a sign of the Resurrection, that we are not bound to the temporal sphere, that individuals can live a life of total self-giving love as did Christ, who gave all and expected nothing in return, who was among us as one who served. Celibacy is not something to be accepted simply because it is a part of the package; this is not a bill in Congress. Neither should celibacy be looked at from a utilitarian perspective: Because this priest is celibate, he has more time to spend on his ministry. Celibacy as a gift from God is first and foremost meant to be a sign that the Kingdom of God is among us, that these men's lives belong in an exclusive way to God and the Church.

Many of those young men who left the priesthood over the issue of celibacy had entered the seminary at eighteen or nineteen, zealous, idealistic, and enthusiastic about their future as priests. Although loving their ministry, some of these seminarians—after ten, twenty years of struggling with their sexuality—were forced to resign their vocation, often with a sense of anguish and guilt. Falling in love, expressing that love for another, was for some of these men a natural part of their lives; denying that vitality was denying something they felt God was also calling them to do and be. An article by Stephen J. Stanley that appeared in the *Stamford Advocate* (Conn.) on October 12, 1995, sums up well the feelings of many of these resigned priests:

> How different the world looked and felt in 1979. I experienced the priesthood as both a challenge and a delight. The vocation for which I had spent nine years preparing was everything I had hoped for and more. . . . In 1988 I resigned from the priesthood to marry. . . . These days 1979 feels like a lifetime ago. I have a wonderful wife, a beautiful baby son, and a job with a local government. I also have the conviction that the call I felt to the priesthood since I was a teenager has not been nullified because I opted out of celibacy. If anything, I feel that I am now better qualified to be a priest than ever before. Family life does wonders for grounding a ministry in reality.

Like this individual, many of these men have found meaningful ways to continue their ministry to the People of God, but their conviction that they have been called to the priesthood remains. Many have organized into groups such as Corpus, an association of married priests, celibate priests, laypeople, and religious who seek ways to establish an expanded priesthood. There are several men in my parish who resigned their ministry and have since married; they still love the Church and attend Mass. These are good sincere men whose theological training and love for the Church could be put to use for the service of the Church at a time in history when the shortage of priests is denying people the sacramental life of the Church. On many Sundays I have looked at one or the other of them and thought what a waste it is to relegate these men to pews, rather than pulpits. What sound advice they could offer on Sundays to the people of our parish about love, sacrifice, and family life.

For years, men who left the priesthood were considered weak, fallen creatures who could not live up to "higher" standards. The guilt, anxiety, and shame associated with leaving the priesthood forced many men to stay on, living lives of emptiness, often turning bitter. The fact that many men were left ill prepared for a life of loneliness, which can be a part of celibacy, led them to turn to alcohol or some other means of filling the void. Some resigned priests suffered for years waiting for the proper dispensation to come from Rome, releasing them from their priesthood so they could marry. When John Paul II was elected Pope he waited eight years before he began granting dispensations. This meant that some of these men were forced into a situation where they had to marry outside the Church, they were separated from the institution they had faithfully served for years. This has caused hurt and resentment among some former priests. Somehow the Church needs to find a way to reach out to these men and to use their talents in a productive way where they feel affirmed in their service to the Church. Barring someone from the altar and ministry to the faithful because he has chosen to marry says a great deal about the attitude of the Church toward marriage, women, and the raising of children, despite what is written in encyclicals and statements.

If marriage and family life are primary values in the Scriptures and if the image of marriage is used to describe the covenant relationship of God to his people, why is marriage off limits to those who feel called to the priesthood? The Eucharist is the sign, the symbol, the *reality* of the intimate relationship God has chosen to have with humankind. How could it be, then, that a married man whose life is a witness to the reality of intimate relationships is not able to stand at the altar and celebrate the Eucharist? Jesus himself is referred to at least metaphorically as a bridegroom in the Gospels, the Epistles, and the Book of Revelation, and even though he may never have been married, it does not seem like such a theological stretch to suggest that a bridegroom in actuality could celebrate God's presence among us in the Eucharist. What if Jesus had been married? Would that have limited the redemptive character of his life? I think not. Jesus' life was one lived unselfishly to its fullness. What we admire about Jesus is not necessarily his celibacy, but his love and concern for others, something we all are called to reflect in our lives. Christ-centered celibacy is a gift for the Church, but it stands in a complementary relationship to marriage. People in either situation are called to be signs of authentic love and giving to others. In the final analysis all Christians are called to live as parents generating new life for the Kingdom of God, which begins now and extends into eternal life.

While in fact many men given the right spiritual formation may embrace a life of celibacy as a sign of the Resurrection and in order to be devoted completely to Christ, many Catholics today feel that a life of celibacy ought not to be so intrinsically bound to the priesthood that if an individual feels called by Christ to the priesthood and also feels called to a loving sexual relationship, the two calls ought not to be seen as mutually exclusive. In the past twenty-five years we have seen a revival of men being ordained to the diaconate, a step of orders just below that of priests. Many of these men are married. Often they have listened to dying people's confessions without being able to officially give them absolution or been in a situation where presiding over a Eucharistic celebration would have been the most meaningful way to open or conclude a meeting. Because married men are not allowed to be ordained they have had to do what is second best, and people have been denied the sacraments of the Church. Many of these deacons would choose to be ordained to the priesthood if it were allowed.

Surely, allowing priests to marry in the Roman Catholic Church would present new challenges and raise a number of questions. Perhaps the Church is just not ready at this point in history to face these challenges. If the clergy were subject to the same problems that Catholic families deal with such as family planning, responsible parenting, and the financial difficulties of raising and supporting a family today, we might see a change in attitude on such issues as birth control. What would happen if a married priest's marriage failed for one reason or another, or if he fell in love a second time and wanted to remarry? Would a married clergy affect the way men would be assigned to a parish or other clerical jobs? How much could their wives and children influence their jobs? One thing is certain, a married clergy would give rise to a systematic theology of marriage, family, and conjugal love that largely has been orphaned by theologians until recently. While there is in fact some excellent theological and pastoral work being done in this area today, it has been only in the latter part of the twentieth century that the Church has admitted officially that even within marriage, there are reasons for sex other than the procreation of children.

One other thing seems certain: Unless the Church changes its position on this issue and moves creatively toward allowing priests to marry, as well as allowing the ordination of women, the Church will be compromising the grace of God to thousands who are without priests, the celebration of the Eucharist, and the grace of the sacrament of reconciliation. Often I read about deacons or sisters in parishes conducting Communion services in the absence of a priest, and while this may satisfy some people, having a Communion service in place of the Eucharistic celebration does not fulfill Christ's words "Do this in memory of me." Unless the Church is willing to radically change the way the Eucharist is to be celebrated—say, by laypeople, which is highly unlikely—the institution is confronted with a choice between its sacramental life and the mandate of celibacy (or a choice between its sacramental life and a male-only clergy). It would be too bad if the Church waited until a crisis moment, when it had no other option for its survival than to begin allowing a married and/or female clergy.

For those priests who do choose celibacy, there is a need for better preparation and formation for such a life. A young person who embraces celibacy must be equipped spiritually and psychologically for the challenge. In many dioceses this is already the case of course. Perhaps celibacy as expressed for a certain period of time in a person's life who devotes himself/herself to service of the Church would be a more realistic approach for some. Those who can remain celibate for a lifetime, graced by God, should be supported spiritually and psychologically throughout by their bishops. But those whose lives take a different direction after a certain amount of time perhaps need to be freed and encouraged to enter another state of life, that of marriage, without being forced to resign their priesthood. We are all called to holiness and wholeness. We are all called to minister to one another in the Church. The call to the priesthood to minister in a special way is a call from the Holy Spirit. As in any issue under consideration, openness to the Spirit is essential in discerning the signs of the times and sorting out what is essential from what is inessential. What has been suggested here is that perhaps celibacy does not have to be linked as irrevocably to the priesthood as it has in the past few centuries. If the apostles and early bishops were married and were able to live effectively holy lives, then men today might also be able to do so.

I recently read a *New York Times* article that described how the archbishop of Canterbury and his wife were going to have lunch with the Pope. It was the phrase "together with his wife" that struck me. The fact that there are good holy men, including the Nobel Peace Prize–winning Bishop Desmond Tutu of South Africa, who are married and ministering to their Churches in other Christian denominations can make the Catholic celibate stance seem somewhat embarrassing.

The call to celibacy is a special charism in the Church; it should be valued in itself. But, there could be a distinction made between the call to celibacy and the call to the priesthood. Not that they necessarily have to be viewed as mutually exclusive, but they are two charisms, neither of which can be mandated. Perhaps one day a theology of a married priesthood may find its way into the Church. Marriage and a priestly calling both can help to realize more fully the Kingdom of God on earth.

5

SEX AND THE CHURCH: BIRTH CONTROL, ABORTION, FERTILITY PROCEDURES

A young friend of mine recently had her first baby. She had a difficult pregnancy and spent twenty-two hours in labor. Her contractions stopped before the baby was completely delivered, and the doctor had to perform emergency surgery to extract the baby and then the placenta. A week later when I went to visit her and her beautiful baby boy, she told me that this prince of a fellow would be an only child because she would never go through another labor. Her husband told me he'd never seen so much blood and feared that his wife would bleed to death, despite the fact that medical personnel had started to give her transfusions and that with modern technology such an occurrence was highly unlikely. He talked about the fact that he had become keenly aware of why so many women in years past had died in childbirth. Both members of this couple have changed their minds about having only one child, but they at least have a choice about preventing a pregnancy, unlike most women in the past. They are both practicing Catholics: she teaches in a Catholic school, he coaches a parish basketball team, they go to Mass most Sundays, and they are generous, caring people. They want to give themselves time before they have another child and will use a reliable means of birth control. The issue is birth control.

Five years ago another friend of mine called with this story: She had three beautiful children, all of whom had been born premature because she was unable to carry the babies to term. The last one had been born thirteen weeks early, weighed only one pound, thirteen ounces, and was deaf and blind. She and her husband spent hours of time and energy to make a fulfilling life for their disadvantaged child as well as their other two children. The previous two years had been especially difficult because her teenage son had started having some "growing pains," as she put it. At forty-four she discovered she was pregnant again. Because of her age, a problem with high blood pressure, and her history of premature births, the doctor feared for not just the life of the new baby but also her own life, and suggested she terminate the pregnancy. She and her husband were practicing Catholics, but she was faced with an agonizing decision about whether or not to terminate this pregnancy. The issue was abortion.

The guidance counselor at a Catholic high school in the area where I live has been trying for eight years to have a child with her husband, who also teaches at a Catholic school. They long desperately to start a family. They've applied for adoption, but because her husband is over forty, they were told that the wait would be very long, and in fact, nothing was guaranteed. They began to see a fertility specialist in their quest for a child. He gave them some hope, but their archdiocesan insurance policy would not cover the cost when they began pursuing a course involving insemination of her husband's sperm and possible in vitro fertilization, which is forbidden by the Church. The cost of the procedures was prohibitive for them without insurance. They are angry and resentful that the Church, which they love and which holds as paramount the procreation of children in a marriage, seems to be betraying them. The issue is fertility procedures.

The issues of birth control, abortion, and fertility procedures are critical for Catholics today, and all three are colored by the Roman Catholic Church's attitude toward sex and sexuality, a major part of human life and relationships. The Church so frequently has spoken out about these matters that its teachings on sex have become a major way that the Church has defined itself in the twentieth century to the world. Objections to the way that the Church seems to have focused on sexual issues in recent times are raised by Catholics and non-Catholics alike, who see this as an obsession on the part of the Church hierarchy to control the sexual lives of its followers. As recently as 1995, in the encyclical *Evangelium Vitae:* "Gospel of Life," Pope John Paul II condemned artificial means of birth control, abortion, and fertility procedures outside of sexual intercourse as gravely immoral and part of the culture of death. Some Catholics have simply tuned out the Church's teachings on these and other issues, seeing them as an intrusion into a part of their lives ultimately personal, unique, and sacred; others wait expectantly for the Church to review these issues with a more open mind to the intimacy involved here and to take into account new scientific information before making judgments.

This chapter presents these issues in an attempt to explain what the Church teaches and why. Given the statistics about Catholics who use some means of artificial contraception (a May 1993 *National Catholic Reporter*/Gallup poll showed that approximately 73 percent of all American Catholic women do so), I had thought that birth control was not that big an issue. Then I started talking to people. While these individuals I talked to at work, in my parish, among family and friends, are practicing birth control with a good conscience, I realized that they still feel some anger toward the Church because what they are doing is not officially approved and in fact condemned by the Church. "It is none of the Church's business what my husband and I do in responsibly planning a family in this day and age" was a frequent response. Others I spoke to and articles I read displayed resentment that the Church's stance against birth control meant that it condemned and thwarted plans for population control in Third World countries where children are being born into abject poverty, misery, and suffering. Such resentment was publically voiced at the Beijing Conference on Women in the fall of 1995.

There are other ramifications to the Church's stance against birth control, particularly regarding the use of condoms. Condemning the use of condoms in countries in Africa means encouraging the spread of AIDS, which has reached epidemic proportions even among heterosexual couples and children, and lowered life expectancy there by almost ten years.

As with other teachings, the Church bases its ideas about sex and sexuality in the Scriptures, both the Old and New Testaments; like other ideas, the Catholic concept of sexuality has been conditioned culturally. Revelation itself, as contained in the Scriptures, is historically and culturally conditioned. The self-disclosure of God as expressed in Scripture is rendered in human language and human images, which were created by a specific group of people at a particular historical time. We see, for instance, that the images in the Old Testament of God as warrior, judge, and shepherd were conditioned by the time and physical environment in which the Old Testament writers lived. These images are limited in terms of a *full* disclosure of God. Jack Miles, a contemporary author and theologian, has shown in his book, *God: A Biography,* that in fact the image of God as presented in the Old Testament evolved over the centuries of Hebrew history. Once the wandering Jews had conquered and settled into the Promised Land and no longer needed the image of God as warrior, this image softened and changed. Similarly, other concepts in the Old Testament, including an understanding of sex, evolved over the centuries. Certainly the common practice of having more than one wife is a case in point. How we understand ourselves as sexual beings is certainly different today from several thousand years ago.

This presents a theological problem, however. If we admit that the Scriptures are culturally conditioned, then how are they to be understood and interpreted today? How are we to understand a theology of sexuality based on a literalist or metaphorical interpretation of the Scriptures? As was discussed in chapter 3, the case against women unfolded gradually. Revelation and theology became so intertwined over the centuries that they were almost indistinguishable. Our study of the Scripture reveals that much of it was written against the backdrop of a patriarchal culture, one that viewed women and sexuality as dangerous and, while necessary to the continuity of life, fearsome. By and large, anything related to sex has been labeled suspect by Christianity; until recently, Christians have been denied any view of sex as something to be celebrated joyously. We can forgive such attitudes in peoples who lived two or three thousand years ago, when the human body and its abilities to copulate and reproduce were thought to be connected to mysterious forces or powers linked to nature and the gods, but not today, when science has dispelled sexual myths and provided us with lots of information.

For the ancients, the male seed was the active principle of life, and women were merely the receptacles, gardens as it were, for the reception and germination of that seed. Since the emission of semen was the source of life, there were prohibitions against masturbation, seen as a means of loss of potential human beings. Greek philosophers believed that sex weakened men because energy went the way of sperm, out of the body. The Greek Stoics, who influenced later philosophies and early Christian writers, taught that the emotions were a form of human expression lower than activities of the mind. Sexual activity, often viewed as giving in to one's emotional life, was viewed as part of man's lower nature.

In the Old Testament the Book of Leviticus places ordinances against the issue of seminal fluid outside of intercourse, as well as ordinances related to a woman's menstrual flow. These bodily emissions, linked to uncleanliness and sin, carried with them commandments for purification (Lev. 15). The wonder, awe, and fear expressed in the Old Testament about anything genitalia-related led to a set of laws and taboos that still have an impact, even after we have unveiled the mysteries involved. Women often are thought to be unclean during their menstrual cycle, referred to by some people even today as "the curse" because God cursed Eve after the Fall (discussed in chapter 3), telling her it was in pain that she would bear children (Gen. 3:16).

The soul/body dualism of Plato's philosophy, mentioned earlier in chapter 4's discussion of Augustine's ideas, also affected thinking about sexuality as it is found in Scripture: Man is seen as defined by his mind and reason, woman by her ability to bear and nurture children, and therefore her attachment to the physical world. In this Platonic dualism it is the soul that gives the person dignity. Since women are connected to the physical world, to nature, they are subordinate to the male, the mind; it is the woman who must be controlled. This is probably where the stereotyping of women as irrational began.

In much ancient thinking—Hebrew as well as Greek—women were linked easily to the introduction of evil into the world and seen as seductresses, luring men to a lower level of existence. This idea is embodied, as was mentioned in chapter 3, in the second creation account found in the Book of Genesis. The Wisdom books of the Old Testament, probably influenced by the Greeks, frequently warn against the seductions by women as well: "And lo— the woman comes to meet him, robed like a harlot, with secret designs" (Prov. 5:1–6, 7, 9ff).

Despite the above, intercourse itself was seen for the most part as a good and a duty in the Old Testament, a part of human biology that protected the Chosen People and their covenant with God because it carried on their lineage through future generations. Marriage and sex were an essential part of the social and religious life of the Jew. Sex was considered a duty for both men and women. Most of the sexual proscriptions arose from the fear that the Chosen People would forget this primary duty of begetting children in the line of Abraham or that they would entangle themselves sexually with foreigners and thus contaminate the line of heritage. Within Judaism the idea of levirate marriages developed: If a woman's husband died, his brother was to marry the wife, ensuring the bloodline of his offspring. So important in the Old Testament is the continuation of Jewish lineage that women are viewed merely as the property of their husbands, like fertile land to which they have rights, in order to beget children. As a result of Israel's patriarchal society, women were kept in an inferior legal and social position, viewed as the possession of first their fathers and then their husbands. In fact, if a young Jewish woman had premarital sex, it was considered a sin not just against God, but also against her father. Both Exodus 20:17 and Jeremiah 6:12 list a man's wife as part of his possessions. The contracting parties in a marriage were not the couple, the man and woman. The *fathers* of the couple drew up a contract. The father of the young woman, in exchange for a payment, gave his daughter away. The young man, the husband (which literally means "owner of the property"), would marry (which also means "to possess") the wife. Her duty was to produce children. It was considered a curse and a humiliation among the Hebrews to be unable to produce children. Sex and marriage took on a fundamentally functional character. Certainly there are great stories of romantic love in the Old Testament, such as Isaac's love for Rachel (Gen. 24:67) and Jacob's love for Rebecca, which led him to work for seven years to obtain her as his wife (Gen. 29). We have to believe that sex was something joyous and freeing for the Old Testament peoples, as is evidenced by the lyrical, erotic Song of Songs. For the most part, however, marriage was prized as a process of providing heirs, preferably male heirs. If a wife was unable to bring children into the world, she would not hesitate to provide a concubine for her husband in order to bear children for him, as did Sarah for Abraham before she was able to conceive Isaac.

From the Old Testament we also inherit attitudes about sex based on the need for cultic purity, which the Hebrews shared with other ancient cultures. It was a common practice among many of the ancient Hebrews' neighbors, like the Babylonians and Chaldeans and later the Greeks and Romans, to go to a temple prostitute, thus ensuring blessings from the gods on crops and their lives in general. The Hebrews often are admonished in the Old Testament about practicing these pagan rituals of their neighbors, considered to be a type of idolatry strictly forbidden to Jews. Prostitution became equated with infidelity to the covenant with God, best expressed by the prophet Hosea: Marriage becomes the image of God's relationship to his people, one of fidelity, and prostitution becomes synonymous with the opposite. Frequently in the Old Testament, when Israel was unfaithful, she was referred to as a prostitute or a whore. Over several thousand years the Hebrews wrestled with questions of sexuality because of the social and economic factors that were a part of their religious customs, beliefs, and identity; many of the prohibitions attached to sex involve these social and economic factors, as well as religious considerations.

In the New Testament, sexual matters are sometimes reflections of Old Testament understandings, since Jesus and his first followers had been raised under the Law. Jesus himself has very little to say about sex.

It is important to remember also that the New Testament is a reflection not only on the life and ministry of Jesus, but on the problems faced by his early followers as they tried to live without his physical presence in a world often at odds with his message. The writings of the New Testament on sexuality are occasional, conditioned by questions arising from particular circumstances. Sometimes statements are taken out of context and applied unsystematically to our present situation to justify a particular point of view—on remaining celibate, for instance. It is necessary to ask when reading the New Testament, what was the occasion or situation or problem that prompted this passage? When New Testament writers tell us that Jesus allowed a woman with a flow of blood to touch him, that he allowed a prostitute to wash his feet, and that he saved an adulterous woman from stoning, they are saying more about his willingness to break with the strict laws of punishment and exclusion than about his attitudes toward sex. That Jesus is said to have performed his first miracle at a wedding in Cana, that he frequently used the imagery of wedding banquets and the bridegroom (Matt. 22:1–14; 25: 1–13; Mark 2:19) to communicate something about the Kingdom of God, gives evidence for the high regard he placed on love, marriage, and even sexual intimacy. (Quite appropriately, these passages are also mentioned in chapter 4's discussion of celibacy and marriage.)

The authors of the New Testament also were influenced by the expectation of the immediate return of Jesus and the establishment of the Kingdom of God. (Chapter 4 described how great value came to be placed on the state of virginity or celibacy for the sake of the Kingdom of God.) Saint Paul encouraged the unmarried to prepare for the return of Christ without the encumbrances of marriage. Biblical eschatology has led to a view of sexual pleasure as problematic (Mark 12:25) because such pleasure is lacking in the afterlife; the happiness of the Kingdom was beyond anything conceived in this earthly life (1 Cor. 2:9). Saint Paul's letters disparage sex because of the imminent coming of the Kingdom, but also because prostitution was rampant during his time; he felt compelled to warn against the weakness of the flesh and giving in to that which is forbidden, including temple prostitution. In defense of Paul, it should be pointed out that he also provides some often-quoted passages in which he exalts married life, viewing it as a symbol of the relationship Christ has with his Church (Eph. 5:25).

But a number of factors contributed to the creation of a negative attitude toward sex in the New Testament. First, because Jesus presumably was not married, he presumably was celibate and so had no sexual relations. Second, Paul was celibate, as he himself states; he and Jesus—both celibates—are held up as role models of Christian living, so celibacy must be good. Third, expectation of the immediate return of Christ made Christians cautious about becoming involved in this world. And finally, because Paul's writings were so influential in the formation of Christianity—he himself having been influenced by Old Testament beliefs and driven by a need to keep Christian converts from resorting back to pagan sexual practices—the understanding of sex that emerges in the first century is that of a barely tolerated human activity.

By the time the early Church Fathers of the second and third centuries began writing, sex had been reduced to something functional—for procreation—in Christianity. Christian teaching by the early Church Fathers on sex, from the second to the fourth century, relied first on New Testament statements taken in a literalist framework, and secondly on Greek philosophies such as those of the Stoics, who viewed celibacy as a noble ideal and marriage as a concession to those who could not live up to the ideal. The Gnostic philosophy also influenced the Church Fathers. Gnostics viewed sex and marriage as intrinsically evil because they were a part of the material world. In fact, they viewed procreation itself as evil for continuing to bring evil into the world, since human beings are a part of the material, fallen world. Christian teachers countered this by writing that sex was good, but only within marriage and for the sole purpose of procreation. They were also influenced by Neoplatonic dualism, seeing the spirit world as superior to the material world. Consequently, a certain incompatibility between sexuality and sanctity found its way into Christian writing.

Augustine (354–430), also mentioned in chapter 4's discussion of celibacy, had perhaps the strongest influence on the developing attitudes toward sex and sexuality. Augustine was influenced by the Neoplatonic dualism of the spiritual world as superior to the material world but also by the Manichean philosophy, in which the world is viewed as though it were in a *cosmic conflict* between the spiritual world and the material world, between the forces of light and darkness, between good and evil. His personal life before his conversion, as he describes it, was lived in darkness, including sexual license and lustful self-indulgence. His conversion symbolized light and goodness, and everything about his former life was rejected as evil and sinful. Augustine wrote that after the Fall, Adam and Eve covered themselves because they were ashamed. He also taught that all sexual acts are in some sense sinful because at least some lust is involved in virtually every one. For Augustine, the sin of Adam and Eve was passed down for generations through sexual intercourse; thus, all humans carry Adam and Eve's Original Sin. Conjugal love was viewed as a duty and a good only insofar as it was directed toward the end for which it was naturally intended, procreation, and continence was enjoined on partners in a barren marriage, though no penalty was given for a violation of this injunction. As the greatest theologian of the first five centuries of the Church, Augustine in his works systematized the influence of Manichean sexual cynicism and early Christian skepticism toward sex and passed it on to successive generations:

> At the end of the Patristic era, the Christian attitude toward sexuality was generally pessimistic. Although some recognized sexuality itself as good because of its procreative function, the pleasure attached to sex was viewed as a consequence of original sin. The experience of sexual pleasure therefore, even indeliberate, and even within marriage for the purpose of procreation was somehow tainted with sin. (Kosnik, *Human Sexuality,* 37)

Since the only valid reason to have sex was procreation, any attempt to prevent conception was regarded as categorically sinful. Sex simply for pleasure was viewed as lustful, selfish, and giving in to one's lower nature.

This attitude characterized the Church for about a millennium. From Augustine's death until the twelfth century, writings and laws on sex and marriage were codified by monks and bishops, far removed from the realities of living an intimate life of sexual love.

The medieval monks of the tenth and eleventh centuries began writing guides, or penitentials, for priests hearing confessions so they would know which punishments to give out to penitents seeking forgiveness of their sins. Every sin imaginable from stealing a neighbor's chickens to sleeping with a neighbor's wife was addressed. These manuals helped ingrain in Church membership an attitude that sin consisted of individual acts, with a penance attached to each act. The list of sexual sins in these manuals, sins of impurity and lust, was long; punishments were harsh. One of the criteria for determining the seriousness of a sexual sin was whether or not the desire to procreate was attached to the act. Sex outside of marriage, adultery, prostitution, masturbation, homosexuality, even a man's withdrawal during sexual intercourse or having sex with his pregnant wife, were all viewed as serious sinful offenses, since the procreative intent was either ignored or not primary.

In 1140, the monk Gratian compiled the first collection of canon laws, official Church laws, accepted as authoritative and binding on Church members. Contraception was declared a sin against God and nature.

The concept of contraception as a sin against nature reached a scholastic high point in the thinking of Thomas Aquinas in the thirteenth century. And while Thomas views favorably the institution of marriage as well as marital intercourse, he is remembered more in subsequent Church teaching for his support of the natural law theory in judging the morality of human acts. Scholastic thought as epitomized in Aquinas considers human reason very important for the determination of the moral order. It says that through reason we observe in the universe that there is a natural order to life at work. Furthermore, there is a relationship between this earthly ordering of the cosmos and the supernatural order, since God has created all that exists and created it good (Gen. 1:31). The natural law theory for judging the morality of an act is based on whether or not an action is ordered toward what is perceived to be its natural end. The natural end of sex, said the Scholastics, is conception. Therefore, if that natural ordering is interfered with by contraception, an act is evil and sinful. The first papal injunction against birth control was made by Pope Gregory IX in 1234, when a list of authoritative decretals was produced to make certain precepts universally binding on all Christians. One of these decretals banned anything hindering the conception of a child during intercourse. Pope Sixtus V went further in a statement issued in 1588, *Effraenatam:* "Without Restraint," comparing contraception to homicide. It must be noted, however, that part of the reason for the statement was the rampant prostitution in Rome in his day and also the scandal that wafted around the Church itself due to the indiscreet sexual activity of its own clergy.

Consequently, the teaching that sex was naturally ordered toward conception and eventually procreation led to a view that the sacrament of marriage itself had a primary end, the procreation of children. It was several centuries later that a discussion of a secondary end of marriage, the love and support of spouses, began to be considered in Church teaching. For centuries marriage was considered to have primary and secondary ends. The secondary end was not stressed in Christian teaching.

Sex for pleasure was looked down upon for the most part, although there were voices of objection, particularly Martin Le Maistre (1432–1481) and Thomas Sanchez, the sixteenth-century specialist on marriage who had the audacity to write: "There is no sin in spouses who intend to have intercourse simply as spouses" (Kosnik, *Human Sexuality,* 44). By the eighteenth century, the growing awareness of the devastating effects of poverty on families, the economic considerations of raising a family responsibly, the change from a rural economy (where a large family was a necessity) to urban centers (where a large family could lead to hardship), and the difficulties in childbearing itself created a consciousness among people that controlling the size of a family was a significant factor in having a family at all. Despite the fact that the Church had always taught that contraception was wrong, people throughout history had for one reason or another attempted contraceptive measures. These attempts began to increase in the eighteenth and nineteenth centuries.

An important scientific development occurred in the nineteenth century—the discovery of the ovum and the realization that there are only a few days a month, depending on a woman's menstrual and ovulatory cycle, during which a woman is actually fertile and therefore able to conceive a child. The realization that every conjugal act is *not* in fact open to procreation sent Catholic moralists into a frenzy, since for centuries the teaching had been that the justification for every conjugal act had been procreation. Now scientists were saying that not every conjugal act is in itself open to new life. Moral theologians for the Church began talking about the importance of at least having the intention to procreate whenever couples engaged in intercourse, even if a couple was timing intercourse *not* to allow pregnancy to occur.

Fuel was added to the fire in 1930 when the Anglican bishops held a meeting at Lambeth, England, approving artificial means of birth control when Christian couples felt a moral obligation to limit the size of families. They did, however, condemn the use of sexual intercourse for selfish reasons such as luxury or mere convenience. Pius XI reacted quickly and strongly to the Lambeth meeting by issuing an encyclical entitled *Casti Connubii:* "Pure Marriage" or "On Chaste Marriage," condemning birth control as intrinsically against nature, deliberately depriving the sexual act of its natural ordering to the generation of offspring. Any use of contraception was to be considered a grave sin. The encyclical did, however, suggest that because of the secondary ends of marriage, "mutual aid, the cultivating of mutual love, and the quieting of concupiscence" (*The English Translation,* 28), a couple could time their sexual relations as a means to regulate births, thus giving tacit permission, but not approval, to the rhythm method of charting one's menstrual cycle and timing intercourse accordingly. This was viewed as a natural form of responsibly controlling births. Many proponents for relaxing the teaching on birth control cite this as an inherent contradiction. For the Church to say that on the one hand every act of intercourse ought to remain open to the possibility of conception and on the other hand that Catholics can plan their sexual acts in a way that would most likely prevent pregnancy is illogical and hypocritical, even if it is under the umbrella of natural family planning.

Another significant aspect of this encyclical was the contribution it made toward a more personalist approach to marriage by stating that marriage is to be "the mutual inward molding of a husband and a wife to perfect each other, and can in a real sense be said to be the chief reason and purpose of marriage, provided matrimony be looked at not in the restricted sense as instituted for the proper conception and education of children, but more widely as the blending of life as a whole and the mutual interchange and sharing thereof" (ibid., 4). This was a real breakthrough in developing the idea that the so-called secondary end of marriage was now moving toward a more prominent position in Catholic teaching. This change in attitude was mirrored in the consequent writings of theologians such as

Herbert Doms, the German priest who published *The Meaning of Marriage* in 1935; these scholars began to insert the personalist values of mutual love, support, and growth into their writings on marriage. These developments set the stage for the Second Vatican Council's statement on marriage, which carefully avoided mentioning the concepts of primary and secondary ends of marriage, but blended the nobility of the conjugal act as an expression of mutual love and respect with the idea of the importance of having children as the "supreme gift" of a marriage (GS, para. 49). The official Church, however, continued to discourage any means of birth control until 1951, when in an address to the Italian Catholic Society of Midwives, Pius XII publicly approved the rhythm method as a means of birth control, but only when serious medical, eugenic, or social conditions prevailed.

Proponents of the Church's teaching on birth control also advocate the natural family planning method of ensuring the desired number of children. Referred to as NFP, this method boasts that it is 90 percent effective, and it claims to be less harmful to a woman's body than the Pill or uterine devices. NFP dictates that women must follow their bodily rhythms and cycles very closely in order to abstain from sex while they are ovulating. There are apparently many women who are satisfied with this method. However, this is difficult for couples who want to give expression to their love spontaneously, when it seems called for in a loving, encouraging, sometimes forgiving relationship. If one has to run to a calendar and check if this is indeed a proper moment, not associated with the risk of pregnancy, before having sexual intercourse, some intimacy could be lost in the process. The NFP proponents would say that there are ways other than sexual intercourse to express love, but most couples argue that there is nothing like the real thing. And attempts to teach and encourage people in Third World countries to use this method provide many challenges and often prove unsuccessful.

By the 1950s the two purposes of marriage were seen as inseparable, suggesting that the human person was the integrating element. The Second Vatican Council also recognized the difficulties that modern life and society imposed on the family and acknowl-edged that there "were circumstances where at least temporarily the size of . . . families should not be increased" (GS, para. 51). How to limit the size of a family without using contraceptives was now the issue, involving decisions to be made by the couple, who were to use, in the words of the Second Vatican Council, "the nature of the human person and his acts" (ibid.) as their compass in the determi-nation of the morality of human sexual acts. The act alone was no longer the focus; the "nature of the human person" was *also* to be taken into account. This was a real breakthrough for the Church, which finally was able to discuss sex openly as an interpersonal rela-tionship between husband and wife rather than as a series of sexual acts resulting in children. Together with a redefinition of the Church as the People of God, and an emphasis on religious freedom and the importance of individual conscience, as outlined in Vatican II's Dec-laration on Religious Freedom (*Dignitatis Humanae:* "Of the Dig-nity of the Human [Person]"), this breakthrough set the stage for a revolution among Catholics—laypeople as well as theologians and bishops—on the issue of birth control and other aspects of sexuality.

Indeed, many societal and religious conditions factored into this revolution. A more person-centered morality, scientific advances, overpopulation, sociological studies on the family, ideas of respon-sible parenting, a new awareness and appreciation of the dignity and freedom of the individual, and biblical research all contributed to an awareness for the need to change centuries-old attitudes toward sex, sexuality, and birth control. No doubt the sexual revolution going on in the sixties in general was also a contributing factor. Not to be overlooked in this list, of course, was the development and use of the Pill. Since the late 1950s the convenient birth control pill had grown in popularity, and many women, Catholic and non-Catholic, were using it as a means of contraception.

Pope John XXIII knew that a discussion of birth control on the floor of the council might bring all proceedings to a halt because of the strong opinions on both sides of the issue. In 1963 he estab-lished a Pontifical Commission on Population, Family, and Birth to examine the issue. Unfortunately, John XXIII died before the members of the commission met, but his successor, Paul VI, carried out his intent. The six men originally on the commission soon realized that the issue, involving theological, sociological, and scientific points of view, was more than they could handle. Seven more members, including laypeople, were added to the commission to examine such questions as what was natural or unnatural in regulating births, what was the place of science in regulating births, and how the Church could change its teaching without losing its credibility. By 1964 more members were added to the commission to deal with the problems, bringing the number to fifty-eight.

Among the new members of the commission were the Crowleys, a Catholic couple, who had been active in the Christian Family Movement, which had developed to support Catholic couples in maintaining a loving relationship and raising children as strong, active Christians. The Crowleys sent out questionnaires to other members of CFM to solicit their opinions and reactions before arriving at Rome for meetings. Most of the married couples who responded urged the Crowleys to present to the commission a case for changing the official teaching policy of the Church on birth control. Relying on the rhythm method, as many Catholics had been doing, had threatened the integrity of many a family. Members wrote letters to the Crowleys telling them how painful was the lack of spontaneity in expressing their love for one another and how ineffective was the method itself. Obviously, having to wait for the right moment of a woman's menstrual cycle to express love was not easy on a marriage and resulted in many rhythm babies. After two years, a solid majority of the commission favored changing the teaching and issued a report of their findings called "Responsible Parenthood," later known as the Commission's Majority Report. Those opposing a change in the teaching also issued their findings, known as the Minority Report. "Several published reports stated that the full commission voted on the two proposals before adjourning and that the result was 52–4 in favor of the Majority Report" (Fox, *Sexuality,* 61). The commission handed over its work to the Pope, awaiting his response.

There was tremendous anticipation on the part of Catholics throughout the world, and most felt optimistic that the teaching would be changed. Many Catholics had already begun to use artificial means of birth control, considering rhythm to be *un*natural, since it inhibited a natural, spontaneous expression of love between a couple and was unreliable. The Pope at first was expected to rule on the Commission's findings quickly, but as time went on and leaks were made to the press about what the teaching would be, people again began to take sides. Finally on July 25, 1968, more than two years after the adjournment of the commission, Paul VI issued his teaching in what was to be his last encyclical, *Humanae Vitae:* "On Human Life." However beautifully worded some of the sections on marriage and love may be in this encyclical, it is known and remembered for one thing: upholding the traditional teaching and ban on the use of any artificial means of birth control. The key statement of the document, "The Church calling human beings back to the observance of the natural law, as interpreted by the constant doctrine, teaches that each and every act must remain open to the transmission of life" (HV, para. 11), was seized upon by people on both sides of the issue. The long-awaited teaching had arrived, but it flew in the face of the commission who had worked diligently for its issuance, trusting that the notion of collegiality promoted at Vatican II would assure that advocacy for change would be considered. It flew in the face of the personalist approach toward sex espoused by Vatican II, which had rooted moral decision-making in *both* "the human person and his acts," by reverting back to the natural law theory and an emphasis on the act in itself. Many considered this encyclical as an affront to Vatican II and to the memory of John XXIII.

The consequences of this document were far reaching. The responses were not simply a matter of dissent or dissatisfaction. They were more disillusionment and disbelief. The general Catholic population simply could not believe that they were expected to keep every act of intercourse open to the possibility of pregnancy. Many critics point to the internal inconsistency of the encyclical, which states that each and every act must be open to the transmission of life but also that "the rhythm system of contraception may be used for appropriate reasons" (HV, para. 16). To say that people like the Crowleys and those who had petitioned them to support the use of birth control were extremely disappointed is an understatement. Many Catholic couples had already been told by their parish priests that their use of artificial birth control could be condoned. And Catholic theologians questioned how such a teaching could be promulgated when it was based not in revelation but in natural law. If ever there was a moment when the Church leadership seemed out of touch with people's lives and daily struggles, this was it. This document, then, helped to bring about a general erosion of the laity's respect for and trust in the teaching role of the magisterium of the Church. As mentioned in the introduction to this book, respected theologian Charles Curran, who was one of my college professors, was removed from a tenured teaching position at Catholic University for his dissent regarding some parts of *Humanae Vitae*. The general public, Catholic as well as non-Catholic, does not see the sense in such a teaching and believes that one can practice artificial means of birth control and still be a good Catholic. Not only do Catholics disagree with the teaching for themselves, but many resent the fact that the Church not only preaches against contraception to its own following but also works publicly, putting pressure on national and international organizations to disallow the availability and use of contraception despite the AIDS epidemic, despite the issues of poverty, famine, ill treatment of women, and reproductive rights in various parts of the world.

Since the encyclical was issued thirty years ago, the official teaching has not changed. In fact, in 1993 Pope John Paul II issued the encyclical *Veritatis Splendor:* "Splendor of Truth," in which he confirmed the longtime teaching that artificial birth control is morally objectionable. Each year some of my students put before me the question "If the Church considers abortion so terrible, then why won't it allow artificial birth control to avoid unwanted pregnancies?" An oversimplified question? Perhaps, but it doesn't take much reasoning to come to the conclusion that there could be fewer unwanted pregnancies if the attitudes toward birth control were not so stringent. Because of this teaching, which makes the magisterium of the Church appear to be removed from the real-life experiences of the faithful, some of the more important teachings of the Church on other social issues are now overlooked by Catholics. Because of the bad blood bred by *Humanae Vitae* and the feeling of many Catholics that the Church in general is out of touch, other encyclicals, documents, or teachings issued by the magisterium are sometimes ignored.

Finally, this teaching on birth control reinforces the centuries-old teaching that sex is something that ought to have one specific end, children, rather than viewing sex as a more general mutual embodiment of love between two people, a perfectly justifiable end in itself. The teaching belittles the meaning of marriage as that covenant relationship between two people intended to help and support one another in the journey of life toward salvation, when it overlooks the real need a couple may have to control the number of births to maintain that covenant relationship. No other sacrament, except the Eucharist, is as Incarnational as the sacrament of marriage. Marriage is also the only sacrament in which the couple themselves are the ministers of the sacrament, a fact that highlights what ought to be the personalist approach to all that these two people share and create in their lives together.

When a couple extends itself through love into the creation of another being, their child, this is a continuation of the Kingdom of God on earth. A precious gift, this symbol of love between two persons needs to be guarded, protected, educated, and loved in a responsible way so that he or she too will be able to continue the Kingdom of God throughout life. Planning, and preparing for children is not something that can be done in a haphazard way today, given the social and economic conditions we face. That some couples will choose not to have children to further their own lives is a given, with or without the teaching on birth control. But that the Church needs to respect and promote a type of responsible parenting to build up the Kingdom also seems to be a given. Until the Church begins to teach a type of joyful, celebratory theology of Christian marriage and family, people will feel distanced from the Church and its teaching on sex.

⟡

OPINIONS ON THE ISSUE of abortion are conditioned by many of the same attitudes and teachings of the Church on sex and sexuality in general, but it is also a far more complex issue than that of birth control or any other issue discussed herein because of its serious moral implications. The Church, and those against abortion, see abortion as the killing of human life, equivalent to homicide. The debate on whether or not abortion is the killing of a person makes this issue a highly emotional and controversial one. At the heart of this issue is the question, when does human life begin?

I count myself among the many Catholics who personally believe abortion is wrong, but support the right of women to make their own decisions and feel divided about the absolutist attitude of the Church in regard to abortion. Few Catholics, or Americans, for that matter, sanction the wanton use of abortion as a customary means of birth control. The mention of abortion often brings to mind visions of protests, bombings, grotesque pictures of fetuses, and even the killing of abortion doctors and/or their patients. People have mobilized and categorize themselves and others as either "pro-life" or "pro-choice"; I for one refuse to be categorized. For people like myself, who try to be open to the particular situations of individuals faced with an abortion decision, this is not an easy issue to take sides on, and yet the Church forces us to take sides. The issue is complicated further by the fact that this is not just a religious issue, but also a political one. Bishops have preached against politicians who support the right of a woman to make that decision for herself, even though those government representatives privately may hold that abortion is wrong. This is an issue both private and public. I find it difficult not to acknowledge that there is a miracle of life occurring from the earliest days of fertilization to birth. On the other hand, I know that the exact moment of conception is difficult to determine, and that differentiation, or the point at which the zygote can separate into twins, triplets, or more, does not happen until sometime around the fourteenth day. So I question whether human life is present at the moment of conception to the extent that we can call it murder if termination occurs. Abortion is also a social issue. It affects millions of women each year, many of whom are lost and alone, living in poverty, without the support of a spouse. There are also many educated, *non*poor, as well as married women who seek abortions for personal reasons that are difficult, if not impossible, to judge.

There are vast numbers of the human population in India or China who do not believe in the concept of an individual, immortal human soul, and who view abortion as a "Catholic" issue because we *do* believe in the immortality of the soul. The soul, Catholics believe, distinguishes humans as created in the image and likeness of God; makes the human person more than just a mass of cells at the beginning of its life; and is, according to the Church, infused into the new life at the moment of conception.

There are many Catholic women who see the abortion issue as yet another situation in which an all-celibate male clergy is dictating what one ought to believe and practice, while it is still *women* who are being victimized by this absolutist attitude. My high school and college students ask the question, "How can a group of celibate men ever imagine what it must be like to find yourself pregnant, alone, and afraid?" The decision to have or not have an abortion is viewed as a woman's problem and the woman's sin because it is her body facing the consequences of pregnancy. Male responsibility for pregnancy and child care is an issue that rarely receives the level of attention accorded to abortion. Because people look to their faith for guidance and comfort, many would welcome on this issue an attitude of loving compassion and concern from the Church. The issue of abortion, like that of sexuality and birth control, is viewed sometimes as part of the Church platform. Because the Church includes millions of members, is highly organized, and has an authoritative head, the Church has been able to mobilize vast numbers of people to its cause—another reason so many people equate the anti-abortion movement with Catholicism. Of course, this is not just a Catholic issue. There is a strong, conservative Protestant coalition that works against abortion as well, along with many fringe elements well known for their extremist measures. Nonetheless, the Church is often the focus of the media in regard to an anti-abortion stance, which makes for bad publicity and poor public relations for the Church among those advocating greater tolerance for other opinions.

While the Church hires scientists, sociologists, and labor leaders to help draw up encyclicals on capital punishment, labor, and war, it operates in a vacuum in terms of its teaching on sex or ignores suggestions when it does invite discussion on sex-related matters, as happened in the case of the Pontifical Commission on Population, Family, and Birth. Despite the fact that scientists and gynecologists had provided input for the commission that investigated birth control for the Church, the majority opinion was rejected, the conservative minority opinion was accepted. It is as if Church leaders do not want help in looking at these issues. Birth control, abortion, and homosexuality remain intrinsically wrong and intrinsically disordered, according to the Church, despite the research of sociologists, scientists, or psychologists. As a result the teachings often are dismissed by an educated populace.

The Church has always maintained, at least in theory, that all of life and any life is sacred, and so debate about abortion began early in Church history. The issue then as now is, when does hominization, or ensoulment, take place? In other words, when does the fetus achieve human status so that abortion could be considered homicide? As early as the second century, some Christian thinkers considered abortion a serious sin. For centuries, however, the Church had relied on Aristotle's philosophy for their theories of "ensoulment" in determining the seriousness of abortion, a philosophy based on a belief in delayed hominization. Aristotle's philosophy included a concept called hylomorphism, the belief that the soul, as the life principle that animates the body, can only animate the sort of body that is appropriate to that soul. The theory of hylomorphism rejects the dualistic notion that the human person is made up of two separate elements, the body and the spirit, but rather indicates that the two are united. While there may be, at the beginning of conception, primal matter, it is not until that matter is developed to a certain point that it is capable of receiving a human soul, says Aristotle. This implies that hominization does not occur until *after* the embryo has taken on the characteristics of the human body. A plant is animated by a vegetative soul, and a human body by a rational human soul. In applying this theory to human fetal development, Aristotle concluded that a human fetus could acquire a human soul, that is be a true human being, only when it had developed human bodily form. Ensoulment for a male occurred, according to Aristotle, after about forty days, and for a female after ninety days (another indication of the shallow regard for women) into development. The fifth-century Augustine held to Aristotle's philosophy, writing, "The great question about the soul is not hastily decided by unargued and rash judgment; the law does not prove that the act [abortion] pertains to homicide, for there cannot yet be said to be a live soul in a body that lacks sensation when it is not formed in flesh, and so not yet endowed with sense"("On Exodus" 21.80, as quoted in Hurst, *The History of Abortion in the Catholic Church*, 7).

Abortion was viewed by some early Church Fathers as a serious sexual sin because it was often used to hide illicit sex, and also because it clearly violated the rule that sex was to be engaged in only for the purpose of procreation. In 1140, when Gratian codified canon law, abortion was condemned, but it was also concluded that the human soul is not infused until the fetus is formed. Until 1869 the church continued to distinguish between the ensouled fetus and the unensouled embryo in determining the gravity of the situation. Even Thomas Aquinas, during the Scholastic period, embraced Aristotle's approach to ensoulment. Each soul is subsumed by the succeeding soul: "This vegetative soul which comes first, when the embryo lives the life of a plant, is corrupted and is succeeded by a more perfect soul, which is both nutritive and sensitive, and then the embryo lives an animal life; and when this is corrupted, it is succeeded by the rational soul, induced from without. Since the soul is united to the body as its form, it is not united to a body other than one of which it is properly the act. Now the soul is the act of an organic body" (*Summa Contra Gentiles,* 2.89.) This hylomorphic theory holds that hominization is delayed until the soul can be received in a body capable of receiving it, one that has developed beyond the earliest stages of development. Proponents of this theory, even today, cite the fact that there are vast numbers of spontaneous abortions or miscarriages that occur within the first four weeks of pregnancy, and that it is hard to believe that each of these embryos has a human soul.

Despite the support for this theory of hominization, the argument continued in theological circles about when hominization occurred and whether or not abortion was murder. As mentioned earlier in this chapter, in 1588 Pope Sixtus V issued the statement *Effraenatam:* "Without Restraint," which indicates that abortion and contraception are murder, that they are both secular and religious crimes by their very nature and merit excommunication. There are no exceptions, not even an abortion to save a mother's life, otherwise known as a therapeutic abortion.

An unrelated theological development in the sixteenth century had an effect on the abortion debate: the increased devotion to Mary that was encouraged by the Church, particularly devotion to the Immaculate Conception of Mary (discussed in chapter 4). In 1701 the Pope declared the associated holy day (December 8) one of universal obligation. Because the teaching on Immaculate Conception holds that Mary was given grace from the moment of conception, which means that she must have had a soul at that moment, the idea of ensoulment at the moment of conception was given support by theologians and Church Fathers. The idea of delayed hominization was losing ground. Many Church thinkers began to argue that since we don't know exactly when hominization occurs, we ought to consider the *possibility* of it occurring at the moment of conception sufficient reason not to perform abortions, "just in case." The idea of "better safe than sorry" began to emerge, and the trend toward the Church's present attitude about ensoulment from the moment of conception became the favored theological teaching, though the idea of delayed hominization still held some influence, particularly in regard to therapeutic abortions. As has been mentioned, some people thought that not even the potential death of the mother justified an abortion, but there was another school of thought that said it would be permissible to abort an unformed fetus if the primary intention was to save the mother, *not* kill the fetus. Furthermore, it was argued, the fetus in this instance could be viewed as an aggressor against the life of the mother; self-defense justifies the taking of this life. Paul VI, however, in *Humanae Vitae* asserted that even therapeutic abortions were wrong: "directly willed and procured abortion, even if for therapeutic reasons, is to be absolutely excluded as licit" (HV, para. 13). (In the early twentieth century the Church backed away from permitting therapeutic abortions. Two exceptions can be made: in the case of an ectopic pregnancy or in the case of a cancerous uterus, even that of a pregnant woman. Neither of these therapeutic types of abortions is considered murder, since in both cases the fetus would die anyway, and the mother's life could be saved.)

Gradually, the debates about when ensoulment takes place and about the distinctions between the unformed and formed fetus were abandoned. In 1869 Pius IX issued *Apostolicae Sedis:* "From the Apostolic Seat," forbidding abortion at any stage of pregnancy, with the threat of excommunication. This statement was made around the same time that the debate on the Pope's ability to make infallible statements was being carried on. This was the first official papal statement on abortion and so was seen by many as carrying additional authoritative moral weight. An aura of papal infallibility has certainly surrounded the issue of abortion since that time, even though there is not an infallible statement on the subject. Canon law was updated in 1917, and this update also ignored the question of delayed hominization by threatening excommunication for the mother and any others involved in the procurement of an abortion.

Pius XII's Address to the Italian Catholic Society of Midwives in 1951 as well as Paul VI's *Humanae Vitae* in 1968 condemned all abortions for any reason as acts of homicide, and also forbade contraception because both practices intend to separate sexual union from procreation.

In more modern times the distinction between human life and potential human life has blurred, further adding fuel to the abortion debate. In 1974, the Sacred Congregation for the Doctrine of Faith issued the Declaration on Procuring Abortion, which states: "In reality, respect for human life is called for from the time that the process of generation begins. From the time the ovum is fertilized, a life is begun which is neither that of the father nor the mother; it is rather the life of a new human being with his or her own growth. It would never be made human if it were not human already" (Fox, *Sexuality*, 100). In this statement any idea of delayed hominization is ignored. But this has not put to rest disputes on the subject. Philosophers, theologians, and even scientists still argue the significant point of when human life as distinguished from potential human life actually begins, thus complicating the issue of whether or not abortion is murder. As has been mentioned in this chapter, science has shown that twinning can occur up to fourteen days or at least through the morola stage from one embryo. Furthermore, it has shown that several embryos may recombine to form one. According to the immediate hominization theory, this would mean that souls can multiply or decrease in number. Also, as cited earlier, between fertilization and complete implantation a large percent of all embryos are naturally discarded by the body; it is reasonable to question whether all of these embryos had human souls. If so, how could they be lost so easily, and what happens to them?

The Catholic teaching on abortion is quite clear. Abortion, except for the therapeutic abortions defined in this chapter, is always wrong, at any time for any reason. However, the hominization debate causes conflicting opinions on this teaching, and they are not likely to go away in the near future. Is a potential human being the same as an *actual* human being? Is a mass of undifferentiated cells to be given the same status as a fully developed human person? Should a funeral mass be said for every miscarriage a woman suffers? Because of these questions and other more personal questions—such as, what about abortion in the case of incest or rape?—the discussion, at least in the minds of many Catholics, is unresolved. The abortion issue is also ensnared in the Church's teaching on birth control. The implication here is that if birth control was not condemned, there would be fewer people turning to abortion, especially in Third World countries. The Church's forceful entry into the political arena on this issue has clouded the feelings of some Catholics on the Church's stance since they see the public condemnation as an intrusion into an area of life that is private and personal for the world community. Their fear is that the Church's anti-abortion influence could lead to pre–*Roe* v. *Wade* conditions, inviting disproportionate suffering on the poor in our country and a return to back-alley abortions, leaving desperate women wounded or dead. These are reasonable concerns, which beg for further discussion on this issue. Finally, there will be another round of debates and questions when the Food and Drug Administration here in the United States approves the use of the abortifacient pill RU-486 (mifepristone) already available in France.

❖

GROWING UP CATHOLIC and entering into a marriage means that we are expected to become parents. When a couple is faced with the challenge of infertility, when after months and years they are unable to conceive, the problem for them can be devastating. Questioning the significance of their relationship, their marriage, and even their individual worth becomes almost inevitable as they try to have a child. In the past, many couples attempted to get on with life, some feeling cheated, others trying adoption. Today medical technology has made tremendous advances in providing reproductive opportunities for couples seeking to have children who have been otherwise unsuccessful in their attempts. Reasons for infertility are many and varied; likewise, the means of overcoming this problem are also varied. Artificial insemination by the husband, by another donor, in vitro fertilization, embryo transfer, and gamete intrafallopian transfer are some of the more common means of reproductive fertility procedures. Other options include surrogate mothers. In all of these procedures, conception comes about outside of the actual conjugal act of intercourse. For this reason alone, some people in the Church argue that such procedures go against natural law. But the issue is more complicated than that.

In 1987 the document Instruction on Respect for Human Life in Its Origin and on the Dignity of Procreation (*Donum Vitae:* "Gift of Life"),* was published as the official word of the Church on this issue. The Congregation for the Doctrine of Faith, which issued this document, rightly recognizes the complexity of the issue and divides its teaching into three categories. After discussing the preeminence that ought to be given to the dignity and integral good of the human person, the document sets forth these three major considerations for assessing the moral validity of reproductive technology. The first is that the preembryo must be "treated as a person from the moment of conception" and therefore given "unconditional respect" (DV, para. 12). If, therefore, there is destruction or freezing of preembryos or nontherapeutic experimentation on preembryos, such treatment would be considered a "crime against their dignity as human beings" (DV, para. 16). Some Catholic theologians would argue that while there ought to be profound respect for the preembryo, it is however questionable, as in the case of abortion, whether the preembryo ought to be considered a person. The possibility of twinning, the recombination of fertilized ova, and the numerous instances of spontaneous loss of life in the preembryo stage all could be discussed with respect to this point. The second issue considered in the document is third-party participation, which is always considered wrong because the man and woman as husband and wife are the collaborators with God in the creation of another human being. Therefore, this creation has to be the

---

*Hereafter cited as DV.

product of mutual giving by the spouses without the introduction of a third party, whether that is by artificial insemination of third-party sperm or the use of a surrogate parent. The document sees all use of a third party as a violation against the unitive and procreative aspects of marriage. The third consideration is that of the nature of marriage itself, which is ordered toward being unitive and procreative. When, therefore, the procreative is separated from the unitive, the marriage is "deprived of its proper perfection." The Church teaching rejects any reproductive fertility procedure that replaces sexual intercourse.

There are theologians, however, who point out that this view concentrates too much on the act of intercourse itself as the unitive element rather than on the relationship of the spouses as the unitive element. They would argue that the love, respect, and devotion present in the shared life of the couple are indicative of the presence of the unitive in the marriage. Intercourse is the symbol of the unity, not the unity itself. These theologians would argue that such procedures as introducing the husband's sperm directly into the vagina or fallopian tubes in an attempt to cause conception certainly should not be considered wrong, or that even the procedure whereby a woman's egg is fertilized by her husband's sperm outside her body and afterward transferred to her womb ought to be considered acceptable. In 1977 the Catholic Theological Society of America did an in-depth theological study of sexuality and concluded that a shift from emphasizing the procreative and unitive values of sexuality ought to be replaced by creative and integrative values as norms for evaluating the morality of sexual acts. Their study suggested that in the past too much emphasis was placed on the objective moral nature of a given act, which led to a kind of impersonalism, legalism, and minimalism. The study proposed that greater emphasis be placed on the interpersonal attitudes and habits of the individuals involved. I think it is important to remember that the Church certainly has the right and responsibility to speak up and out about matters related to guaranteeing the sacredness of human life and of marriage. Problems, however, arise when the principles and laws take priority and are more important than the individual lives. When the Second Vatican Council mentioned "the nature of the human person and his [her] acts" (GS, para. 51) as the standard involved in determining the morality of life choices, it was redefining our ways of seeing and categorizing the "good" and the "bad." To speak about an act as always intrinsically evil, as sinful, apart from individual lives, does not seem to accord them the dignity they deserve as human persons and harks back to a pre–Vatican II assessment of morality.

While there are many parish priests and bishops who offer compassion and understanding to women and couples using birth control, or considering abortion or fertility procedures, the perception by many within and outside the Church is that her unshakable moral teachings about these issues leave little room for responsible individual choice and create an image of the Church as a self-contained and increasingly isolated institution. Catholics continue to think of themselves as the People of God and practice their faith despite the conflict they feel between what the Church officially teaches and what their consciences tell them, especially about married life and living that out in loving sexual expressions.

6

MARRIAGE, DIVORCE, REMARRIAGE, ANNULMENT

❖

My father's parents were married in the rectory of Saint Margaret's Church in Buffalo, New York. I have a picture of my grandmother Ryan in a lavender dress and matching hat with a little veil that covered only her forehead. My grandmother told me how afterward they went out to lunch with some friends. My grandfather's family did not attend because the woman he was marrying was Protestant. Her religion also was the reason they could not get married inside the Church itself but rather had to marry in the rectory. In those days it was a common understanding among Catholics that there was no salvation outside the Church. Because my grandmother was a Methodist, as I mentioned in chapter 1, I suspect that my grandfather's family thought that she would somehow carry the whole family to Hell with her, and so they disassociated themselves from her. She mentioned on numerous occasions that she felt like an outsider in her husband's family. So many family and social events centered on religious events like baptisms, First Communions, confirmations, weddings, she always felt like an observer, rather than a participant, even when they were her own children's sacramental events.

My Grandmother Ryan was an exceptional person. Her favorite season was autumn, and the yellow and crimson leaves matched the warmth of her heart. She packed wonderful picnic suppers of fried chicken and crunchy kirbys, played with us grandchildren in the sprinkler on hot summer days, and swayed with us in the glider on the back porch while telling us scary stories to the sounds of katydids on hot nights. All of the grandchildren adored her, and not for one minute did we believe that she deserved to go anywhere but Heaven. There were so many people at her funeral remembering her good deeds, it seemed quite strange to me that she had to be buried in the Protestant cemetery instead of in the Ryan family plot, which was in the Catholic cemetery where only Catholics in good standing could be buried. Even in death she remained somehow outside the family.

When I was twelve, in seventh grade, my mother sat my brother and I down in the living room one day to tell us that she and my father had been granted a divorce. Stunned, I remember tracing the pink peonies on the slipcover of the couch we were sitting on. I was unprepared for this announcement, and when my father moved out of the house and down to Georgia, where he remarried, I felt shame and resentment. Now I had to worry about my parents getting to Heaven as well as my Methodist grandmother. In 1960, I was the only person in my Catholic school class whose parents were divorced; I was now from a "broken" family. In those days Catholics stayed in their marriages unless conditions were truly unbearable. It wasn't until several years later that I mustered up the courage to ask her why she and my father had divorced. "The real question," she responded, "was why we had gotten married in the first place." She told me how handsome my father had been in his army uniform, and how getting married and starting a family had seemed like such a romantic idea for her at age eighteen. She was married at nineteen, and the marriage continued for fifteen years, but she told me it actually had ended long before it was formally terminated. During all my growing-up years, my mother was never a part of the "couple" things our parish sponsored: the parties, dances, meetings. She went to Mass every Sunday but would not take Communion. When I look back I realize what a lonely life she led for so many years before in her late fifties she met a man and remarried, outside the Church. She died a few years later and of course could not be given a Catholic funeral or buried in the cemetery with the rest of the family because she was outside the Church for divorcing and remarrying without an annulment. Once my brother had suggested to her that she get an annulment, but she'd said that she had neither the money or the strength to go through the process, which was confusing and degrading. She would take her chances, she told my brother, that God would judge her on the merits of her life and her attempts to be generous and kind to others, rather than on her inability to be a practicing Catholic.

The day of her wake a young obese woman came to pay her respects. My mother, who had been a seamstress for a bridal salon, had helped her with her bridal gown the previous year. She told me that all of her life she had been made to feel like some kind of a monster for being so large. But not your mother, she said to me. Your mother made me feel like a princess, like I was going to be the most beautiful bride in the world, and that's how I did feel because of her. Your mother was a very special person, and when I read that she had died, I knew I had to come and say thank you and good-bye.

The Church holds a hard line on the sacredness and significance of marriage. The marriage bond is indissoluble. Once a Catholic couple is married within the Church and consummates their marriage, that marriage bond cannot be broken. The Church does not recognize a legal divorce as breaking the bond, and if one or another of the spouses chooses to remarry, it cannot happen within the Church. A divorced and remarried Catholic cannot receive Communion at Mass, though a Catholic who is divorced and not remarried may receive the sacraments. However, if the couple or one of the spouses so chooses, an annulment of their marriage may be sought, basically nullifying the validity of a Catholic marriage bond from the beginning. This does not mean that the marriage never existed *legally* but that it never existed as valid in the eyes of the Church and therefore in the eyes of God.

Sociologists are quick to tell us that marriage today is in a state of crisis, that one in three marriages ends in divorce, and that Catholics are just as likely to get divorced as non-Catholics. In the past, there was often the tacit understanding between Catholic couples that they would stay in a marriage that wasn't working well unless the situation became intolerable, or unless one of the spouses had fallen in love with another person and desired to remarry. Often people stayed in marriages that weren't working "for the sake of the children." This is no longer the case, and the divorce rate among Catholics now equals that of the general population. Many divorced Catholics, particularly those seeking to remarry and to be able to continue practicing as Catholics, are seeking annulments. At the time of my parents' divorce, back in the sixties, getting an annulment was a rare occurrence, and simply not an option for my mother. It was commonly thought that this could be done only if one had the right connections and a great deal of money. The Church is quick to disperse these two myths today, and as a result the number of annulments has risen dramatically. The subject was most poignantly brought to the public's attention in Sheila Rauch Kennedy's book, *Shattered Faith,* already mentioned in chapter 2. The former wife of Congressman Joseph Kennedy II gives a personal account of her reaction and the responses of those around her when she received in the mail a petition to have her marriage annulled. She admits that her marriage failed in part because she could not embrace fully the political scene in the manner expected of her as the wife of a Kennedy; she also describes the anger and pain she felt for herself and her twin sons over the possibility of having it stated that her marriage had never existed in the eyes of God.

As it stands today, if a couple gets married and the marriage fails for one reason or another, neither party may remarry within the Church without an annulment, and if they do remarry outside Catholicism, they are cut off from the life of the Church by being denied Communion at the Eucharistic celebration. Congressman Kennedy had fallen in love with another woman and wanted to have his new marriage blessed by the Church, which could happen only if his first marriage was annulled. Sheila Rauch Kennedy is not a Catholic; and when she started doing research on the annulment process, she was horrified to discover that it meant that first her marriage was never legitimate in the eyes of God and the Church and that her two sons were offspring of a union that never had existed, despite the fact that their legitimacy was assured. For her this was a matter of moral dishonesty; she was determined to fight back. She writes: "To me were the Church to declare my children the offspring of a marriage that never existed, it would be abdicating its sacred and historical role to protect and promote their moral well being" (*Shattered Faith,* xiv). She decided to contest the annulment and also to illuminate the process in the pages of her book. She contacted and spoke to many people who had gone through annulments, finding the process degrading and dishonest, but who had felt helpless to do otherwise. She met many people who felt betrayed and whose faith in the institutional Church and in themselves was shattered.

The Church is caught in a type of duplicity in its annulment process today. On the one hand, the Church is upholding its long tradition of witnessing to the sacredness of marriage and its indissoluble character. Since the twelfth-century formulation of canon law by Gratian, Church law has ruled that the bond of marriage is indissoluble. The Council of Trent (1545–1563) strongly reaffirmed this stance. And while there have been times in the Church when, for one reason or another, the Church has allowed a couple to divorce and a remarriage has been recognized, its constant teaching has been the indissolubility of marriage. On the other hand, the Church recognizes that some marriages do not work, and upholds a process by which they will nullify a marriage—annulment. Without an annulment, an innocent party in a failed relationship can be expected to live celibate for the rest of life or risk being cut off from the sacramental life of the Church. People are having to make a decision between living a fruitful, fulfilling life in a second marriage or living outside the sacramental life of the Church. More and more people are choosing the first option, believing God to be more understanding and welcoming than the institutional Church. The process of getting an annulment is timely, costly for some and for many a humiliating experience they would prefer to avoid. A college friend of mine who went through the process had to answer, before a Church tribunal, the most intimate questions about her sexual life with her husband in order to get an annulment. And in spite of the fact that probably many Catholics feel as Joseph Kennedy II does, that the process as he described it to his ex-wife, is "Catholic gobbledygook" (ibid., 10–11), more people are applying for annulments than the Church tribunals can hear in a given year. Many individuals misunderstand what an annulment is, thinking that it is some kind of a Catholic divorce, and are therefore scandalized by the way the Church rules on annulments and how they are granted, or they wonder about this magical power of the Church to say that a particular marriage was never a marriage at all. There is a great deal of criticism about the process and even allegations that this process is hypocritical, since on the one hand the Church proclaims the indissolubility of marriage and on the other hand will pronounce that a marriage was never valid as a sacramental marriage within the Church for reasons that can seem pretty flimsy, such as "lack of due discretion of judgment" on the part of the couple before they were married, which was the case with Sheila Rauch Kennedy. As I mentioned briefly in the introduction to this book, a colleague of mine recently told me that her sister's former husband, after twenty-two years of marriage and three children, was able to get an annulment so he could marry a nurse at the Catholic hospital where he is a physician. It is politically correct for him to attend all hospital functions as a Catholic in good standing, which he wanted to continue to do even after remarrying. My colleague mentioned also that her sister had helped put this man through medical school, working full-time so he could pursue his studies and career through residency. She was outraged that her sibling had been put through the humiliation of the annulment process solely for the advantage of her former husband. He also was able to get an annulment on the grounds of "lack of due discretion."

That marriage is sacred and ought to be entered into with the intent of making a lifetime commitment is an ideal to strive for and one that the Church confirms. In fact, the ideal in most societies and in all religions is that marriage is an enduring bond between two people in which they pledge their love and loyalty "till death do us part." On a purely social level, it seems to be for the good of society itself that people can feel rooted and grounded in a constant relationship, especially when children are involved. A stable family life appears to be the best environment for children, one in which they thrive and grow, eventually able to contribute to society. I think most people hope as they enter into marriage that it will last forever and that the two will live happily ever after.

In the Judeo-Christian tradition the Old Testament gives witness to this ideal. Genesis describes Adam and Eve as complementing and completing one another, "That is why a man leaves his father and mother and clings to his wife and the two of them become one body" (Gen. 2:24). Within Judaism marriage has always been considered a sacred event symbolizing God's love for his people, as is expressed in Isaiah 54, Jeremiah 2:2 and 3:20, and Hosea 2: "I will espouse you to me forever. I will espouse you in right and in justice, in love and in mercy; I will espouse you in fidelity and you shall know the Lord" (Hos. 2:21, 22). Marriage within Judaism also assumed the overtones of a contractual relationship, one that was made, as it was in many cultures, between the parents of the marrying couple. Children were betrothed, sometimes at a very young age, to ensure that the right lineage would result. The marriage contract took into consideration property, household duties, and of course the begetting of children.

In the New Testament marriage is not only a sign of God's love for his people but also a symbol of Christ's love for the Church. It is often pointed out that while it seems that Christ himself was never married, his first miracle according to the Gospel of John was performed at a marriage feast in Cana (see chapters 4 and 5) and that he frequently made use of marriage imagery to describe the Kingdom of God and his relationship to it, thus showing his high regard for marriage. The sacramental value of marriage is further enhanced by Paul, particularly in his letter to the Ephesians, where he writes: "Husbands love your wives, even as Christ loved the Church and handed himself over for her . . . He who loves his wife, loves himself. For no one hates his own flesh but rather nourishes and cherishes it, even as Christ does the Church, because we are members of his body . . . This is a great mystery but I speak in reference to Christ and the Church" (Eph. 5:25, 28–32). Paul was probably trying to distinguish Christian marriage from the cultural milieu of his time, giving such marriage the character of divine love. He linked marriage to the fundamental religious symbol of Christianity, Christ's selfless, faithful love. The incorporation of marriage into the larger vision of the Church as the beloved bride/body of Christ in Ephesians creates a unique image of what Christian marriage is meant to be. The Church has held to this image for two thousand years. Marriage is shown to reflect and participate in the very mystery of salvation.

According to the Church, then, Christian marriage is meant to make present the reality of unconditional love that Christ lived. Because of this, marriage itself brings salvation to the couple, just as celibacy does for those who receive that gift. It is an expression of humankind's highest potential of love and therefore a reflection of the creative power and grace of God. Ritual enactment of this vision of marriage takes place within the Eucharistic celebration. The Church means to lift marriage above the conventions of the legal and social world. Because marriage points to Divine love, to Christ's love for the Church, it takes on the character of indissolubility; Christ could never dissolve his love and bond to the Church: "Behold I am with you always, even to the end of the ages" (Matt. 28:20).

The Church further looks to the words ascribed to Jesus in three of the Gospels to promote the teaching on the indissolubility of marriage. Theologians do not agree that the passages used to defend the indissolubility of marriage and the forbidding of remarriage without annulment by the Church actually do support this teaching because the passages are not in agreement themselves. There is a great deal of debate about what occurred historically to instigate Jesus' words in these passages; and the theologian Theodore S.J. Mackin devotes forty-six pages of his book *Divorce and Remarriage* in an attempt to unravel the contradictory interpretations accorded to them.

For the purposes of the argument here, Mark's Gospel will be quoted at length; the differences in Matthew and Luke will be referred to as is appropriate.

> The Pharisees approached and asked, "Is it lawful for a man to divorce his wife?" They were testing him. He said to them in reply, "What did Moses command you?" They replied, "Moses allowed him to write a bill of divorce and dismiss her." But Jesus told them, "Because of the hardness of your hearts he wrote you this commandment. But from the beginning of creation, 'God made them male and female.' For this reason a man shall leave his father and mother and be joined to his wife and the two shall become one flesh. Therefore what God has joined together, no human being must separate ... Whoever divorces his wife and marries another commits adultery against her." (Mark 10:2–11)

It is important to look at the words of Jesus within the context in which they were probably said. Mark's teaching on divorce, which is lengthier than in the other Gospels, occurs within what is referred to as an entrapment story, a situation in which the Pharisees or another group are trying to trap Jesus into saying something that could be held against him. In this situation Jesus' enemies attempt to catch him in a compromise, either in regard to the Jewish Law, or in regard to one of his former teachings. The Law allowed a man to divorce his wife by writing a bill of dismissal. But according to one Jewish school of thought, the Shammai, such a note could be drawn only for a very serious reason. According to another school of thought, the Hillel, divorce was allowed on almost any grounds that a man deemed suitable. Because women had no rights, no privileges without a husband, divorce meant great shame, and destitution in some cases. Divorce put women at a great social, religious, and economic disadvantage and was clearly an injustice. Jesus' teaching here on divorce is most certainly a commentary on the practice of divorce in his day and the hardship it placed on women. That he is commenting on the sacredness of marriage is a given, but he also is reacting to the social injustice of divorce at the time.

Jesus uses strong language when he states that if a man divorces and remarries, he commits adultery against his wife. The Church uses this statement to justify its teaching that divorce and remarriage in the Church is not permitted except under specially controlled situations, such as getting an annulment or the dissolution of a nonsacramental marriage for the sake of living out the faith, known as the Pauline Privilege and the Petrine privilege. The context in which these words are spoken is not clear. From a reading of Mark and Matthew, one could suppose that presentation of divorce as a secular, contractual phenomenon prompts Jesus to address the issue. Jewish Pharisees approach Jesus, saying in effect, "Tell us the conditions, give us laws and guidelines on when we can divorce our wives," and Jesus responds, "Marriage is more than a contract, it involves two people in a relationship. We are not going to reduce this relationship to something less, to a legal contract. What God intended is that these two people become one in a permanent union of husband and wife." Jesus presents to them the ideal of a loving relationship and is unwilling to discuss such shallow topics as the conditions under which man can dismiss his wife. Perhaps he was rejecting their "hardness of heart" at a time when women seemed to have no rights and deserved justice. Matthew's version of this event has Jesus saying "whoever divorces his wife, except for unchastity [some translations say "except for adultery"], and marries another commits adultery" (Matt. 19:9). Matthew here points out an exception—unchastity—to Jesus' ruling on divorce, an exception that might render a particular divorce justifiable to him. Luke has only a short statement, leaving out the section quoted from Genesis: "Everyone who dismisses his wife and marries another commits adultery, and he who marries a woman dismissed from her husband commits adultery" (Luke 16:18).

That all three of the Gospels at least have similar teachings shows that the problem of divorce was a concern at this time; apparently Jesus was intent on letting his listeners know how important he considered marriage as an event joining two people in a relationship that shouldn't be cheapened by allowing a man to treat his wife as an object to be dismissed at will. Jesus was reminding his listeners that marriage involved love and commitment. It was not just a matter of contracts and legalities. For the people questioning Jesus at this time, marriage was caught up with laws and social expectations and obligations. As with so many other instances in the Gospels, Jesus seems more concerned with the *people* involved in a situation rather than with a strict interpretation of law. As always, when Jesus is questioned about laws and technicalities, he takes his listeners beyond the law to the heart of the matter, a call to holiness for husband and wife. It is reasonable to suggest, as some theologians have, that using these passages to justify a particular theology of marriage is not fair to the circumstances today, which differ from the context in which Jesus was speaking.*

Following Jesus' death, Saint Paul and the other apostles had little to say about marriage, in part because of the expectation of Jesus' imminent return (the eschatological perspective that influenced Paul's writing is referred to in chapter 4). Paul only grudgingly gives permission to marry, acknowledging that it is better to marry than to be on fire with passion. Paul believes that marriage is something of a distraction (1 Cor. 7:32), though he does mention that bishops should be successful in marriage and family life before their election (1 Tim. 3:3). Paul's frequent warnings about the need for self-control are rooted in the Stoic philosophy that took hold in early Christianity, characterizing sex and passion as base. It is no wonder, then, that marriage as a sacrament, as a call to holiness, gets scant treatment in the writings of the time, many of which portray

---

*See *Why You Can Disagree and Remain a Faithful Catholic* by Philip Kaufman.

such a union as functional, geared toward procreation. Other writings present a consideration of what was sinful within the marriage contract; still others get caught up in the legal wrangling of trying to decide what did and didn't constitute a valid marriage.

First, the issue of sin within marriage. Early Church Fathers wrote of how a married couple could be guilty of sexual sins if the desire to procreate was not present when they were having intercourse; that it would be unreasonable, not natural, for instance, to engage in sexual intercourse if a woman was pregnant or beyond her childbearing years. Sexual desires were viewed as the effect of the Fall (discussed in chapter 3): ". . . in pain shall you bring forth children. Yet your urge shall be for your husband and he shall be your master" (Gen. 3:16). The ideal society for Augustine was one without passion, where male and female would join for reproduction not "through the eager desire of lust, but the normal exercise of the will" (*City of God,* 14.26). Augustine went so far as to write that the genital organs were bodily instruments for the transmission of Original Sin ("On Marriage and Concupiscence," as quoted in Hugo, *St. Augustine on Nature,* 61). Ironically, the conjugal act of intercourse was and still is considered to the validating character to marriage. The conjugal act was considered good only when it was fulfilling the end toward which it is meant, continuing the life of the human race.

The idea of marriage as a covenant relationship was lost to an understanding of it as a juridical, legalistic act with duties and obligations. For example, some writings from the first few centuries of the Church indicate that if two unbaptized persons get married and later one converts to Christianity, the baptized person does not have to stay in the marriage. This is referred to as the Pauline Privilege, based on 1 Corinthians 7:10–16. Another legal procedure, called the Petrine Privilege, permitted the Pope to dissolve a marriage into which two people had *entered* as a Christian and a non-Christian. Marriage began to be referred to as an institution, and little was done to create a person-centered theology. With the exception of only a few scholars (such as Thomas Aquinas in the thirteenth century, who taught the natural goodness of sex), the bulk of theological opinion supported the thought and rigorism of Augustine as theologians drew selectively from his more pessimistic writings. It does seem ironic that Jesus' attempts to rescue marriage from the legalistic structures of Jewish life during his time would eventually become more burdened by legalism within the developing Church.

In the eleventh century the early Scholastics fixed the number of sacraments at seven; while marriage was one of them, it was viewed as a lesser sacrament—not as grace-giving, which the others are, but as a necessary remedy against sin. It was better to enter into marriage than to be ravaged by passion and desire. The later Scholastics of the thirteenth century begrudgingly conceded that God's grace could come from marriage, but continued to state that marriage was a state of life secondary to that of vowed celibacy.

By the time Gratian codified Church law in the 1100s, the duties and obligations of the two parties indissolubly linked in marriage were defined by laws. For the most part these laws were drawn up by celibate men who created the illusion that marriage was an objective reality unconcerned with the two persons actually involved. That sexual intercourse was an expression of mutual love and support, of self-giving, was an idea quite foreign to the celibate monks of the Middle Ages who were creating a theology that endured for many centuries.

By the thirteenth century, the Church's teaching on marriage was still impersonal, indicating that it was ordered toward "ends": procreation and the salvation of the couple. This thinking dominated Catholic thought on marriage well into the twentieth century.

Even devotion to Mary (discussed in chapters 4 and 5) had an effect on our view of marriage, if only indirectly. Mary conceived immaculately, the pure, unspotted, virginal Mother of God, was a model for behavior. Mary was revered as Virgin, and so the visual impact of Mary as unattached to any man began to grow. To be sure, there were pictures of Mary with Joseph, but he was generally placed in the background, sometimes pictured as an elderly man and certainly not as someone sexually appealing. Even as I grew up, the statues of Mary and Joseph were kept on opposite sides of the Church. To suggest that they may have been sexually attracted to one another was almost blasphemous. What Mary and Joseph had was a marriage of convenience to allow Jesus the benefit of having a foster father. We all knew they never had sex and probably didn't want to! Their asexual nature was a given. Even though the Gospels make mention of Jesus' brothers and sisters, their existence was explained away in statements indicating that they were his cousins, in order to safeguard the teaching of Mary's perpetual virginity.

In 1854 Pope Pius XI proclaimed as Catholic doctrine the Immaculate Conception—that Mary from the first moment of her existence was without the stain of Original Sin. This and the Virgin Birth, Jesus' conception without male intervention, were deemed as miraculous events. The perpetual virginity of Mary was made much of in prayers and hymns written to remind the faithful of this fact. The emphasis on purity and the miraculous only enhances the traditional dichotomy in the Church between purity and chastity on the one hand, and marriage and sexuality on the other. Only two kinds of women exist: the Madonna and the whore, the good and the bad. As Catholics, we are expected to model ourselves on Mary, the virgin mother of God. Women especially have been taught that to experience sexual desire is wrong, making us loose or cheap. When I was growing up, sexual fantasies were something to be confessed, in the course of acknowledging our impure thoughts and deeds, on Saturday afternoons. We were told that all sexual feelings were temptations from the Devil. It is unrealistic to think that a young woman brought up with these thoughts and feelings was going to shed them upon marrying. One has to wonder, how many women entered marriage unable to give themselves freely and joyously to their spouse because of this attitude toward sex and the general lack of a real theology of marriage? With the exception of a few lone voices such as Thomas Sanchez (1550–1610), who wrote that there was no sin in spouses who intend to have intercourse simply as spouses, or Alphonsus Liguori (1696–1787), who echoed this sentiment, little was done theologically to sacramentalize sex or to bring a more personalist approach to marriage.

The Protestant Reformers of the fifteenth century upheld the sacredness of marriage though rejected it as an actual sacrament, and encouraged their ministers to marry. It was thought that they could minister better to their people if they were married; also, since they viewed human nature as flawed, they felt the weaknesses of the flesh would be bridled within the legal, contractual relationship of marriage. Since marriage was not viewed as a sacrament by Protestants, divorce was permitted, though it was discouraged because of Jesus' words in the New Testament.

Protestantism and Eastern Orthodoxy have long interpreted Jesus' words on divorce less stringently than the Roman Catholic Church. The tradition of the Eastern Church has been to rely on Matthew's Gospel, which adds the phrase "except for unchastity" to the admonition against divorce. Within Eastern Orthodoxy, then, adultery is considered grounds for divorce. Either one of the couple also may remarry, although the second marriage is not considered a sacrament, as was the first, and the individuals are allowed full participation in the sacramental life of the Church. There are some theologians who would encourage this approach to divorce and remarriage for Roman Catholics.

As was mentioned in chapter 5, "Sex and the Church," in 1935 the German diocesan priest Herbert Doms published a book called *The Meaning of Marriage*. In it he questions the "primary ends" theory of marriage (Fox, *Sexuality,* 36). His approach is personalist and relational, indicating that the first value of marriage is rooted in its vitality as a loving relationship between two people. This view understands procreation as a natural part of the fulfillment of the relationship, not as an end in itself. This book allowed a small movement of a more personalist approach to sex and marriage, which had begun earlier, to expand. It found its first formal expression from the Church at the Second Vatican Council, where for the first time the concepts of primary and secondary ends of marriage were not spoken of separately but blended together. Marriage was described as a "sacred bond," an intimate union of two persons and their actions, a mutual self-giving (GS, para. 51). The constitution intertwines the ideas of the fruitfulness of marriage and the procreation of children, giving the impression that there is no hierarchy or ordering. Whereas prior to Vatican II, the teaching on marriage tended toward a discussion of the procreative and unitive elements, after Vatican II the emphasis shifted to the creative and integrative aspects of marriage. Expressing conjugal love is done with such ease in this document that one might have expected that it had been a part of the Church's writings for centuries: "This love is an eminently human one since it is directed from one person to another through an affection of the will. It involves the good of the whole person. Therefore it can enrich the expressions of body and mind with a unique dignity, ennobling these expressions as special ingredients and signs of the friendship distinctive of marriage. This love the Lord has judged worthy of special gifts of healing, perfecting, and exalting gifts of grace and charity" (GS, para. 49). The sacramentality of conjugal love was being explored, and since the Second Vatican Council great efforts have been made to elevate the status of marriage in the Church. Married love is seen as rooted in divine love; Christ is present and abiding in this community of persons. Marriage is viewed as a sign of God's presence among us as a couple lives out their self-giving to one another and continues the creative power of God by building up the Kingdom of God. Theologians today talk about how the conjugal act brings grace and healing, an idea foreign in centuries past. I think present-day theologians are also reacting to the ideas of free love and uncommitted relationships, which are so prevalent, in an attempt to say that for Christians sexual intercourse is more than a biological act.

But now the Church is, so to speak, caught between a rock and a hard place. As it extols the importance and beauty of marriage as a communication of God's grace and stresses the other personalist aspects of marriage, more Catholics have begun to question the reality of this ideal in their own lives and, where it is lacking, are choosing to leave marriages that are not supporting and life-giving. Fewer individuals are willing to stick it out, to stay in a marriage that does not meet the Christian ideal. For many people in their thirties or forties, staying in a marriage for another forty or fifty years with a partner less than faithful and loving is not an option they feel they can endure—or ought to. The idealization of marriage and the personalist approach have left some individuals feeling cheated out of a genuine marriage relationship. It is no wonder, then, that the divorce rates among Catholics are as high as they are among the rest of society. There is a burgeoning attitude in general that marriage, like the rest of life, is to be lived to the fullest, that the dignity and potential of the individual, regardless of station in life, demands that his or her relationships be satisfying. When love cannot be realized in one relationship, with or without attempts at reconciliation, many people move on.

The Catholic Church has continued to maintain the permanence of the marital bond, despite the fact that ours is an era of tremendous impermanence. We live in a time when not only does change occur constantly, but also the *dissemination* of changes occurs rapidly. It is little wonder that the impermanence of life in general affects our relationships and attitudes toward them. In the Church's tradition Jesus' word on the indissolubility of marriage is the unconditional ideal for every Christian marriage, but is it meant to be so in the juridical way that it has always been interpreted? Could Jesus have been able to foresee the changes that have occurred since his time in regard to the understanding of the human person or the extended life expectancy of people? Is an absolutist statement appropriate in our time?

As has been stated, there is little doubt that Jesus was trying to raise the concept of marriage to a new level of understanding, to a new level of holiness, bestowing dignity to those involved in that relationship. Seeing marriage as an indissoluble bond in a cooperative relationship overlooks the very real struggles and problems in some marriages, which cannot always be overcome: addiction, the inability to relate to another in a meaningful way due to a past experience such as rape or incest, or other psychological problems. Reasons for terminating a marriage are many and most often traumatic for those involved. A failed marriage is very often the point at which an individual needs the Church the most; having to choose between a celibate life or denial of the sacramental life of the Church in a second marriage without an annulment is hardly the support needed.

Among all the pastoral problems faced by the Church today, few have the same widespread impact as the issues of divorce, remarriage, and annulments. In 1995, Pope John Paul II reinforced the ban against giving Communion to Catholics who have remarried without an annulment. Priests were warned against knowingly giving Communion to such people because it could bring scandal to the rest of the faithful. But as Jim Bowman writes in his book, *Bending the Rules: What American Priests Tell American Catholics,* many priests choose in their best judgment to offer such parishioners Communion anyway. Since Vatican II made "the nature of the human person and his [her] acts" (GS, para. 51) the norm for evaluating the morality of an action, this same principle can be used in determining who should receive Communion. Real life tells us that there are many Catholics who benefit not from condemnation but from support and encouragement. Many of these people believe in their heart of hearts that if Jesus were around today, he would be much more forgiving than they find the institutional Church to be. The reality is that many divorced Catholics feel shut out of the Church and simply stop going to Mass, believing that they are tainted in some way because they have not lived up to the ideal.

There are theologians who are quick to say that we ought to be using the life experience of individual believing Christians and their communities as one of the starting points for theological reflection on this issue. While other sources of revelation such as those described in chapter 1—Scripture, tradition, the magisterium, and the liturgy—enter as principles of interpretation, it is the action of God in people's lives that provides the immediate "word" of revelation with which we must deal as theologians. Consider a Catholic Christian who says, "Look, I tried hard to make my marriage work, we went for counseling, but the past marriage failed. I want to try again." Are we always, in every case, to say, "Sorry, laws are laws. Go through the annulment process, and if that doesn't work, too bad"?

Is it just and compassionate to expect the injured party in a marriage, after the contract has been broken, when love has been revoked by the other through infidelity or dishonesty, to go through the annulment process in order to marry again? Can we say, for instance, that a betrayed person in a marriage, a person who has clearly been deserted, is still bound by a one-sided contract and must live this out? Can a person be expected to remain committed to live out a sacramental relationship that is existentially over?

At a 1980 synod of bishops, Archbishop Derek Worlock of Liverpool urged his fellow bishops to consider carefully the pain that divorced and remarried Catholics carry with them. He asked the synod to listen to the voice of knowledgeable priests and laity pleading for consideration of this problem for their less happy brethren, spiritually destitute Catholics whose first marriages perished and who have a second and more stable (if only civil) union, in which they seek to bring up a new family. Often, such persons, especially in their desire to help their children, long for restoration to full communion with the Church and its Lord. Archbishop Worlock asked, "Is this spirit of repentance and desire for sacramental strength to be forever frustrated? Can they be told that they must reject their new responsibilities?" (as reported in *Origins*, Oct. 9, 1980). He and Cardinal Basil Hume (England) called for a study of the Eastern Orthodox practice, which in consideration of human weakness tolerates remarriage and continuing reception of Communion, although it does not consider the second marriage a sacrament. The Pope, however, rejected Archbishop Worlock's plea, stating that such Catholic Christians should not be readmitted to Communion because of the scandal and confusion that would result and because their condition of life objectively contradicts what is signified and effected by the Eucharist. In 1994 Bishops Karl Lehmann of Mainz and Walter Kasper of Rottenburg went to Rome three times to discuss a more lenient attitude, suggesting that perhaps a bishop could review the cases of remarried divorcés who want to receive the Eucharist, stating that the care of divorced and remarried Catholics was one of the key questions in pastoral work, but the Pope remains steadfast in upholding the present teaching. In 1993 a Gallup poll found that 62 percent of Catholics believed that you could be a good Catholic without obeying the Church's teaching on divorce and remarriage. The question of scandal in the minds of many Catholics is related more to the lack of compassion and understanding on the part of the magisterium with regard to this issue than to the issue of remarried Catholics receiving Communion.

For a marriage to be declared invalid and therefore annulled, there are two sets of laws considered. The first set are disqualifying laws, which render a person ineligible to have been married in the Church in the first place. There are twelve major disqualifying laws, referred to as impediments, which include underage, prior bond, disparity of worship, Holy Orders, prior vow, abduction, murder of a spouse, consanguinity, affinity, public propriety, adoption, and impotence. The last is not in the strict sense an impediment. It means that if there is some sort of natural reason why one or another of the partners cannot consummate the marriage, the marriage could be annulled. Let us say, for instance, that one partner is homosexual and could not consummate the marriage; this would merit an annulment.

The second set of laws are the invalidating laws, which render a marriage invalid because of the situation in which the marriage took place. For instance, if the marriage was not witnessed by at least two people, or if it was performed by someone other than a validly ordained priest, the marriage would be invalidated in the eyes of the Church. Since consent is absolutely essential in a marriage, there are also considerations that could be used to invalidate and annul a marriage based on consent—or lack thereof—at the time of the marriage. Defective consent could include a lack of genuine freedom at the time of the marriage, or an incapability because of psychological reasons to consent to the duties and obligations of marriage. If a young man consented to marry a woman because she discovered that she was pregnant and convinced her boyfriend that her father would come after him with a shotgun if they did not get married, this could be defective consent. There are a number of other consensual defects recognizable in invalidating a marriage such as fraud, dishonesty about some important aspects of one's life (e.g., a criminal record), or force or grave fear compelling a marriage. Of course, because the Church considers the desire to have children as central to marriage, if one or another of the couple refuses to procreate, this is also a reason for obtaining an annulment. I had a roommate in college who, several years after she was married, asked if I would testify to a marriage tribunal that she had often spoken about never wanting to have children. This was in fact the case, and my testimony helped her to get the annulment she desired. At the time, twenty years ago, this seemed like the good Catholic thing to do; today I would feel somewhat hypocritical agreeing to testify in an annulment hearing.

The formal procedure one must go through to get an annulment is long and tedious and can be humiliating for one party or both of the people involved. The Church tribunal that officiates over such pronouncements, made up of priests and sometimes laypeople who have been trained in canon law, relies on pages of testimony to decide the validity of a marriage. Even after a great deal of time is spent doing groundwork, filling out papers, and finding witnesses, Church tribunals are so overwhelmed that only a fraction of the cases are heard in an expedient time. There are other Catholics who become overwhelmed with all that has to be done, and give up. Some Catholics have to wait patiently for many months, even up to a year, for the annulment process to be completed and their case heard. Others choose to go ahead and get remarried before the annulment is granted and so are considered by the Church to be living in sin. Whether or not the above objections are based on fact or colored by subjective opinions, annulment is widely misunderstood by the average Catholic. Defenders of the annulment process, however, see it as a compassionate way to help divorced Catholics heal, reaching out to people who otherwise would leave the Church.

What is to be done in this regard? Since marriage serves as the root of the human community, it will always be important to testify to its sacramental character, to lift it beyond the purely functional to the level of a sacred event, a sign of God's love. In this sense marriage in the Church ideally ought to be entered into as an indissoluble union of persons, a life commitment of love and learning. The Church has made great strides in the last twenty years to expound on the beauty of conjugal love and marriage and ought to continue to do so, but at the same time it has to be remembered that the Church is a community of persons, with human weaknesses and failings and that the ideal is sometimes a long reach from the reality we live. Anyone who has been married can testify to the hard work it takes for two people to make their marriage work on every level. The question can honestly be asked whether *any* human union is capable of witnessing fully to the union of Christ and his Church. The ideal is there for us to strive toward, we try, sometimes we succeed, but often we fail.

Jesus Christ as the Son of God could make an unconditional commitment to remain always with us until the end of time, but can this be true of every young couple who approaches the altar to promise love and fidelity? Human relationships are complicated, fraught with human need and shortcomings. Can human marriages always represent existentially a divine love that never fails? How often is it possible for two people to be totally open, honest, true to self and one another, committed to each other's growth unselfishly so as to have a marriage that reflects and sacramentalizes God's relationship to his people, especially when the majority of marriages take place early in life?

Perhaps indissolubility is something that a marriage grows into, rather than something that is—or should be—imposed upon it from the beginning. There is marriage, which is a juridical bond, and there is a relationship between two people, which grows and changes with each child, each sickness, each success, each job setback, each move to a new city or town, each failure. The ideal is that these two faces of marriage are not separate realities, but even the Church admits that this dichotomy exists when it grants annulments. The indissolubility of the personal, relational bond between two people is a goal in marriage; it is not automatic. Marriage is indeed a juridical act, but it is first and foremost a personal relationship that does not always "work"; to suggest that it is always supposed to be indissoluble for Catholics, who are not immune to any of the human weaknesses and failings of all God's people, is to expect the impossible.

Another important aspect of this discussion about divorce is the Vatican's stance about not allowing divorced Catholics who have remarried access to the Eucharist. In a 1980 encyclical entitled *Familia Communitatae:* "The Community of the Family" the Pope wrote, "They are unable to be readmitted thereto from the fact that their state and condition of life objectively contradicts that union of love between Christ and the Church which is signified and effected by the Eucharist. Besides there is another reason: if these people were admitted to the Eucharist the faithful would be led into error and confusion regarding the Church's teaching about the indissolubility of marriage" (para. 7). Many people feel that this is a harsh and even un-Christian punishment. "Don't you think Jesus would invite my mother to the Eucharist if he were making the decision?" a young Catholic once asked me about this attitude. If the two parties in a second invalid marriage seriously want to live as faithful Catholics and asked to be readmitted into the full sacramental life of the Church, the presumption that they are sincere and well intentioned is certainly reasonable. Consequently they would not be a scandal or detriment to the Church. However, when people move out of a relationship where love has ceased to exist, or perhaps never existed in the first place, and find love in a new relationship, they are made to feel guilty and are deprived of the grace and healing of Christ in the Eucharist unless they go through the annulment process.

Many Catholics are resentful of the fact that if they do enter a new marriage, which in fact is more loving and stable than the first and therefore more salvific for all members of the family, without an annulment, they cannot share in the full sacramental life of the Church. Divorce is not always a matter of sin and should not always be punished as such by denying individual access to the Church's life. Human weakness can be forgiven in every other act that a Catholic Christian commits, even murder.

Punishing the divorced and remarried, as well as the children of divorced and remarried couples who provide a loving environment in which to grow and develop into Catholic adults, is a great injustice. These children more likely will turn from—rather than toward—a Church that rejects their parents' remarriage.

There is no doubt that Jesus' words on divorce ought to be taken seriously and that he holds up an ideal to be pursued from the beginning of a marriage. Society and the Church depend on such an approach. The Church can and ought to have laws that bear witness to how seriously it considers the indissoluble character of marriage, and how seriously marriage bears witness to a larger truth about Christ and his Church. In many places the Church does an excellent job of preparing couples for the meaning of their marriage as Catholics through the Pre-Cana Program, named after the city of Cana where Jesus performed his first miracle of changing water into wine while attending a wedding (John 2:1–11), and through retreats provided for engaged couples who come together and prayerfully reflect on their upcoming life together. The Church also needs to continue to support married couples all along their journey.

Perhaps some kind of program similar to the Pre-Cana Program—for divorced Catholics whose previous marriages have been annulled, and for their partners seeking to remarry within the Church—could be created where individuals are helped to understand the sacredness and seriousness of what they are about to do in relationship to the failed marriage they have left. There are always going to be people, Catholics as well as non-Catholics, who do not consider marriage as a sacramental activity; those who blithely enter into the contract with the attitude of "well if it doesn't work I'll get a divorce," should not marry in the Church because the Church has a very specific teaching about marriage. Certainly a more relaxed attitude toward divorced and remarried Catholics may give the appearance that the Church is weakening its teaching, but with the proper preparation and a clearly defined rubric for such occasions this could be avoided. What is important is that after people make mistakes they be given the opportunity to find an honest and fully participative way to practice their Catholic faith. The annulment process does not always provide this, since it often requires attesting to such excuses as "lack of discretion" to end the marriage. Individuals often feel that they have to compromise the honest true love they felt early in their marriage.

Any discussion of marriage, its goodness, and the character of its indissolubility needs to take into account the individuals most intimately involved in the topic, the married couple themselves. It is paramount that the Church invite and seek out the experience of married couples for its theological reflection. Without this involvement, the magisterium is working in a vacuum. It seems that we need a somewhat new, though traditional, respectful look at the issue of marriage and indissolubility. We also need married men and women to help create a reflective theology on the importance of sexuality in marriage, one that emphasizes the creative, the joyous, and the life-sustaining. Married couples have the lived experience of giving expression to an incarnated self, giving love in a way that celibate persons do not know. Little attention is paid to the importance of sex and sexuality in marriage by the Church. Intercourse is an act of giving life to another, affirming the other as an invaluable, unique person. It is an act in which one recognizes one's incompleteness and need for community. It is an act that admits that one's whole being is meant to be involved in a loving relationship, and in this way it is sacramental. What celibate bishop can give expression to the concept that one's whole being, body and soul, longs to reach out in total self-giving to another; can describe that early morning awakening when a touch, a sound, can cause a response in a spouse from a place so deep within one's life that the body longs to move into the other? What a perfect analogy lovemaking is for the Incarnation—that God longed to take on the flesh of man to give expression to his love. That the act of intercourse, unlike in the days of Augustine, ought to be able to be viewed as an act sometimes of healing and reconciliation, sometimes as a celebration of life, as well as a continuation of the creative presence of God in the world, is something that any married couple can testify to and that ought to be a part of Catholic theology on marriage.

7

GAY AND UNHAPPY:
LIFE AS A CATHOLIC
HOMOSEXUAL

In October of 1994, Bishop Thomas Gumbleton, an auxiliary bishop of Detroit, donned a miter and proceded down the aisle of the Basilica of Saint Mary's in Minneapolis to celebrate the Eucharist. This was not an ordinary celebration, just as the miter he wore was not ordinary: It bore a cross with a pink triangle and featured a wide border of multicolored stripes, representing the gay/lesbian rainbow. Furthermore, it had been presented to him by the gay/lesbian community, who had invited him to celebrate the Eucharist at a meeting in Minneapolis because he had lent a sympathetic ear in the past, even speaking out publicly on their behalf. The celebration was a "Eucharistic liturgy of liberation," one of five events scheduled by a coalition of Twin Cities parishes working with the Catholic Pastoral Committee on Sexual Minorities. The events of October 1994 provided sessions at which the bishop could listen to stories of gay and lesbian Catholics as they related their anguish, hopes, and expectations of life as homosexuals and Catholic Christians.

Besides listening, Bishop Gumbleton, as is his style, gave words of compassion, understanding, and affirmation to those gathered, in hopes of being, as a representative of the Church, a sign of the unconditional love that Christ showed to everyone he encountered, as evidenced in the Gospels. Bishop Gumbleton, though not alone as a sympathetic member of the hierarchy, knows the pain of homosexual Catholics in the Church. Because of the experiences of his own brother who is gay, he must find it difficult to balance official Church teaching—that homosexual acts are depraved, unnatural, and evil—with the knowledge of homosexuality that social and basic sciences have recently afforded us.

Growing up Catholic was not so different from growing up Jewish or Protestant in regard to our attitudes toward homosexuality in our country: *Catholic homosexual* was an oxymoron. Words such as *queer* or *faggot* commonly were used to designate homosexuals. Such words kept these people at arm's length so that we didn't have to think of them as full persons, but merely as members of an odd group. It is easier to be discriminatory toward a group of unknowns rather than toward individuals with whom we are acquainted. Only a generation ago, most gays stayed "in the closet" because prejudice against them was so rampant, even acceptable.

As a human community the Church has always worked within the boundaries of what it knows and understands at a particular time. Though the Church is led and inspired by the Holy Spirit, it is human persons who interpret issues for it from a particular historical and cultural vantage point. Saint Paul, as a man of his age, believed that women should not be heard at Church services. As mentioned in chapter 1, the Church at one time tolerated slavery and overlooked the persecution of Jewish people, as was the case during the Inquisition. Likewise, any examination of the issue of homosexuality is conditioned by an historical, social perspective. As we have moved forward in time and learned new things about ourselves and the human community, it is important that we keeping reading the signs of the times, as Pope John XXIII suggested before convening the Second Vatican Council. This enables the Church to make room for the Holy Spirit to continue inspiring the Church. It is important to reassess controversial issues because they affect thousands of Catholics who in good faith and right reason find themselves questioning various teachings of their Church. The teaching of the Church that homosexual acts are intrinsically evil and always sinful seems to go against what modern science is telling us.

One of the first questions to be asked about the issue of homosexuality and the Church is not *what* is a homosexual, but *who* is a homosexual. This is an issue about *people* who often feel alone and estranged. He or she is my brother, my sister, my friend, my neighbor, my son. Whoever a homosexual is, he or she is first of all a person with a face and freckles, a hand for holding, a shoulder for crying on, and a heart for loving. As Bishop Gumbleton discovered, he is a brother. Aside from a specific sexual orientation, they are persons with the same hopes for happiness and aspirations for love and acceptance as any other person. We don't define heterosexual persons by their sexual activities, and we should extend the right of wholeness to homosexual individuals as well. The connotations of the word *homosexual* box the individual homosexual in stereotypes and expectations that deny them their humanity and unique personhood. Unfortunately, the Catholic Church is not alone in its discriminatory and homophobic attitudes. Whole societies and cultures have created constructs about homosexuals that have engendered fear and mistrust, not just of homosexuals but of ourselves in terms of our own sexuality. Too often the heterosexual has to prove his/her own sexuality in order to affirm to himself and others that heterosexual orientation. How often has a heterosexual man withheld a hug or an affectionate pat for fear that the gesture would be misconstrued?

In years past, most homosexuals preferred to remain anonymous, hidden. There was, and in many cases still is, so much shame and guilt attached to being homosexual that it has not been dealt with openly and honestly. It was not until 1973, in fact, that the American Psychiatric Association voted to remove it from its list of psychiatric illnesses, the *Diagnostic and Statical Manual*, as something to be cured, and even today many people naively think it can and/or should be "fixed." Although many homosexual individuals are involved in self-hate because of the onus placed on their lives, most are involved in the search for full humanity and spirituality that is the birthright of everyone.

The simplistic belief that homosexuality is some kind of chosen sexual deviancy is no longer acceptable among the educated. Empirical sciences have discovered that homosexuality in itself is not harmful to human persons and that a same-sex orientation in some people is as "natural" as heterosexuality in others, if by natural we mean a human characteristic that cannot be changed without doing violence to one's physical or psychological well-being. One only has to listen to the life stories of homosexual men and women to realize how difficult the awareness of their same-sex orientation can be for them. A friend of mine told me that for seven years she had fought against her own human nature, trying to make it something it was not—heterosexual—until one day, totally drained psychologically, she let herself *be* herself and admitted her homosexuality. Since then, while there is still struggle in her life, it is not *against* herself, and she has discovered an inner peace and strength she never thought possible. Another friend of mine, who is very active in AIDS education, asked me this question when we were discussing whether or not homosexuality was a biologically determined orientation or a choice: "Do you think for one moment that I would *choose* to be this way, when it has cost me rejection from family members and friends; when I have to be on guard constantly about what I say and to whom; when I have to face discrimination and attitudes of disgust? I don't think so." He said, "This is who I am. Years ago I thought I could change that, but now I know that this is the way I was created and the way I am called joyfully to live out my life. So here I am!" A homosexual orientation is natural to some individuals. While the statistics are still being debated, it is thought that around 10 percent of the population has a homosexual orientation. If homosexuality is in fact an orientation and not a choice, the Church has a problem because where choice is absent, sin does not exist since freedom of choice is a condition for sin. If homosexuality is not a choice, could it be a part of God's plan? While the Church does not condemn the homosexual person, it does condemn the acts; separating the acts from the person is difficult, however.

In some cultures and in different historical periods, homosexuality has been acceptable, but for much of Western history, being homosexual has been a matter of shame and embarrassment vis-à-vis the larger heterosexual community and within the Judeo-Christian tradition. The Church has taught that homosexual acts are intrinsically evil and mortal sins.

Our knowledge of homosexuality as a permanent, innate condition is a modern understanding, one that simply did not exist in the ancient world, even among the Jews. It is not surprising, then, that there is no biblical text that adequately addresses this issue. It is naive to expect biblical texts to provide detailed answers for all of our modern concerns such as drug use or homosexuality. The Bible has very little to say about homosexual behavior and nothing about a homosexual orientation because this was not understood as a possible human condition.

The specific texts used to condemn homosexuality in the Old Testament include the story of the destruction of Sodom and Gomorrah (Gen. 19:1–11). In this text, Abraham has settled in the city of Sodom, and two visitors come to see him. The townsmen of Sodom arrive at Abraham's house, knock on the door, and demand that the visitors come out of the house so townsmen might have "intimacies" with them. The townsmen are quite rude and insistent, but Abraham's brother-in-law, Lot, is able to keep them out. That night, God commands that Abraham's family leave Sodom and not turn back because he is going to destroy the city. Almost everyone is familiar with the part of the story in which Lot's wife looks back and is turned to salt. The Israelite tradition ascribes the destruction of Sodom and Gomorrah to the wickedness of the cities. The common understanding of their great sin is that of homosexuality (ergo, the term *sodomy*), but according to Isaiah (1:9–16; 3:8–11), the sin is a lack of social justice. Ezekiel (16:46–51) describes their transgression as a disregard for the poor, and Jeremiah (23:14) sees it as general immorality. So it is not at all clear that the sin of Sodom is that of homosexual practices. A number of biblical scholars suggest that the real sin was that of inhospitality, a very serious sin in the Jewish tradition. In fact, even when Jesus makes reference in the New Testament to Sodom, it is in relationship to a lack of hospitality: "Whatever town you enter and they do not receive you, go out into the streets and say, 'The dust of your town that clings to our feet, even that we shake off against you.' Yet, know this: the Kingdom of God is at hand. I tell you it will be more tolerable for Sodom on that day than for that town" (Luke 10:10–12).

The only other specific Old Testament text dealing with what we consider homosexuality is a part of the Holiness Code in Leviticus that reads, "You shall not lie with a male as with a woman; it is an abomination" (Lev. 18:3). Taken at face value, this text seems clear. However, considering this text in the cultural context from which it arises allows another light to shine on it. The key to understanding this text lies in the word "abomination," used in the Hebrew Scriptures to designate something as ritually unclean, like eating pork, which was also a part of the Holiness Code. The condemnation in this text is directed toward idolatry: Since the People of Yahweh are not to be involved in the unclean idolatrous practices of their neighbors, and lying with the male temple prostitutes is one of those practices, then this homosexuality is a forbidden abomination. The fact is that the homosexual reference in Leviticus is related more to unbelief and idolatry than to homosexuality as we think of it today. (Oddly there is no reference to a woman lying with another woman in the Old Testament.)

This is not to say that Jews of biblical times would accept homosexual practices. We have seen that the entire Hebrew Scripture is given over to institutionalizing family and procreation, essential for the survival of ancient tribal peoples. Children were considered to be the fulfillment of the promise God made to Abraham (Gen. 12:1–3). They were the future, the sign of immortality, and so to be involved in a relationship that could not produce children was a type of heresy in ancient Jewish thought. Wasting the male seed was wrong. Fidelity, love, compassion, filial obedience all helped to establish the order of creation. One would be hard-pressed to find Old Testament passages *condoning* homosexual love, but to use the above cited story of Sodom and Gomorrah or the Leviticus passage, as is often done, to condemn all homosexual activity and homosexuals themselves is an injustice to the Scripture itself.

Other factors that influenced Jewish thinking about homosexuality involve their patriarchal ordering of life. In a patriarchal society in which men dominated women, for a man to assume the social or sexual posture of a woman was out of line. This is an attitude prevalent even today; for a man to assume feminine habits or ways is considered degrading, a denial of one's manliness and the power associated with that prized position. No man should identify with the lower half of human nature, that which is feminine, nurturing, feeling. His place is to be rational, the predator, dominator. The common stereotype, though not of course true, is that in a homosexual relationship one of the partners always assumes a traditional female role. Another cultural factor that could have influenced the attitude toward homosexual sex was the common practice in the ancient Mideast of mounting one's enemies sexually after a conquest as a tactic of further humiliation for the conquered. It was a statement of the superiority of one nation over another. Israel was conquered many times throughout her history, and her people may have had to endure this humiliation; the Hebrew mind may have understood this activity as necessarily punitive, one in which force is used against another person.

In the New Testament, Jesus himself says nothing about homosexuality. He does of course speak at length about love and relationships being based in justice and mercy. As noted, his reference to Sodom relates to inhospitality, not to homosexuality. Saint Paul, on the other hand, reminds his early Christian communities that they are to remain pure and blameless before the Lord's coming; this includes refraining from the sexual practices of their pagan neighbors. Paul also is concerned with cultic purity and reminds the recently converted Roman followers in his letter to them that they are not to engage in the idolatrous activities of their past, including visits to temple prostitutes, some of them male, and other idol worshipping acts. "Therefore God handed them over to impurity through the lusts of their hearts, for the mutual degradation of their bodies. They exchanged the truth of God for a lie and revered and worshipped the creature rather than the creator, who is blessed forever. Therefore God handed them over to degrading passions. Their females exchanged natural relations for unnatural and the males likewise gave up natural relations with females and turned with lust to one another. Males did shameful things with males and thus received in their own persons the due penalty for their perversion. And since they did not see fit to acknowledge God, God handed them over to their undiscerning mind to do what is improper" (Rom. 1:26–28). This is the only extended reference to homosexuality in the New Testament, and it clearly refers to idolatrous acts.

What does Christian Tradition communicate to us about homosexuality? Christian Tradition as it emerges out of the late Hellenistic age, influenced as it was by Stoicism and the dualism of Gnosticism, regarded any sexual desire, as has been discussed in previous chapters, as originating out of the lower levels of human nature. Only by bringing sexual desire under the control of reason, a superior attribute, with a set purpose in mind could any sex be justified. All sexual activity was measured against the order seen in the natural world law; procreation became the goal of all sexual activity. Marriage gave such activity a framework in which childbearing could be achieved most successfully. Marriage became the Christian state of life for those who could not meet the ideal of sexual abstinence through celibacy in the priesthood or religious life. Sex outside of marriage was always sinful, and even within marriage having sex could be sinful, mortally so if the intent for procreation was not present. As mentioned in chapter 5, having sex with one's pregnant wife or a wife past childbearing years was a surefire way of getting a ticket to Hell. Saint Augustine catapulted these ideas into mainstream Catholic thinking, which endured through the centuries.

In the fourteenth century, Thomas Aquinas espoused similar thoughts when he systematized Catholic theology. He asserted and "proved" through natural law theory that procreation is the natural end of sex and therefore that homosexual behavior is a lustful self-indulgence. In fact masturbation as well as oral and anal sex are sinful for the same reason: They spring from sinful desires that did not have procreative intention. Understanding sex as relational, as a means of cultivating and expressing human love, and as a reflection of divine love, was not a part of the theological thinking of an Augustine or an Aquinas. It would be many centuries before the unitive, creative, and integrative approach to sex would be explored. Until then, pastoral practice viewed not just homosexual acts but the persons engaged in them as depraved and sinful. If homosexuals were not reformed, then they were condemned.

So embedded into the religious ideals of Christianity were these concepts that they found their way into civil laws. In some countries, including the United States, laws made oral or anal sex between homosexuals *or* heterosexuals illegal. Such sexual activities, then, were not only sinful but also criminal. Any form of nonreproductive sex was viewed as sexually and socially deviant. It is no wonder that homophobia developed and that homosexuals were viewed as spiritually and morally decadent, chipping away at the established social order of society. Hitler had them branded and exterminated. Laws were written to reduce their subversive numbers. It was acceptable, and still is in some places, to discriminate against them in housing, hiring, and admittance into social and educational establishments.

Psychologists and others tried to establish homosexuality as a sickness to be cured. Freud promoted this idea, charging that homosexuality was a developmental failure, a fixation on an infantile stage of sexuality, a perversion to be overcome. As was stated earlier in this chapter, it was not until 1973 that the American Psychiatric Association removed homosexuality from its list of illnesses. Today, most psychologists tell us that homosexuality in itself is not a disease that needs to be cured. To be sure, there are homosexual persons with various psychological problems, but the same can be said of heterosexuals. The stress that many homosexuals feel because of the social alienation they experience must be extremely difficult.

And how damaging Church teaching about sexual orientation has been for most homosexuals, telling them that their acts are sinful.

In the broadest sense, Tradition enjoins us, as does Scripture, to live and love as Jesus did. That the Church Fathers were conditioned by their cultures is apparent in Church Tradition and teaching. The influence of Stoicism, the duality of Gnosticism, and reaction to pagan practices have left imprints on virtually everything related to sex, gender, and sexuality in Roman Catholicism. It is apparent that the shaping of Catholic theology by the Church Fathers was done in good faith in an attempt to create a responsible ethic for their time. In our day, it is easy to use 20/20 hindsight to be critical. But one works with the knowledge and understanding one has in any historical period, however shortsighted such comprehension might be. Few of us have the vision to see beyond our own time. However, once we become aware of our shortsightedness, through biblical research and analysis, historical evaluation, and the findings of psychology, sociology and other sciences, we become responsible for changing not only our attitudes but also our practices and the enlightened thoughts we pass on to future generations.

As was discussed in previous chapters, there is much about sex and sexuality in general that has baffled the human community. It has been only in the last half of the twentieth century that researchers such as Masters and Johnson have undertaken serious studies to better understand sexuality, which have enlightened and informed the public. New information on social conditioning, the psychological effects of child rearing, chromosomes, hormones, and the brain has helped us understand how and why some individuals diverge from heterosexuality, which we assume to be the norm. Still, there is no conclusive evidence as to why homosexuality occurs, though it has become more clear that this is not a choice individuals make but rather a biological identity.

The official teaching of the Church does not seem to recognize the value of this point. It was inevitable that the sexual revolution of the sixties would help to liberate the gay community as well as the heterosexual one. Organized and confident, gay men and women worked toward acceptance into the larger community. The impact on religious groups was tremendous. They were forced to take a public stand. Armed with new scientific research suggesting that homosexuality was a natural orientation rather than something chosen, members of this minority began speaking out and laying claim to the rights and freedoms to which they felt entitled. Many homosexuals who had felt shame and guilt about their sexual orientation, who had been shunned by and alienated from religious gatherings, had stopped practicing their faith; they now demanded recognition from their various religious traditions. By the 1970s they were saying, in effect, "You can't deny my experience of God, my call to holiness, my contribution to the life of the Church, and I am not going away."

What is the official teaching of the Church on homosexuality? In 1975 the first official contemporary statement on homosexuality by the Vatican was released a Declaration on Certain Questions Concerning Sexual Ethics, which states, "According to the objective moral order, homosexual relations are acts which lack an essential and indispensable finality i.e., procreation" and identifies homosexual acts as "intrinsically disordered" (para. 5); under no circumstances are they to be condoned by anyone in the Church. The declaration was in part a reaction to the new stance of the American Psychiatric Association, no longer identifying homosexuality as an illness. The declaration accepted the medical conclusion that homosexuality in general is a condition that is constitutive of a given person and encouraged pastoral sensitivity toward such people, but the declaration also lashed out at people who had been accepting of the homosexual condition and lenient about related behavior. It states that such an attitude had resulted in "erroneous opinions and resulting deviations which are continuing to spread everywhere" (para. 2), thus making it necessary for the Church to reaffirm its traditional teaching on sexual ethics. Grounding this teaching in what it describes as the divine law of human nature, it condemns homosexual acts as pathological and essentially disordered because they lack an essential finality in procreation. Because it also requests that pastors counsel homosexual against forming relationships analogous to marriage—secure and permanent relationships with a beloved partner—far from extinguishing discussion on this issue, the declaration became a catalyst for further debate and was condemned for its close-mindedness.

Individual theologians, scholars, educators, and bishops began an intense and thorough study of the issue. Bishop Francis Mugavero of Brooklyn issued a pastoral letter in 1976 that, while upholding the norm of heterosexuality, judged other orientations mildly, stating not that they were disordered, but that they "less adequately reflected the full spectrum of human relationships" (as quoted in Gramick and Nugent, *The Vatican and Homosexuality*, xiv.) The U.S. bishops in 1976 also issued a pastoral letter, To Live in Christ Jesus, adopting a strong stance toward ensuring the civil rights of homosexual individuals and encouraging them to take an active role in the Christian community. The bishops further asked that they be granted a "special degree of personal understanding and care" (Kosnik, *Human Sexuality*, 71).

The year 1976 also saw the publication of John McNeill's *The Church and the Homosexual*, which was the focus of much debate, in which he asked the Church to reconsider its position on homosexuality. (He was silenced for speaking about the subject and was eventually expelled from the Jesuits in 1987, when he decried the teaching on homosexuality from the Vatican, which had come out in a 1986 letter.) A year after the publication of NcNeill's book, in 1977, the Committee on the Study of Human Sexuality of the Catholic Theological Society published a report suggesting support for committed homosexual relationships as consonant with the book's criteria for genital expression, which involved being creative and integrative.

In 1980 a young medieval historian at Yale University, John Boswell, published his findings in a book, *Christianity, Social Tolerance, and Homosexuality,* suggesting that homosexual persons found a much more accepting environment in the Middle Ages than is evidenced in the twentieth century. He argues that the Church's attitudes and policies on homosexual relations have not always been as rigid as present-day policies might lead one to believe, rather, homosexuals had been acknowledged and religious life had provided a supportive environment for homosexual people. Boswell further contends that the scriptural texts used to condemn homosexuality cannot bear the theological weight accorded them. In 1981 the archdiocese of Baltimore issued a statement that homosexual orientation "is in no way held to be a sinful condition" and that like heterosexuality it serves as a starting point for one's response to Christ (as quoted in Gallagher, *Homosexuality and the Magisterium,* 39). The Baltimore archdiocese also began officially sanctioned diocesan ministries for gays and lesbians.

Meanwhile, organizations for gays and lesbians had been multiplying, even within the Church. Dignity, formed in 1969, began by offering support and advice to the gay community. New Ways Ministry, founded in 1977 by Jean Gramick and Robert Nugent, two leaders for gay rights in the Church, in 1981 sponsored a symposium on homosexuality in the Catholic faith, at which noted scholars and theologians presented papers calling for a more compassionate understanding of homosexuality. These were later published in the book *Homosexuality and the Catholic Church*.

In 1983, another significant book of essays and papers on homosexuality and the Church, entitled *A Challenge to Love: Gay and Lesbian Catholics in the Church*, edited by Robert Nugent, was published. The introduction was written by Bishop Walter Sullivan of Virginia. Sullivan therein challenges the Church community to continue to reassess and reflect on its teaching in regard to homosexuality:

> Yet we cannot remain satisfied that once we have clearly articulated the official Church position on homosexuality, nothing else remains to be done in the area of pastoral care for homosexual people and education on this topic for the larger human community, including the families and friends of homosexual people. This is especially true in those cases where the teaching of the

Church itself has been presented in such a way that it has been the source or occasion of some of the pain and alienation that many homosexual Catholics experience. We cannot overlook those injustices, including rejection, hostility, or indifference on the part of Christians, that have resulted in a denial of respect or full participation in the community for homosexual people. We must examine our own hearts and minds and consciences and know that each of us stands in real need of conversion in this area. (*A Challenge*, xii)

During this dialogue within the Catholic community, AIDS was already beginning to take its toll, particularly among gays. For some, this justified the condemnation of homosexual behavior, but some religious leaders encouraged *greater* pastoral care and support. The hierarchy was not always thrilled with their efforts. When Archbishop Raymond Hunthausen of Washington welcomed the Gay and Lesbian Organization to celebrate its biannual Mass in Seattle's Saint James Cathedral in 1983, the Vatican stripped him of some of his episcopal authority, allegedly for failing to uphold Catholic orthodoxy; other bishops also were investigated about whether they were complying with the Church's hard line against condoning homosexual practices. The Catholic community should have been prepared but was left dumbstruck when, in 1986, the Vatican's Congregation for the Doctrine of Faith released the document Letter to the Bishops of the Catholic Church on the Pastoral Care of Homosexual Persons. The letter insists on the orthodoxy of its previous 1975 statement, that describes homosexual acts as "intrinsically disordered," though it does suggest that a homosexual person is not necessarily culpable because such an individual is constitutively inclined toward a homosexual orientation. The letter had been billed as one about the pastoral care of homosexual persons. What was heard loudest and clearest, however, were the following words, which seem anything but pastoral: "Although the particular inclination of the homosexual person is not a sin, it is a more or less strong tendency ordered toward an intrinsic moral evil; and thus the inclination itself must be seen as an objective disorder. Therefore special concern and pastoral attention should be directed toward those who have this condition, lest they be led to believe that the living out of this orientation in homosexual behavior is a morally acceptable option. It is not" (para. 3). The letter met with shock, disbelief, and anger from the homosexual community and those working with them.

Shock, because the fact was that since the beginning of this century when the institutional Church began turning its attention increasingly to social issues such as the economy, warfare, peace, labor relations, and capital punishment, Vatican encyclicals and pastorals had reflected the magisterium's reliance on the laity and "experts" in these fields. These parties had given them guidance, with accurate scientific and sociological information to support the Vatican's position. This newest statement on homosexuality, however, overlooked all such expert advice on this complex issue. The letter overlooks even the suggestion made in Vatican II's Pastoral Constitution on the Church in the Modern World (*Gaudium et Spes*), which states, "In pastoral care, appropriate use must be made not only of theological principles, but also the findings of secular sciences, especially psychology and sociology [in order to] blend modern science and its theories and the understandings of the most recent discoveries with Christian morality and doctrine" (para. 5). The 1986 Letter to the Bishops of the Catholic Church on the Pastoral Care of Homosexual Persons suggests that present-day Rome is able to leap over the former Vatican II statement by stating: "The Church is in the position to learn from scientific discovery but also to *transcend* the horizons of science and to be confident" (para. 2). Many saw this as an example of magisterial self-righteousness. After all, the documents of the Second Vatican were endorsed by the entire body of cardinals, whereas this statement came from one office of the Church. It convinced some that the hierarchy was less concerned with the pastoral care offered to homosexual persons than with its own hierarchical position and teaching. The letter leaves no room for the Church to suggest that the issue is still open, that greater understanding of the homosexual condition is possible, as most anthropologists, psychologists, and sociologists hold.

By suggesting that one ought *not* live out one's natural sexual orientation, the authors of the letter seem to ignore the fact that sexuality is a fundamental dimension of every human being. Sex is reflected in a person's identity psychologically, physiologically, and relationally. To dismiss the interrelationship between one's sexual identity, in this case homosexual, and one's sexual acts is not to respect the person for who he or she is; this seems philosophically incoherent and theologically hypocritical, since the Book of Genesis clearly states that all that God created was good.

What is also bothersome is that a moral evaluation is being made of a condition that the Church clearly states is not a choice but a natural inclination. How can a moral evaluation be made of something "natural"? Moral theology holds the freedom to choose as central in judging the morality of a situation. Should a couple unable to conceive children choose not to have intercourse because the finality of procreation is not possible for them? Granted, the issue of homosexuality is a little more complicated than this, but in this day and age few would be so harsh in judging an infertile couple. Why, then, the seeming hardness of heart toward homosexuals?

There was anger by biblical scholars over the fact that despite the years of study that had gone into the texts traditionally used to condemn homosexuality—which now are interpreted within a larger context—their research is nowhere evident in the 1986 letter discussing the treatment of homosexuals, which is based on fundamentalist biblical interpretation and prescientific church tradition. As was discussed in previous chapters, scriptural texts on celibacy, divorce and remarriage, sex and marriage, and now homosexuality have to be read and interpreted against the historical/religious values of the times in which they were written. After all, an epileptic seizure was interpreted as possession by a demon spirit at the time of Christ. It would be naive to think that homosexuality and homosexual acts would be understood two thousand years ago as they are today.

The dismissal of our present understanding of homosexuality given to us by the scientific community with the words, "Increasing numbers of people today, even within the Church, are bringing enormous pressure to bear on the Church to accept the homosexual condition as though it were not disordered" (ibid., para. 2), displays a self-righteous attitude that many find regrettable. For reform-minded Catholics who believe the Church has made great strides in support of other minorities, including the physically and mentally challenged, this was a great setback and another instance in which the windows and doors opened during Vatican II were being closed.

Shock gives way to anger when words of the letter give tacit approval to discrimination against homosexuals:

> But the proper reaction to crimes committed against homosexual persons should not be to claim that the homosexual condition is not disordered. When such a claim is made and when homosexual activity is consequently condoned, or when civil legislation is introduced to protect behavior to which no one has a conceivable right, neither the Church nor society at large should be surprised when other distorted notions and practices gain ground, and irrational and violent reactions increase. (para. 10)

This last statement invites hate-filled discriminatory activity against homosexuals. And while the letter on the one hand asks the bishops to provide counseling and pastoral care to homosexuals, on the other hand it says that any Catholic gay or lesbian group not adhering strictly to the Church's teaching on this matter should have Church support withdrawn and be denied the use of Church buildings or Church property, since such accommodations to the homosexual community would be "misleading and often scandalous" (para. 17). These words were directed particularly at the Catholic gay and lesbian organization Dignity, which had been growing in membership as a powerful voice for that community and had been meeting at Catholic facilities.

In retaliation for being denied access to the institutional Church, homosexuals took action, as in the case of the "cathedral project." In 1989 gay Catholics and other members of ACT UP (the AIDS Coalition to Unleash Power) attended a Mass at Saint Patrick's Cathedral in New York City, stood throughout Cardinal O'Connor's homily in defiance, and otherwise disrupted the service. The frustration had hit a high point. The anger intensified six years later when the Vatican issued another directive to the American Bishops only months before the 1992 elections; gay rights legislation was to be voted upon in several state ballots. The document, Some Considerations Concerning the Catholic Response to Legislative Proposals on the Non-Discrimination of Homosexual Persons, stated that discrimination against homosexual persons in areas of employment and family such as teaching, coaching, service in the military, adoption, and foster care of children was justified because support of their participation in such activities was an attack on family values and condoned a homosexual lifestyle. The statement was considered an affront not only to the gay and lesbian community but to many educated Catholics of good faith, who simply could not accept discrimination toward any group of people. The Conference of Major Superiors of Men, superiors of the priests and brothers in religious communities in the United States, issued their own response, "This statement clouds the institutional Church's stated views on justice and human rights. We view this statement as a hindrance to the Church leaders of the United States in this most difficult and sensitive area of human living. . . . We are shocked that the statement calls for discrimination against gay and lesbian men and women" (as reported in the *National Catholic Reporter*, Sept. 2, 1992). Supporters of the official Church would argue that this is not discrimination but protection against a lifestyle that is immoral.

Other Catholic groups and individuals, such as Bishop Thomas Gumbleton of Detroit, spoke out against the statement but such voiced opposition did little to mend the rift between the institutional Church and the gay community. In fact the letter suggested that the mothers, fathers, siblings and friends who supported and encouraged their homosexual relatives or acquaintances could also be objects of discrimination, which may have led some of those loved ones to remain silent or take little or no action.

There was also disbelief about this official teaching position for other reasons. Since Vatican II, the emphasis in Catholic moral theology has been on a person-centered rather than an act-centered morality. The letter seems to imply that in evaluating homosexuality, one can exclude the person and look just at the acts, an approach that contradicts the efforts of Catholic moral theologians over the past twenty years. In one sense it is natural to assume that heterosexuality is the norm and therefore the good for everyone, since this is the experience for the majority of us. It is difficult for most heterosexuals to imagine sharing an intimate sexual relationship with anyone of the same gender. Nevertheless it is still important that we open our minds to the possibility and reality that a homosexual relationship can be creative and integrative for the people involved, a real expression of human love. One only has to move among the homosexual community to discover how many loving, committed homosexual relationships there are and how many more there could have been except for the shame and condemnation homosexual persons experience from the community at large. A close friend of mine has been in a stable homosexual relationship for eighteen years, longer than some of my heterosexual friends' marriages. Any human relationship should be judged by the self-giving, loving concern, trust, and respect for the other embodied in its acts. To judge the acts apart from the individual is an injustice. To suggest that all homosexual love and acts cannot achieve the depth and relevance of heterosexual love is an injustice.

Many questions have been raised about the nature of making love. What is the real value underlying sexual acts, and must they be ordered toward some specific end, as the Church has suggested in the past? If the procreative intent or ability is not there among heterosexual couples when making love, why is it wrong if the intent and ability for procreation is missing between same-sex couples when they make love? Is the moral quality of sexual behavior defined biologically in terms of certain body parts, or is it defined in terms of personal love and commitment? If the Second Vatican Council suggested that the moral evaluation of sexuality be conducted according to the harmonizing principle of "the nature of the human person and his acts" (GS, para. 51), and if some people are *by nature* oriented toward same-sex relations, then on what grounds does anyone condemn their embodied love? I do not have the answer to these questions. I raise them because they are real questions in the minds of those who minister to the homosexual community and because the present teaching on homosexuality in the Church causes them to be raised but does not provide adequate answers.

An affirmation of sexuality as a good, whether ordered toward a same-sex partner or other-sex partner, ought to involve the same values and norms. For many homosexual partners, an expression of love may not be procreative but is creative and integrative, the values stressed by the Catholic Theological Society of America for judging the morality of sexual acts in its study on sexuality. Sexuality, within either a heterosexual relationship or a homosexual relationship, would be judged against that which fosters a creative growth toward integration, concomitant with a call to holiness and wholeness. Respect, service, honesty, compassion, fidelity—all are values that are at the heart of the Christian message and norms against which any acts are judged. Heterosexual acts such as rape or incest or molesting children are reprehensible because these values are entirely missing. There is a context and intentionality within which sexual acts ought to take place. To say that heterosexual acts are good but homosexual acts are always morally wrong is simplistic. Much of the anger toward and frustration about the Church and its teaching from the gay community arises out of this discriminatory nature of the Church's judgments. It is difficult to believe that the Jesus of the Gospels, who sides with the weak and the outcasts judged harshly by the Jewish leaders of his day, would dismiss homosexuals as some kind of aberration and ask them to forgo any kind of loving relationship in which they could grow into full human persons. According to the Church, homosexual love is not to be embodied if such people want to be saved. Homosexuals see their lives as gifts from God, as part of the ordering of creation, as made in the image and likeness of God.

In a May 1993 interview in *America* magazine, Andrew Sullivan, the editor of *The New Republic*, had this to say:

> I am drawn in the natural way that I think all human beings are drawn to love and care for another person. I agree with the Church's teachings about the natural law in that regard. I think we are called to commitment and fidelity, and I see that all around me in the gay world. I see as one was taught to see in the natural law, self-evident activity leading toward this final end which is commitment and love: the need and desire and hunger for that. That is the sensus fidelium, and there is no attempt within the Church right now even to bring that sense into the discussion of the teaching. . . . Being gay is not just about sex, but about who one can love. It is about one's emotional identity and what makes him whole as a person.

Andrew Sullivan has been an exceptional spokesperson for gay Catholic men and the pain and frustration they feel about having been rejected by the Church they love. Church leaders would argue that *homosexuals* have not been rejected, but rather their *acts*. But to have their acts demeaned and to be required not to give sexual expression to their lives *is* a rejection of their persons, they believe. While it is certainly not the whole of life and no one should define his or her individual life by sexual identity or practice, sexual expression is the way we as humans give and accept the love of another intimately. Celibacy is a gift that can be prayed for but ought not to be exacted on others.

Homosexuality is not going away. If it is true that homosexuality is something that occurs naturally in some persons, as it has throughout history in all civilizations and societies, perhaps it is time for the Church to address homosexuality as a way to live out one's call to holiness rather than trying to frustrate homosexual love and the possibilities for creative growth for homosexual persons. The bottom line is that the Church's teaching about homosexuality, particularly as it is stated in the 1986 letter on the topic, is not the meaningful pastoral address that it could be for people who are ministering to those with AIDS or for anyone in the Catholic homosexual community. Few people are aware of the many wonderful individuals within the Catholic community and the Church establishment, such as Bishop Gumbleton, who are more sympathetic to the gay community than this letter would indicate. Unfortunately, in our society, AIDS and homosexuality are sometimes believed synonymous; this misunderstanding has led rise to more homophobia and greater discrimination. The already-serious stereotype of homosexuality as a sickness was further embedded in people's minds. As the media seized upon the news of the HIV virus and AIDS, the gay community was often their focus. As gays and lesbians have become more politically active, the one issue that many people associate them with is AIDS research and education.

However, the positive upshot is that as AIDS went public, so did individuals in the gay and lesbian community, and awareness of homosexuality grew. People found that they had brothers, sisters, sons, daughters, aunts, and uncles who were gay. Some were forced out of the closet because they had AIDS, and others came forward desiring to dispel the many myths about homosexuals that existed. Listening to people was a lesson in humanity itself. I heard stories about everything from out-and-out rejection of friends and relatives who were gay to warm and embracing love and acceptance by family and acquaintances. A friend of mine recently told me that her Catholic mother still tells friends three years after the fact that her homosexual son died of kidney failure rather than admitting that he died of AIDS. Another friend came to visit me in the New York area when her brother was dying of AIDS; she stayed with me for the three days, never mentioning the word *homosexual* or the cause of his death. She had to lie to her mother about where she was going because the family had disowned him when they discovered he was gay. However, I know another woman whose brother died of AIDS; she invites his mate of fifteen years to all her family gatherings. Her children call him Uncle Steve.

There of course were and are Christians of every denomination who view AIDS as a punishment on the gay community for their sins. On the other hand, many denominations, the Catholic Church included, have established means of pastoral support. The AIDS epidemic forced everyone—Catholics, Jews, Protestants, Muslims—to face the issue of homosexuality. For many of us homosexuality took on a name and a face. It made us examine the cultural values and constructs we had inherited from the past. At the same time, researchers and writers from the scientific community, from the fields of psychology and sociology, were forced to examine the issue more closely. They have since contributed to a growing body of knowledge on homosexuality and continue to educate us. Prejudice and bigotry, at least in educated circles, has given way to compassion and acceptance. Even among many of the clergy in the Roman Catholic Church a new sense of understanding about homosexuality has begun to emerge, and we can find compassionate, understanding, and supportive members there.

Two statements by the American bishops have been issued, "The Many Faces of AIDS: A Gospel Response," issued in December 1987, and "Called to Compassion and Responsibility: A Response to the HIV/AIDS Crisis," in November 1989. Both of these documents attempt to disengage the disease from the homosexual community by pointing out that it also affects heterosexuals and children. Both documents encourage attitudes of compassion and understanding, as well as concerns about justice toward those with HIV/AIDS. The rights and dignity of each member of the human community are underscored, and the documents encourage education of the public and support for research to find a cure. However, it is clear in the 1989 statement that moral evaluations are still being made against the larger context of traditional Catholic teaching on anything of a sexual nature: "Sexual intercourse is appropriate and morally good only when, in the context of heterosexual marriage, it is a celebration of faithful love and is open to new life." From this vantage point the American Bishops use these statements to reaffirm and promote the traditional Catholic program of sexual abstinence before marriage, heterosexuality in general, as well as the ban on contraception.

I suspect strongly that the day will come when the moral certitude of the Church on this issue will soften. With clergy and their relatives dying of AIDS and the realization that many priests are homosexual, the awareness that this is an issue about people, compassion, and justice will take hold. The many ways that the homosexual community has enhanced the human community through its art, scholarship, and leadership is testament to the creative powers that lie within this group of people. Perhaps one day we will look back on this issue too and wonder how we ever could have been so lacking in understanding and love.

8

GROWING UP

RESPONSIBLY CATHOLIC:

FREEDOM AND LOYAL DISSENT

*Only in freedom can man direct himself toward goodness.
For its part, authentic freedom is an exceptional sign of
the divine image within man. For God has willed that
man be left in the hand of his own counsel so that he can
seek his creator spontaneously, and can come freely to
utter and blissful perfection through loyalty to him. Hence
man's dignity demands that he act according to a
knowing and free choice. Such a choice is personally
motivated and prompted from within. It does not result
from blind internal impulse, nor from mere external
pressure.* (GS, para. 16)

One of the things that makes reading the Old Testament so
exciting is its unpredictability. God always seems to do the unexpected. He promises Abraham a son, from a woman who is past
childbearing years. He delivers on the son, but then asks Abraham
to sacrifice the child. Fortunately, this is just a test, and the son,
Isaac, grows to be a man and has two boys. The younger of the two,
Jacob, with the help of his mother, cheats his older brother out of
his birthright and goes on to become the next great patriarch of the

Chosen People. The favorite son of Jacob is sold off into slavery by his own brothers to the Egyptians and ends up becoming a powerful governor in Egypt. He then has the opportunity to save his brothers and father from famine and does so. Moses, who has a speech impediment, becomes the spokesperson for Yahweh, and the great king of Israel, David, falls prey to one of the greatest sins imaginable, betrayal of a loyal friend. All of this teaches us to expect the unexpected. It shows us that God is beyond our ordinary categories of thought and anticipation, that we can never quite get a handle on God. As soon as we think we have God all figured out, the unpredictable happens. God is free, and as the epigraph to this chapter reminds us, freedom is our inheritance, created as we are in the image and likeness of God. I often tell my students that God had to make us free, for without freedom we would be unable to come spontaneously to God in love. He created us free, not perfect, I tell them, because if we were perfect we would have no need of one another or God. Not being perfect means we always have room to grow, discover, and learn. It means we are in process. God created us with the unique ability to make choices and decisions in regard to our relationship with him, one another, and the world. Being free forces us to continually make use of our gifts of intellect and reason to shape our lives.

This chapter is about our use of freedom and the place of the Church in the life of Catholics. Obviously, we are not talking about license, the ability to do whatever we want regardless of the consequences or a type of freedom motivated by wanton self-gratification. That's not really freedom. Freedom here involves our ability to be informed, responsible, aware of freedom vis-à-vis dignity as humans in relation with others. Freedom here encompasses love and loyalty to the past and traditions as well as the capacity to move forward.

In the years before Vatican II in the early sixties, there had emerged in the Church a way of thinking that went something like this: "There are truths in the Church that are 'guarded truths' grounded in the life and teaching of Christ that endure and are not subject to change—that Jesus is the Son of God, that he manifests

God in a unique way, that he meant for us to memorialize him in the Eucharist, that he promised his Holy Spirit to be present always, that he suffered, died, and rose from the dead and ascended into Heaven—these are some of the enduring, eternal, irrefutable truths. But on the other hand, the language and conceptualization we as humans have used to communicate those truths are limited and often in need of change. There are other things about the Church that are true but not necessarily guarded truths. I remember heated debates around the table at Sunday dinner when three generations of family members would argue about whether or not the language of the Mass ought to be changed from Latin to the vernacular, in our case English. The argument extended to school and outside our parish church after Mass. There were people who thought that if the language of the Mass changed, it would not be the sacrifice of Christ, that it would lose its mystery and respectful worship, that it would not be a true form of Catholic worship. This one issue stirred up some division, with talk from people threatening to form their own Church. Today most see that change from Latin to the vernacular as a necessary change that has made the Eucharist more understandable to the people and hence more relevant in their lives.

Discoveries and inventions in science, technology, and communications have altered our world. As the world's people progress in self-understanding, as we have evolved as a human community, our whole frame of reference has undergone dramatic transformation. Some matters in and about the Church are being questioned today because the human experience we bring to those truths in the late twentieth century has changed, altering our perceptions and understanding of those truths as well as the way we give expression to them. Many people argue for the use of more inclusive language in the liturgy as well as in the workplace, as a sign of our growing awareness of the contributions of various members of the human community. To use the word *man* or *mankind* in discussions of women as well as men has become politically incorrect. Twenty years ago the term *inclusive language* was almost an unknown. Life and human experience have changed that.

As was stated in the first chapter, the measure of our ability to adapt to change is related to the confidence we have in Jesus' word that he will remain with us always, even to the ends of the earth, and that he will send us his Spirit, "the Spirit of truth [who] will guide you to all truth" (John 16:13). So we continue to strive to give expression to the truths of our faith for each succeeding generation. It is always possible that we could err in the expression; our language is limited and never can convey finally and ultimately the mysteries of faith. Words are always symbols that point beyond themselves to greater realities. The reality of our Christian beliefs far exceeds the words we use. While it is the Church's duty to guard these truths, it is also the Church's duty to refine its expression in such a way that it is able to illuminate the truth to every generation of the People of God. This is a pastoral consideration, which means that the hierarchy must respond to its charge to care for and support the faithful in their search for God. The truths are meant not to be hermetically sealed entities held out before the People of God, but to involve and touch their lives in such ways that they become living truths, that they speak of their experience and to their lives. John XXIII said as much on October 11, 1962, in his opening speech at Vatican II:

> . . . the Christian, Catholic, and apostolic spirit of the whole world expects a step forward toward a doctrinal penetration and a formation of consciousness in faithful and authentic doctrine, which, however, should be studied and expounded through the methods of research and through literary forms of modern thought. The substance of the ancient doctrines of the Deposit of Faith is one thing and the way in which it is presented is another. And it is the latter which must be taken into great consideration, with patience if necessary, everything being measured in the forms and proportions of the magisterium which is predominantly pastoral in character. (Abbott, *Documents and Speeches,* 715)

That the responsibility for teaching the truth of the Catholic faith lies primarily with the magisterium is one of the guarded truths. It is also a guarded truth that the Holy Spirit guides and acts through the entire people of God. The 1964 Dogmatic Constitution on the Church (*Lumen Gentium:* "Light of Nations") reads: "Thus it is evident to everyone that all the faithful of Christ of whatever rank or status are called to the fullness of the Christian life" (para. 40). The aforementioned concept of the *sensus fidelium* means that the creative power of the Holy Spirit can be experienced by the whole People of God, the whole Church. Their experience is legitimate and worthwhile in giving expression to the faith. More and more Catholic Christians are beginning to feel that it is a type of pride that leads to the belief that only a few people in the Church have a handle on the truths and the ways in which they are expressed. This does not mean that the *sensus fidelium* should be an opinion poll or a popularity vote on different issues, but it does mean that the experience of the whole People of God—priests, theologians, and laity—should be considered legitimate and worthwhile in an expression of the truths of our faith. Neither am I saying that people other than the bishops should dictate what is being taught, but surely more dialogue, collegiality, and shared vision should be a part of this process of formulating statements and deciding issues. Cutting off discussion on a particular issue does little to acknowledge the call to holiness of the whole People of God.

There is a great deal of evidence that from the time of the New Testament Church until the collapse of the Roman Empire in the fifth century, the mind of the people was an important factor in the way the Church conducted its business. It is clear that at the Council of Jerusalem, as recorded in the Acts of the Apostles, all of the people took part in the discussion and the entire community chose the seven who were to assist the apostles when the number of Christians began to grow (Acts 6:5). Throughout the first three centuries of the Church the people had input and in some instances elected those who would lead them, the bishops. There is a famous story about the fourth-century election of Ambrose to be bishop of Milan. Ambrose was the governor of Milan, known to the people as a just and fair man. He had not yet been baptized, but when he showed up at the cathedral to prevent a disturbance from occurring over the election of the bishop, the people started shouting, "Ambrose for Bishop, Ambrose for Bishop." He tried to flee from town, but the people were so insistent that he was their choice that he was baptized, and ordained through the various ministries in six days, and then consecrated bishop on December 1, 373. The clergy had to concur in such elections; nonetheless, the people were heard and considered.

Catholics in Austria and Holland have come out in large numbers to sign petitions asking for change and a greater say in Church matters. Some of the Catholic bishops have recognized that structures need to change and systems need to be established or expanded so that the People of God may be heard on the issues we have discussed in this book. Chicago's recently deceased Cardinal Bernardin announced in 1996 an effort to find a "common ground" among Catholics of different opinions in order to decrease polarization in the Church—the Catholic Common Ground Project. This group, comprised of twenty-three prominent Catholic laypeople and theologians, would support conferences in order to create a forum for discussion of important issues in the Church, such as birth control and expanded roles for women, in an atmosphere of openness and trust. His idea has been criticized by some other cardinals and bishops. But when three-quarters of Catholics believe that you can be a good Catholic and practice birth control, and the Church continues to hold out on its official position with a resounding "no" to birth control, this is not a simple matter of disobedience on the part of the Catholic population. It is a statement that the magisterium is out of touch with the experience of the people they are shepherding.

In the spring of 1997 an article appeared in the *New York Times* stating that the Church was going to withhold a symbolic gift of two thousand dollars to UNICEF on the grounds that this money was going to an organization increasingly involved with birth control as a means for population control and improved health care for women. Because the Church teaches that any form of artificial birth control is wrong, and this money was going to an organization that taught women in Third World countries how to use birth control, the money was withheld. At lunch that day at the Catholic school where I teach, this became the topic of discussion. By and large my colleagues were appalled that the Church would be so small in its thinking that it would try to intimidate an organization that had done so much to save the lives of women and improve the lives of infants in Hindu, Buddhist, and Muslim countries, by suggesting that the Church's standard of morality on this issue was to be enforced upon the entire world population or it would withdraw its support from charitable causes.

It is interesting to note that it took less than fifteen years for the major reforms of Vatican II to take effect in the parishes and lives of Catholics throughout the world. Architects were called into virtually every parish to make churches more community-oriented, new Eucharistic prayers were written, a new rite of reconciliation came about, and the laity were given roles to play in administering their parishes with the formation of Church councils. The People of God were focused and ready for further reforms and changes. For a while it seemed we were on a roll, things were moving forward. There was a sense of creativity and dynamism everywhere in the Church that could not be extinguished in the late sixties, even with the promulgation of *Humanae Vitae:* "On Human Life." A new mentality in the Church was emerging. People had begun to take seriously the belief that we are the Church, that our prayerful insights would be heard. An example of this occurred when people realized that the Pope had rejected the recommendations of his own commission in issuing *Humanae Vitae.* Reasoned thoughtful dissent was immediate and dramatic. Within thirty-six hours theologians from all over the country, under the leadership of Father Charles Curran, signed a petition respectfully dissenting from the teaching of the encyclical that states: "It is a serious error to think that a whole married life of otherwise normal relations can justify sexual intercourse which is deliberately contraceptive and so intrinsically wrong" (HV, para. 15). The theologians basically agreed that those parts of the encyclical upholding the sanctity of marriage and the importance of the family were to be lauded as representative statements about values that Catholics should strive to incorporate into their lives. But they also felt that statements such as the one just cited indicated a retreat to the past, a return to a static, exclusively act-centered morality, despite the progress made at Vatican II in regard to the importance of a morality centered on the human person as well as his or her acts. Since the Pope had ignored the experience and statements of married Catholic couples, including those on his own commission, and the advice of many other well-intentioned people, these theologians felt that they had a moral responsibility to dissent from this authoritative but not infallible statement.

The furor that followed this act of loyal dissent reverberated throughout the Church. Here were prominent people, highly schooled in theological disciplines, opposed to a Church teaching and saying so publicly.

For some the idea of loyal dissent may sound like a contradiction in terms. How can one be loyal to the Church, a Church known to the world for its positions of authoritative teaching, primarily through the Pope and the magisterium, and also dissent from a teaching? This is not done with a cavalier attitude. For someone to be loyal to the Church, one must love the Church and find in it a source for life and strength. Someone who is loyal to the Church respects the Tradition, its sacramental and communal life, and even the structures that uphold all of this. Someone who is loyal to the Church seeks to live out the message of Jesus in its personal and social implications. Church loyalty suggests that one sincerely searches for the truth out of motives that support the common good and not individual gain. A loyal Church member is one whose conscience has been guided and formed within the Church to do good according to the Gospel values of faith, hope, and love. Dissent such as that which arose over the birth control issue, or any other issue presented in this book, springs from deep loyalty and concern for the Church, the body of Christians in the world. This dissent is not so unlike what occurs in the human body. When an organ sends a pain message to the body's brain, it is requesting a change in the body's behavior that is causing the pain, yet the organ could not leave the body and survive on its own.

The Second Vatican Council, in fact, had some extraordinary things to say about the individual conscience and stated that Catholics had a moral obligation to live according to conscience, even if it means standing alone:

> In the depths of his conscience, man deflects a law which he does not impose upon himself, but which holds him to obedience. Always summoning him to love good and avoid evil, the voice of conscience can when necessary speak to his heart more specifically: do this, shun that. For man has in his heart a law written by God. To obey it is the very dignity of man; according to it he will be judged. Conscience is the most secret core and sanctuary of man. There he is alone with God, whose voice echoes in his depths. In a wonderful manner conscience reveals that law which is fulfilled by love of God and neighbor. In fidelity to conscience, Christians are joined with the rest of men in the search for truth, and the genuine solution to the numerous problems which arise in the life of the individuals and from social relationships. (GS, para. 16)

Our consciences are formed via the human community, family, friends, educational opportunities, and of course the Church. The good in life is placed before us, guidelines are established, laws are set forth, and hopefully a conscience is developed. Environmental influences work upon those inherited and acquired capacities in the human psyche, our emotions, intellect, and will, to aid this development. The social, religious, political, and economic milieu all enter into our consciousness and formation of conscience. As a teenager, I was deeply affected by quotations from two famous people: John F. Kennedy's "Ask not what your country can do for you; ask what you can do for your country," and by Martin Luther King Jr.'s "If a man hasn't discovered something that he will die for, he isn't fit to live." Their lives affected mine and the formation of my conscience. I have since believed that being deeply committed and willing to sacrifice whatever it takes to realize the truth are what makes life challenging and fulfilling.

It is simplistic to think of conscience as some little voice inside of the individual that says, "Do this, don't do that." Nonetheless, Saint Paul and Saint Thomas Aquinas tell us that there is a natural capacity for us to know what is good and what is bad, a law written on our hearts (Rom. 2:15). It is of course because of environmental influences and perhaps inherited qualities that an individual can grow to adulthood with an ill-formed conscience. When one does not have the influences in life to foster a healthy self-image, our consciences are affected. Even in the best of situations, our consciences are always a bit faulty as we struggle against normal pride, insecurity, and selfishness. In the end, however, most of us are free agents in our life choices. At the core of the human person, with the aid of conscience, there is a radical freedom allowing one to choose between the good, the not so good, and the evil.

Loyal dissent, then, takes into consideration the importance of living according to my conscience and choosing freely what I believe to be the best choice. As Catholics our consciences are aided in their formation by centuries of tradition and Scripture. For the present generations, who have been raised under the historical-critical approach to understanding the Scriptures, this involves reassessing the underlying values in various Scripture passages written two or three thousand years ago. We look at the admonitions in Scripture, for instance, with a different understanding from that of previous generations. We are not willing, nor should we be expected, to make an overly simplistic interpretation of a Scripture passage to prove a point. If in the past the Church used a particular scriptural passage to justify slavery, or to imply that women were the formal cause of introducing evil into the world, then today we are compelled to say, let's look at these passages in the context in which they were written. The Scriptures must be interpreted in the *Sitz im Leben*— the life situation in which they arose. All of this comes to bear on the formation of conscience and loyal dissent. This is not to suggest that my own individual interpretation of a given Scripture quote can be used to justify any action. What is being suggested is that a thoughtful, informed reading of the Scripture could lead one to loyally dissent from a teaching—for example, the teaching on homosexuality.

The post–Vatican II mentality among laypeople, one characterized by more critical thinking, has evoked fear in the magisterium and in many Catholics who cling to the past. The fear largely stems from the idea that any major Church changes are a challenge to the certainty of the Deposit of Faith, those teachings passed down through centuries of tradition, to be held as definitive in order for one to be considered Catholic; such changes are believed to be an erosion of what it means to be Catholic. This is a legitimate concern because those guarded truths and sacred practices define us as Catholics. Throughout Church history, speculative thinking that could interfere with what the Church taught was quelled—the most famous instance being, perhaps, the suggestion by Galileo (1564–1642) that the earth circled the sun instead of the other way around. For this he was excommunicated; as mentioned in chapter 1, he only recently was pardoned by the Church. In 1950 Pope Pius XII tried to quell speculative thinking on various matters in an encyclical entitled *Humani Generis:* "On the Human Race," in which he demanded the same assent to papal encyclicals as to solemn declarations of ecumenical councils and infallible definitions of Popes. In the encyclical he declared that once the Popes have expressed "an opinion on a hitherto controversial matter, it is clear to all that this matter, according to the mind and will of the same Pontiffs, cannot any longer be considered a question of free discussion among theologians" (para. 21). In fact, Pius XII expressed in this encyclical the view that the Pope and the magisterium had sole control over the Deposit of Faith and its interpretation: "Indeed, the Divine Redeemer entrusted this Deposit of Faith not to individual Christians, nor to the theologians to be interpreted authentically, but to the magisterium of the Church alone" (ibid.). This of course was challenged privately by theologians, who wondered on what basis such an autocratic view of the papacy could be held. It was not until Vatican II that this idea of all wisdom and teaching flowing from the Pope was formally reexamined. Vatican II asserted that it was the bishops, as pastors of the people, united with the Pope, who held responsibility for the Deposit of Faith and teachings of the Church. Vatican II also complimented and extolled the importance of the theological community in helping the bishops. Thus, a more collegial, conciliar approach to the teaching office of the Church was established. At the same time, there were more people, including laypeople, becoming involved in learning and teaching religion and theology. More study meant more theological input and opinion.

This threatened some in the Church. Liberation theology, as it developed in the sixties in South and Central American countries, was considered suspect. This theology demanded a reexamination of the ways that the poor and the oppressed had been denied their basic freedom and dignity as human beings, and the establishment of a more just social order that would encourage their growth and potential. Since colonialization the Church in South and Central America had been closely identified with the oppressive social order, and liberation theologians called for radical reforms in the political arena as well as in the Church's conduct. Liberation theologies began to expand to other minority groups within the Church, including women and African Americans. This further fueled the practice of questioning, searching for the truth, and putting that truth into practice.

Despite the encouragement of a more conciliar understanding of the Church at Vatican II, the present Pope, John Paul II, has confused the situation by issuing statements and declarations that are emphatically absolutist and leave the impression among most Catholics that all wisdom does flow from the papacy. This stance is highlighted in his encyclical *Evangelium Vitae:* "Gospel of Life" issued in March 1995. Falling just short of infallible, statements such as these reverberate with a rhetoric that leaves little room for questioning or doubt: "I confirm that the direct and voluntary killing of an innocent human being is always gravely immoral. . . . I declare that direct abortion, that is abortion willed as an end or a means, always constitutes a grave moral disorder" (EV, para. 62). The suggestion here is that further study or comment on these issues by theologians or pastors that is not in accord with the Pope is not permissible. The Pope calls such questioning "grievously irresponsible," and says about those doing the questioning that they "betray the truth and their own mission by proposing personal ideas contrary to the 'Gospel of Life' as faithfully presented and interpreted by the magisterium" (EV, para. 82). This seems to be in almost direct contradiction to Vatican II's Pastoral Constitution on the Church in the Modern World, in which it is stated, "In order that such persons may fulfill their proper function, let it be recognized that all of the faithful, clerical and lay, possess a lawful freedom of inquiry and of thought, and the freedom to express their minds humbly and courageously about those matters in which they enjoy competence" (GS, para. 25).

Furthermore, the "Gospel of Life" suggests that all of those not in accord with the magisterium's statements, questioning such issues as birth control or reproductive technologies are a part of the "culture of death." Most of the questioners consider themselves very much on the side of life rather than death and, in good conscience, make what they consider to be responsible choices, but the process is often confusing. In general, Catholics don't want to be at odds with Church teaching. A couple struggling to meet the financial and other responsibilities of parenting in the twenty-first century who use birth control, or couples trying to bring a child into the world as a fulfillment of their love and using some forms of reproductive technology, would hardly consider themselves to be part of a culture of death. Obviously, for a couple trying to have a child, the ideal is for conception to happen naturally, as it does for most couples. The "Gospel of Life" states that the unitive and procreative be upheld in every act of procreation; in reproductive technology this is not always possible. The justification for the use of reproductive technology that focuses on the love relationship of the couple rather than on the act itself is not a mere rationalization. It comes from looking at the nature of human persons and their acts: their deep love for one another, the natural desire to procreate and extend their love to another human person, and their conviction in that sacred center of themselves that this is the "right" thing to do. They know it is second-best, but the desire to bring life into the world overcomes their misgivings. Are these people really to be considered a part of the culture of death? Even though thousands of people line the street for a papal visit, an erosion has occurred between the people and the teaching authority of the Church, in part because of the tone in which such teachings are delivered.

American Catholics and Catholics in other parts of the world have grown up in environments where loyal opposition and dissent are acceptable, and thinking responsibly and reasonably are the norm. Human dignity and freedom of expression are rights that we have come to expect and act upon. It is difficult when the Church seems to pull back from its former Vatican II position of according greater collegiality to a stricter, more absolutist way of teaching and governing. In 1993, in the encyclical *Veritatis Splendor:* "Splendor of Truth," Pope John Paul II states that he alone as Pope, as supreme instructor, knows and has the right to dictate moral attributes. As mentioned in chapter 2, individuals were disbelieving when Sister Carmel McEnroy was removed from her teaching position without due process for signing a petition asking the Pope to reconsider his position on not allowing discussion about women's ordination. Individuals were disbelieving when the book *Catholicism*—which has been used in classes for fifteen years and was written by the respected theologian Richard McBrien (former chair of the Theology Department at Notre Dame and author of the *New Encyclopedia of Catholicism*)—was suddenly ordered out of seminary classes in spring 1997 because there are sections in it that don't make perfectly clear the absolute teaching of the Pope on various issues.

Today the old structures that have been a part of the Church since the time of Constantine are being questioned. It was inevitable that as numbers were added to those who believed and followed the teachings of Christ in the first two centuries, a model for governing this group would have to be adopted. As cited in chapter 2, the model used was what the people at that time knew best, that of the monarchical-style Roman government. But the Church has arrived at another moment in history, when a monarchical model no longer works. Successful parishes throughout the United States are moving toward a structure with a team approach, where more people are responsible for the life of the Christian community. Thinking of new ways of structuring and decision-making does not have to mean compromising the truth or endurability of the Church. Thinking about new structures does not have to mean disvaluing the significance of the Pope as a sign of unity and strength in the Church. There are religious leaders of other denominations who envy the unifying power of the office of the Pope over a group of people scattered throughout the world, evidenced almost everywhere John Paul II visits. Change could mean that the Pope and the magisterium would do more listening to all of the People of God, encourage input and dialogue before making statements. Even among some clergy the suspicion is that the Roman curia simply does not understand the real problems that people have to deal with and therefore their expectations are unrealistic. Many lay Catholics have distanced themselves unwittingly from the teaching authority of the Pope, relying instead on their belief in a personal relationship with Christ and rationalizing that this is enough to be "good" Catholics, when in fact an acknowledgment of the teaching authority of the Church is a hallmark of being Catholic.

Bishops too have suggested that papal reform is necessary. In 1996 in a speech delivered at Oxford University, retired Archbishop John Quinn of San Francisco suggested that an atmosphere of greater collegiality, in which important issues such as contraception, the ordination of women, a married clergy, and general absolution could be discussed and evaluated openly, was important to the survival and unity of the Church. He was quoted as saying, "Far from signaling a lack of loyalty or defect in faith, raising such questions respectfully and honestly is in reality an expression of both faith and loyalty" (*National Catholic Reporter* [July 12, 1996]:11). The concerns the Pope and the magisterium have about open discussion on these issues are valid. Desiring to maintain a strong stance on the sanctity of life, the sacredness of marriage, the value of celibacy, the importance of the role of the priest in the Church is a serious matter. But allowing these issues to be discussed openly and better understood seems to be the only way that they ever will be taken seriously.

Some more conservative members of the Church believe that if the faithful are not willing to give consent without dissent, then they should just leave the Church and go somewhere else. Those dissenters, they believe, have forfeited their right to belong to the Church. What they refuse to see is that, in the words of Vatican II's Declaration on Religious Freedom *(Dignitatis Humanae)*, "Truth can impose itself on the mind of humans only in virtue of its own truth" (para. 1), and people "must not be forced to act contrary to their conscience, especially in religious matters" (para. 3). Truth makes itself known. Truth and intellectual freedom, which leads to wonder and questioning, belong together. The human mind searches for truth almost independently, which has allowed the human community to progress through history. We cannot say to the mind, do not think thoughts like that, do not question ideas like that. It will anyway. Groups like Call to Action and Corpus actually have been banned from some dioceses because they are in the process of questioning and calling for reforms on the contemporary issues mentioned throughout this book. The good that the Church does in the world, its fight against injustices, its promotion of peace, its insistence on the sacredness of all of life are sometimes overlooked because of the institutional face presented to the world.

The Church is not a fortress with walls to keep the enemies out. The Church is the People of God on pilgrimage, in process through life. Being open to the world and its problems has always been a hallmark of the Church. Certainly, in his own day Jesus was seen as a dissenter, but his mission was to bring people to a loving relationship with God his Father and to inspire in them a concern and love for one another as children of God. He often had to do this *in spite of* the religious leadership of the time. If the Church is to continue to be a beacon of light and truth in the world, then it is important that an atmosphere of mutual respect, trust, and dialogue be created so that the truth can set us all free.

9

MAP FOR THE FUTURE:
MOVING TOWARD
A NEW MILLENNIUM

In the South of France, nestled in green hills where goats and sheep graze, is the village of Taizé, perhaps best known for an ecumenical monastery simply called Taizé. Each year thousands of people, especially young people, journey to Taizé in search of a spiritual adventure. Roger Schutz founded the monastery after the devastation of World War II with the hope of restoring unity to Christianity by bringing together people of many different faiths to live in a communion according to the Gospels. There are Lutherans, Presbyterians, Methodists, Anglicans, and Roman Catholics who belong to this monastery and who open their hearts and their home to the thousands of pilgrims who come here each year. Several times a day the monks and their guests come together for prayer. The community supports itself through a variety of works such as a book bindery and a cheese-making operation. Because Taizé has become such a popular place for the spiritual traveler, the monks organize discussions around themes such as the following: How do we live as signs of the Risen Christ amidst the struggle for human rights? How do we use our imagination and courage to create a world where man is no longer victim of man? They put out a short newsletter every few months with articles and comments from young people around the world, which gives inspiration to thousands who struggle to live a Christian life in an increasingly secular world.

On any given day at Taizé clusters of young people sit in the sun or under trees listening and contributing their thoughts and ideas to the discussion at hand. They join the monks for their times of prayer, and at night there is singing and celebration of who we are as human and Christian. During the summer and at Easter, tents in which visitors stay dot the hillside, and a huge tent is added to the monastery church, the Church of Reconciliation, to accommodate all the people gathered there. Twenty-four years ago I went to Taizé to attend what was called the World Council of Youth. Over two hundred thousand young people from all over the world attended, and it was an event that would change my life forever. Never had I felt so much a part of the Church. Never had I felt like I was living and trying to put into action Gospel values of faith, hope, and love. Never had I felt so at one with others in a search for God and a search for common ground among people. And never before had I felt so happy to be Catholic, with my rich heritage of faith, ritual, and sacraments. I decided then and there to be a committed Christian. Recently I had a delightful chat with a twenty-three-year-old Catholic woman who had just returned from Taizé, and I was happy to hear that little had changed in the past twenty-four years as she enthusiastically recounted the events and feelings she had experienced, so much like my own. She told me about young people from Germany who were concerned about the plight of migrant workers from Eastern Europe, about young people from South Africa who were still fighting for the deinstitutionalization of apartheid, even though on paper it no longer exists. She described the evenings of prayer and moments of quiet contemplation and delightedly announced that she had found God. What most impressed me, though, was how excited and enthusiastic she was about trying to continue this adventure here in the United States. "Where can I go?" she asked me. "Where I can get that kind of support and encouragement to live my faith? At Taizé," she said, "the brothers and others really listen to our hopes, fears, anxieties, and needs as young people. There I felt like I really mattered, like my ideas were good ones, as though I really was a gift to the Church." She *is* a gift to the Church, and I encouraged her to *create* the space in her parish.

I think it is time for a World Council of Youth in the Catholic Church. Not a gathering of young people listening to grown-ups speak, but a council where *their* ideas and hopes and questions are listened to carefully, where *their* experiences of God are accepted, and where *their* lives as gifts to the Church are affirmed. After teaching high school and college for many, many years, I have learned more from my students than I ever could have hoped to teach them. Young people are the future of the Church, and their talents, enthusiasm, and contributions need to be tapped and encouraged. Many young people today are really on a journey to discover what is best about the world and themselves, and include God in that search. Most young people today also have a keen sense of justice and can sense dishonesty and hypocrisy immediately. They will tell you that prejudice is something they have learned from adults and that inequality has no place in the world of the future, whether the targets are women, minorities, or gays. Once they become involved in something, they can become fiercely loyal. Many of the young Catholic people I teach, however, do not attend Mass on a regular basis and find some of the teachings of the Church, principally those discussed in this book, difficult to accept. They find the institutional Church outside their experience. I know that youth ministers and others throughout the world are worried about this situation, and many dioceses have made great efforts to reach out and involve young people in the Church. But for many young people the Church, with its all-male celibate clergy and a hierarchy they perceive as unwilling to listen, is not appealing. They long for a "family" faith where they feel at home, nurtured, and encouraged to grow. How to create such an environment for the future members of the Church is a real challenge involving time and genuine concern, a sorting-out of the essentials from the nonessentials, and a promise of full participation on every level of ministry so that they can be responsible for taking the Church into the next millennium. We have to believe that Jesus' promise of the Holy Spirit to guide the Church forever is not an empty promise even in the midst of change.

Another growing concern on the part of many Catholics, especially here in the United States, are the numbers of Central American and South American Catholics increasingly turning to Protestant Churches for their spiritual needs. At a parish in my neighborhood there is Mass for Spanish-speaking Catholics said on Sundays by a Latin American priest. My husband loves to go to this Mass because it is a real celebration of life, complete with a mariachi band and singing that can be heard a block away, even in the winter when the doors are closed. The time spent for the Sign of Peace extends well beyond what occurs in most other parishes because everyone feels the need to greet as many people as possible. Often there is a baptism at the Mass, which is cause for more kisses and good wishes. My husband, who speaks almost no Spanish, comes home from these Eucharistic celebrations smiling and humming the hymns. Where the Church has adjusted to the very real cultural differences and needs of the various peoples of the world, she has survived. There are in fact many parishes, particularly in the southwestern United States and in New York City, that have vibrant Spanish-speaking populations *because* these parishes have placed a priority on the peoples' cultural values. But there are many areas where this is not the case, and Spanish-speaking people, not feeling welcome and at home in the more traditional Roman Catholic ways, are flocking to Pentecostal and Baptist Churches. The same probably could be said for the growing Haitian communities in the United States; upon coming here, they do not feel at home spiritually and are attending Protestant churches to sustain their spiritual lives.

Since the Church is the People of God, efforts need to be made on every level to affirm people within their culture and include them in the Faith. Certainly in the Gospels Jesus' attention to the stranger and the outcast, as well as his commandment to go to all nations teaching and baptizing, set an example for the Church to follow. Globalization, with national lines giving way to a more international human community, is well on its way. Similarly, the days of colonialization are over. The time when we expected people from South America, Africa, or nations in Asia to conform to Western European culture is well behind us.

Since the Eucharistic liturgy and other liturgical celebrations from which we hope to be nourished and renewed in our faith are what draw us together as Catholics, vital liturgical reform is critical. It is not only young people or people of non–Western European descent who are in search of a more meaningful way to celebrate and practice their Catholicism, many of those who have been brought up in the traditional ways are also feeling spiritual neglect from liturgies. There is growing concern over the liturgical renewal effort itself. The use of more inclusive language in the liturgy, which would make women feel more a part of salvation history, is just one example of the need for reform, but a new lectionary approved by the American bishops that attempted to provide such wording is now embroiled in a debate between the bishops and the Vatican. Recently, at a liturgy conference held at Notre Dame, the issue of liturgical reform was addressed. Bishop Donald Trautman of Erie, Pennsylvania, was just one of the people who expressed concern about the fact that there are voices in the Church calling us back to liturgical theology and practice that predate the Second Vatican Council, rather than forward to a much needed renewal. There is a group in the Church, Adoremus (Latin for "we adore"), based in Arlington, Virginia, which advocates such practices as returning to Latin to recite the Eucharistic Prayer, restricting Communion to receiving just the host, having the priest and people facing in the same direction for the liturgy, and barring women from all liturgical ministries. The televised Mass of Mother Angelica on the Eternal World Television Network, where nuns prostrate themselves during the Eucharistic prayer and Latin is used in some prayers instead of English, provides a sympathetic support for these practices.

One thing is certain, and that is dissatisfaction with the way the liturgy is being celebrated in many places. The celebration of the Eucharist and other sacraments are the heart of Catholicism because they provide us with a lived experience of what is sacred in our lives, and when this degenerates into repetitious words and actions, lacking a real soul, we are being deprived of something essential to our life of faith. I listen to too many Catholics, young and not so young, who complain that the liturgy does not really touch their lives or that homilies are shallow and don't enhance the readings at Mass. Many Catholics still have the feeling that they are spectators at a show, rather than active participants at their liturgical celebrations. At Fordham University, and I am sure this is true at other universities, there is a Sunday evening liturgy geared directly to the college students that is warm, inviting, and unifying. The students play their own music, the homilies are well prepared, and everyone participates. I have talked to many of the students attending this liturgy who say that it gives them spiritual fuel for the week ahead. They feel strengthened and supported in their Catholic faith in ways that they do not find at their home parishes.

Certainly the shortage of priests has taken a toll on liturgical celebrations. In some areas of the country and throughout the world, there are not enough priests to celebrate Mass on a weekly or even monthly basis. This sacramental starvation will have a great effect on Catholicism because people will choose to go elsewhere to satisfy their spiritual hunger. In a small town in Kansas, where a former classmate of mine lives, there is no longer a resident priest. A priest comes once a month; in between his visits, many of the town's Catholics have begun to go to Church services at the local Lutheran Church, rather than attend a Catholic communion service, which to them seems like a quasi-celebration of Mass. *Married* clergy or *women* priests would have positive, practical, and spiritual results in such places. This should not be the reason for recalling clergy who have left the priesthood to marry, for allowing priests to marry, or for ordaining women to the priesthood, but it certainly would put more people in touch with their faith as Catholics.

I am amazed when I walk into bookstore supermarkets today and browse through the huge selection of religious books. The number of books on prayer, meditation, and religious reflection present on the shelves is quite a statement about modern people's search for a spiritual life despite the crime and violence that gets front page coverage in the news. The fact that the *Chicken Soup for the Soul* series has extended to six books, including one for teenagers, in numerous printings over the past two years, and that books like *Conversations with God: An Uncommon Dialogue*, volumes 1 and 2, by Neale Donald Walsch, or *Simple Abundance*, by Sara Ban Breathnach, which is about helping women find God in their everyday life, have been on the best-seller lists for months suggests that the need for God is everywhere. Recently, while picking my way through the hot sand on a beach, I passed a bikini-clad young woman reading *The Cloister Walk* by Kathleen Norris, which is a contemplative, prayerful book of stories and memories based on a woman's experience at a monastery.

Last spring when I tried to book a retreat for a group of students and was negotiating with the retreat master for dates, I discovered that retreats were being offered for myriad groups, including the physically handicapped, divorced Catholics, widowed Catholics, bereavement groups, young professional singles, and the hearing impaired, so I missed out on the dates I wanted and was put on the waiting list. The good news here is that on all accounts the Church has extended its concern and outreach in its ministries to many groups in the Church and world who were previously overlooked by society in general. Like the prophet Amos in the Old Testament, who stood in the marketplace and berated his countrymen for their mistreatment of the poor, the oppressed, and the stranger, the Church has been acting as a voice of support and comfort on behalf of those same people in our world today. The Church's teaching on social justice for laborers and immigrants, though often unnoticed by Catholics as a whole, has served as a conscience for modern society in asking and answering the timeless questions, "Am I my brothers' keeper?" and "Who is my neighbor?" The Church needs to continue this mission.

Pope John XXIII saw the need for change and was quick to remind people that the Church had already survived the winds of many turbulent changes. It is worth repeating the words from an address convoking Second Vatican Council, already quoted in chapter 1. He therein talked about the upcoming meetings, stating: "This will be a demonstration of the Church, always living and always young, which feels the rhythm of the times and which in every century beautifies herself with new splendor, radiates new light, achieves new conquests, while remaining identical in herself" (Abbott, *Documents and Speeches,* 706). This is one of my favorite quotes, filling me with hope, because it reminds me that every age has brought new challenges and somehow the Church has survived and offered to the world a message of love. This is what is central and what is expected from the Church today.

In our current fascination with violence, sexual promiscuity, dishonesty, conditions of human oppression and abuse, all of which have been addressed by the Church in recent years, it has become commonplace to expect the Church to take a firm moral stance on safeguarding the rights of humankind. Because the Church has a strong, united voice in the Pope and the magisterium, her words are frequently heard and looked upon as a moral compass that demands of all of us an examination of our motives and actions. I think we as Catholics have become more sensitive to the less fortunate. Everywhere I look in the New York City metropolitan area, there are food pantries and soup kitchens, Church-sponsored hospice and AIDS programs, support for unwed mothers and homeless children, like Covenant House.

Recently, John Cardinal O'Connor of the New York archdiocese made a surprise visit to a large Church-sponsored gathering of Mexicans who had come to the United States to find a better life. This followed upon the heels of the disclosure in New York newspapers that scores of deaf Mexicans had been exploited, brought here by a sponsor to sell dollar trinkets. They were housed in barracks-style living quarters and had been virtually enslaved. The Cardinal's generous gift of himself that day, his comments of compassion for their country and people, and support for their future well-being are evidence of what is best about the Church, extending the life and ministry of Jesus. This type of attitude and action that reaches out, touches, and acknowledges the sacredness of every human person is part of the seamless garment of life that the late Cardinal Bernardin tried to encourage. The archbishop had witnessed the festering debate and struggle between the pro-life and pro-choice groups over abortion. Discouraged by the idea that Catholics increasingly were being seen as a one-issue Church, he encouraged a seamless-garment-of-life philosophy emphasizing the importance of all life—the imprisoned sitting on death row, the homeless, the terminally ill, AIDS patients, and not just that of the unborn. Because of efforts and statements like this, Church leaders are speaking out more about all life issues. The Pope's many journeys and his genuine concern for those he visits bear witness to the significance of his role in the Church as the Vicar of Christ. His office and presence do bring unity to the Church as people rally to greet him and wait on his word. When he visited the United States several years ago, I remember a Jewish commentator saying that he wished there was someone who could speak for the whole Jewish community the way the Pope speaks for Catholics.

However, if the Church is to continue this mission of hope in the world, it is inevitable that it will have to include more and more laypeople to continue these ministries affirming human life in the world. It has been a joy to watch students I have taught—Allison, Sheila, Beth, Bernadette, and Moria—give a year of their lives to serve the less fortunate in the Jesuit Volunteers. Since we rely on laypeople for these ministries—which include men and women in religious orders giving themselves to issues of social justice and charity—the Church should also include laypeople in the formulation of documents and decisions. The situation with the Crowleys and the birth control issue, and how their work and input were virtually ignored by the promulgation of *Humanae Vitae*, did little to gain support for the Church's teaching against birth control. Many laypeople felt disenfranchised by their Church, which seemed to care little for their real marital needs or their contributions of thought. Similarly, in 1997 at the United States bishops annual spring meeting in Kansas City, the bishops voted, albeit 113 to 104, against allowing persons other than bishops to have voting rights on final decisions, even if they had served on the committees suggesting a particular study or document. Henceforth, these people will serve only in an advisory capacity without voting rights on final outcomes or suggestions. Despite the fact that the Second Vatican Council called for greater inclusiveness, this move sends a message of greater *ex*clusiveness as we move toward the third millennium and discourages people from wanting to participate in the life of the Church, since the end result is that their voice does not really matter. This seems to be a strange ecclesiology when there are people willing and eager to participate fully in the life of the Church. Not long ago I read about a parish outside of Chicago that has about 60 percent of the parishioners actively involved in its ministries. Besides the usual director of religious education, there is a paid staff of five who coordinate liturgical celebrations, teach religion, and run an extraordinarily active senior citizens program, a youth ministry program numbering two hundred teenagers involved in volunteer services and other activities, a food pantry, a meal program for the homebound elderly, and prayer and theological study groups. Coordinators and organizers of all these activities meet biweekly for prayer and support from one another so that no one feels as if he or she is working in a vacuum but rather knowing they are part of a larger picture of the Church. Two thousand years later, this parish sounds like the early Church written about in the Acts of the Apostles. The pastor of this parish believes in sharing his ministry with his people and really listens to and cooperates with his parishioners. Vital parishes like this are critical for the future.

Besides all the issues discussed in this book—the reconsideration of a married clergy, remaining open to a continued dialogue about the possibility of ordaining women to the priesthood, a greater acceptance of individuals whose sexual orientation is homosexuality, allowing divorced and remarried Catholics the opportunity to receive the sacraments, and a less judgmental attitude toward those who find themselves in the position of having to make decisions about pregnancy and reproduction—there is also the issue of searching for a more broadly based collegiality in determining some Church policy. The *sensus fidelium* this book has discussed means that many more Catholics have come of age in regard to their knowledge and understanding of their faith and desire to take on more responsibility for it. They have come to believe that their experience of God is legitimate and that their gifts to the Church should be considered and accepted more fully. The magisterium needs to be more sympathetic in this regard.

Following upon this suggestion, I believe that more has to be done to affirm Catholics in their faith through a better system of religious education. As Catholics grow to maturity, their knowledge of what the Church teaches and why ought to be commensurate with that growth. Over the years I have discovered that most of my students end up being grateful for required courses in theology at the university level. It causes them to think more deeply about their faith, raise questions, and search for answers. Generally, they are delighted to learn more about the Scripture and history of the Church, and love to tackle relevant moral questions in a guided atmosphere. I have also discovered that even high school students are prepared for a more in-depth approach to their religious enlightenment than we sometimes expect of them. Many Catholics leave a formal religious education by age twelve. While their minds continue to be broadened in the areas of mathematics, psychology, history, science, computers, and other areas of study they pursue, their religious education ceases. This is unfortunate and means that there are Catholics with immature understandings of the Church and often many unanswered questions. Obviously, Catholics are among that group of people searching for an in-depth experience of God and a spiritual life, and it needs to be provided for them by the Church. Perhaps making more use of the media and computers can enrich our knowledge. It already has to some degree: Even the Vatican is now on-line! But greater use of both could enhance this area of our lives. With a captured audience on a Sunday, homilists could educate parishioners in a more in-depth way than is currently done. At present only priests are allowed to deliver homilies at Mass, but perhaps in the future experts in certain theological areas, clergy as well as laypeople, could be called upon to share their knowledge and help deepen the faith of the community. There are many parishioners who would gladly pursue a course of theological study in a particular area if offered on the parish level and encouraged. The Church needs to be creative and imaginative in conveying the breadth of the Christian message.

The year 2000 is just around the corner. I am one of those people who believes that the Church is still at the beginning stages of its growth and life. We are still *becoming* the People of God.

When someone asked me not long ago what the title of this book would be, I responded, "Practicing Catholic."

"What? After all these years you've just been practicing to be a Catholic? When do you get to do the real thing?" he asked.

"Well, this is the real thing!" I replied.

In this situation, practicing means more than rehearsing. It means participating in the rituals, learning the script, studying the rules, and doing things like acts of loving kindness over and over again until they are really yours, a part of who you are. Practicing Catholic means that I strive to become all I am called to be by God, through baptism, in the Church.

APPENDIX

Church Documents

Documents of the Second Vatican Council

	1964	*Lumen Gentium:* "Light of Nations" (Dogmatic Constitution on the Church)
	1964	*Unitatis Redintegratio* (Decree on Ecumenism)
	1965	*Dei Verbum:* "Word of God" (Dogmatic Constitution on Divine Revelation)
GS	1965	*Gaudium et Spes:* "Joy and Hope" (Pastoral Constitution on the Church in the Modern World)
	1965	*Optatam Totius* (Decree on Priestly Formation)
	1965	*Dignitatis Humanae:* "Of the Dignity of the Human [Person]" (Declaration on Religious Freedom)
	1965	*Christus Dominus:* "Christ the Lord" (Decree on the Bishops' Pastoral Office in the Church)
	1965	*Nostra Aetate:* "In Our Age" (Declaration on the Relationship of the Church to Non-Christian Religions)

The above documents can be found in their entirety in *The Papal Encyclicals* (Raleigh, NC: McGrath Publishing Co., 1981) and *Speeches and Documents from the Second Vatican Council,* edited by Walter M. Abbott (New York: American Press, 1966).

Selected Bibliography

Abbott, Walter M., ed. *Documents and Speeches from the Second Vatican Council*. New York: American Press, 1966.

Aquinas, Thomas. *On the Truth of the Catholic Faith: Summa Contra Gentiles*. New York: Doubleday and Co., 1955.

Aquinas, Thomas. *Summa Sacrae Theologia*. Venice, 1581.

Augustine. *City of God*. New York: Random House, 1950.

———. *Confessions*. New York: Penguin Books, 1961.

———. *Letters of Saint Augustine: Volume 2*. Washington, D.C.: Catholic University Press, 1966.

Boswell, John. *Christianity, Social Tolerance, and Homosexuality*. Chicago: University of Chicago Press, 1980.

Bowman, Jim. *Bending the Rules: What American Priests Tell American Catholics*. New York: Crossroad, 1994.

Callahan, Sidney. *In Good Conscience: Reason and Emotion in Moral Decision Making*. San Francisco: HarperSanFrancisco, 1991.

Carr, Anne E. *Transforming Grace: Christian Tradition and Woman's Experience*. San Francisco: Harper and Row, 1988.

Casti Connubii: The English Translation. New York: Barry Vail Corp., 1931.

Catechism of the Catholic Church. California: Benziger, 1994.

Coleman, Gerald D., S.S. *Homosexuality: Catholic Teaching and Pastoral Practice*. Mahwah, NJ: New Paulist Press, 1995.

Curran, Charles E. *Faithful Dissent*. Kansas City, MO: Sheed and Ward, 1986.

Dulles, Avery, S.J. *Revelation Theology*. New York: Herder and Herder, 1969.

Fox, Thomas C. *Sexuality and Catholicism*. New York: George Braziller, 1995.

Gallagher, John, ed. *Homosexuality and the Magisterium: Documents from the Vatican and U.S. Bishops 1975–1985*. Mt. Rainier, Maryland: New Ways Ministry, 1986.

Gramick, Jeannine, and Robert Nugent, eds. *Homosexuality and the Catholic Church*. New York: Crossroad, 1982.

——. *Homosexuality in the Priesthood and the Religious Life.* New York: Cross-road, 1989.

——. *The Vatican and Homosexuality: Reaction to the "Letter to the Bishops of the Catholic Church on the Pastoral Care of Homosexual Persons."* New York: Crossroad, 1988.

Gunzel, Raymond J., S.J. Celibacy: *Renewing the Gift, Releasing the Power.* Kansas City, MO: Sheed and Ward, 1988.

Gutiérrez, Gustavo. *A Theology of Liberation.* Maryknoll, NY: Orbis Books, 1973.

Harvey, John. O.S.F.S. *The Homosexual Person: New Thinking in Pastoral Care.* San Francisco: Ignatius Press, 1987.

Hugo, John J. *St. Augustine on Nature, Sex, and Marriage.* Chicago: Scepter Press, 1969.

Hurst, Jane. "The History of Abortion in the Catholic Church: The Untold Story." A Series Published by Catholics for a Free Choice, Washington, D.C., 1990.

Jung, Patricia Beattie, and Thomas A. Shannon. *Abortion and Catholicism: The American Debate.* New York: Crossroad, 1998.

Kaiser, Robert Blair. *The Politics of Sex and Religion: A Case History in the Development of Doctrine, 1962–1984.* Kansas City, MO: Leaven Press, 1985.

Kaufman, Philip. *Why You Can Disagree and Remain a Faithful Catholic.* New York: Crossroad, 1995.

Kennedy, Sheila Rauch. *Shattered Faith.* New York: Pantheon Books, 1997.

Kosnick, Anthony, et al. *Human Sexuality: A New Direction in American Thought.* New York: Paulist Press, 1977.

Kung, Hans. *Infallible? An Inquiry.* English translation by Edward Quinn. Garden City, NY: Doubleday and Co., 1983.

Kwitny, Jonathan. *Man of the Century: The Life and Times of John Paul II.* New York: Henry Holt and Co., 1997.

LaCugna, Catherine M., ed. *Freeing Theology: The Essentials of Theology in Feminist Perspective.* San Francisco: HarperSanFrancisco, 1993.

Mackin, Theodore, S.J. *Divorce and Remarriage.* New York: Paulist Press, 1984.

McBrien, Richard P. *Catholicism.* Rev. ed. San Francisco: HarperSanFran-cisco, 1994.

——, gen. ed. *Encyclopedia of Catholicism.* New York: HarperCollins, 1995.

McCormack, Richard. "Personal Conscience." *Chicago Studies* 13 (3), Fall 1994.

McNeill, John. *The Church and the Homosexual.* Boston: Beacon Press, 1996.

Miles, Jack. *God: A Biography.* New York: Knopf, 1995.

Noonan, John T., Jr. *Contraception: A History of Its Treatment by the Catholic Theologians and Canonists.* Enlarged ed. Cambridge: Harvard University Press, 1986.

Nugent, Robert. *A Challenge to Love: Gay and Lesbian Catholics in the Church.* New York: Crossroad, 1983.

Papal Encyclicals. Raleigh, NC: McGrath Publishing Co., 1981.

Rahner, Karl, and Joseph Ratzinger. *The Episcopate and the Primacy*. New York: Herder and Herder, 1962.

Ranke-Heinemann, Uta. *Eunuchs for the Kingdom of Heaven: Women, Sexuality, and the Catholic Church*. New York: Penguin Books, 1991.

Ruether, Rosemary Radford. *Women-Church: Theology and Practice of Feminist Liturgical Communities*. San Francisco: Harper and Row, 1985.

Rutledge, Rev. Mrs. Fleming. "Women's Ordination: Six Responses." *Commonweal*, July 15, 1994.

Schoenherr, Richard. *Full Pews and Empty Altars: Demographics of the Priest Shortage in the United States Catholic Diocese*. Madison, WI: University of Wisconsin Press, 1993.

Sipe, A. W. Richard. *Sex, Priests, and Power: Anatomy of a Crisis*. New York: Brunner/Mazel Publishers, 1995.

Smith, Richard L. *AIDS, Gays, and the American Church*. Cleveland, OH: Pilgrim Press, 1984.

Tanner, Norman P., S.J., ed. *Decrees of the Ecumenical Councils*. Washington, D.C.: Georgetown University Press, 1990.

Tierney, Brian. *Origins of Papal Infallibility, 1150–1350: A Study on the Concepts of Infallibility, Sovereignty, and Tradition in the Middle Ages*. Leiden, England: E. J. Brill, 1972.

Worlock, Archbishop Derek. "Results of Presynodal Consultation with Priests and People of the Diocese of Liverpool." *Origins* 10 (18), October 9, 1980.

Index